American Idolatry

American Idolatry
Celebrity, Commodity and Reality Television

CHRISTOPHER E. BELL

McFarland & Company, Inc., Publishers
Jefferson, North Carolina, and London

LIBRARY OF CONGRESS CATALOGUING-IN-PUBLICATION DATA

Bell, Christopher E., 1974–
    American idolatry : celebrity, commodity and reality television / Christopher E. Bell.
        p.   cm.
    Includes bibliographical references and index.

    ISBN 978-0-7864-4824-1
    softcover : 50# alkaline paper

    1. American idol (Television program)   2. Reality television programs — United States.   3. Popular culture — United States.   I. Title.
    PN1992.77.A56B35   2010
    791.45'6 — dc22   2009049615

British Library cataloguing data are available

©2010 Christopher E. Bell. All rights reserved

No part of this book may be reproduced or transmitted in any form or by any means, electronic or mechanical, including photocopying or recording, or by any information storage and retrieval system, without permission in writing from the publisher.

Cover images ©2010 Shutterstock

Manufactured in the United States of America

McFarland & Company, Inc., Publishers
  Box 611, Jefferson, North Carolina 28640
  www.mcfarlandpub.com

For Sean James,
Lisa Ann Bell,
Leonard Trajano,
Pauline Augustin,
and Denise Hawkins.
But mostly for
Russell Bell, Jr.

Table of Contents

Acknowledgments ix
Introduction: Famous for Being Famous 1

    I. Ideas and Cabbages 15
    II. Dude! I Met Elway! 47
    III. Jay-Z Is One of Us, Only Not 73
    IV. When Someone's Down on the Floor, Kick Them 101
    V. What's a Ballsy? 115
    VI. You've Got the X Factor 126
    VII. Sugarfoot and Babyface 136
    VIII. Wear the Least Amount of Clothes Possible 148
    IX. Why Is She Special? 154
    X. Are You Drunk? 164
    XI. I Want to Break Free 173
    XII. Look at This! I'm Unique! 178

Chapter Notes 201
Bibliography 207
Index 217

Acknowledgments

The next couple of pages are directed to people who are probably not you. If you, dear reader, are the type for whom these sorts of lists are tedious or bothersome, by all means, feel free to skip ahead to the beginning of Chapter I. You won't hurt my feelings. I promise.

At the Oscars, a particular phenomenon occurs: people often, in the excitement and haste of having finally realized a career goal (and, likely, childhood dream), babble off a stream of thanks and forget the most important person of all. I made a promise a long time ago that I would never, ever do that. So, first and foremost, above all others, I want to thank Megan Elizabeth Bell, for standing by me, for believing in me, and for being the sunshine on my darkest days. You're the most beautiful person I have ever known, inside and out. Three and four and five.

Special thanks to Dr. Elizabeth Skewes, who took me under her wing early in my doctoral career and provided opportunities, knowledge, support and motivation. You are dedicated and brilliant, and everything a doctoral advisor should aspire to be for their student — be it the first time she is a doctoral chair or the fortieth.

Thanks to my doctoral committee: Dr. Peter Simonson, Dr. Jan Whitt, Dr. Kendra Gale, and Dr. Robert Trager, each of whom played a special part in the formation of this book in particular and my doctoral career as a whole. I am grateful for the expertise of each and the insightful questioning that put me on the right path to successful completion of this work.

I owe a particular debt of gratitude to Kyle Kontour, who weathered some pretty nasty storms alongside me (we came out on the other side stronger people), and who became, over the years, my partner in crime (especially in the late-night email wars). Thanks to Dale Bridges for his

Acknowledgments

eternal friendship and brotherhood. Thanks to Ginna Sanprie, for being my sounding board and voice of reason. Thanks to Shalauna Miller, Marcy Wells, Christina Bertsch, Marisa Lubeck, Colin Lingle, Leasa Weimer, Monica Garcia, and friends far too numerous to thank individually for the love and support. But you know how much I love you.

Thank you to Gloria Bell, Eric Bell, Nicole James, Sari Mills, Brandon James, Courtney, Kevin, Davis, and Brady Armitage, Dennis and Sonja Howe, Tom and Cindi Whalen, Courtney Linde, Matthew, and Grayson Lee Cassidy, Joshua Whalen, Michael, Karin, and Kyra McMurray, Jeremy Whalen, Kellyn McMurray, and the rest of my family for letting me be me and accepting me as I am in my weirdest moments.

Special thank you to Cynthia Mary Augustin Bell, who worked and sacrificed in ways I cannot even imagine to get me to where I am.

Thank you to Dr. J. Richard Stevens, who has become a mentor, a colleague, and a friend to me over the past year.

There is empirical research to prove, medically, that pet therapy helps people heal. I truly, truly believe that I would not make it through many of my days without Hermione and Kilimanjaro, because they give unconditional love like no human being is capable of giving. Yes, I am thanking my cats. No, I am not ashamed.

Often times, over the course of a project, people will contribute in ways they will never know, and are usually unaware that they are doing so. In particular, I owe an enormous debt of gratitude to Dr. Cari Skogberg-Eastman, who has no idea how much she contributed structurally/mechanically to the skeleton of my dissertation (the original version of this book), and whose own dissertation I regard as straight-up genius. Thanks to Dr. Michelle Miles, for paving the way in my home department. Thanks to Mona Tavakoli, Becky Gebhardt, Chaska Potter, and Mai Bloomfield for providing the soothing soundtrack to many a long and stressful writing session.

Thank you to Dr. Joan Clinefelter and the Ronald McNair Scholars Program for seeing in me the seeds of a lifelong career of teaching and learning back when I could not see them myself, and for encouraging me to continue my academic pursuits past undergrad graduation.

Thank you, maybe more than all of these other thank yous, to Russell Bell, Jr., for always making me feel that it was not only okay, but actually *cool* to be smart.

Acknowledgments

One final piece here. I didn't write it, and I don't know who did, but this is the way I remember it told. The person to whom it is dedicated knows who he or she is. As the saying goes, if you have to ask, it ain't you.

A man approached a painter in the park one day, and stood behind him, watching over the painter's shoulder. For nearly thirty minutes the painter sat there, staring at a blank white canvas. The man bounced on his heels in expectant excitement; the possibilities of the empty canvas were endless.

Finally, the painter slashed a single black stroke across the canvas, nodded, and signed his name at the bottom. The man threw his hands up in exasperation.

"That's it?! That's all you're going to paint?" The man was furious. "How can you possibly call that art?"

Without a word, the painter reached down, grabbed his sketch pad and a pencil, and dashed off an immaculate drawing of the park. Every person, every leaf, every blade of grass was represented exactly as it existed in real life. It was almost perfect. He handed the sketch to the man.

"This is beautiful," the man said. "Stunning!"

"My painting is art because although I can *do that," the painter said, pointing at his sketch of the park, "I* choose *to do this."*

The painter handed his canvas consisting only of a single black line to the man, packed up his tools, and walked away.

Introduction:
Famous for Being Famous

> *"In the future, everyone will be famous for fifteen minutes."*
> Andy Warhol

In 1962, in his book *The Image: Or, What Happened to the American Dream,* Daniel Boorstin came up with what has become, in some ways, the defining (and completely tautological) aphorism of the study of *celebrity*[1]: "The celebrity is a person who is well-known for his well-knownness." Labeling the Celebrity (i.e., the actual human person) "the human pseudo-event," Boorstin's aim is clear: define the Celebrity as a product of manufacture rather than merit. Boorstin pointedly distinguishes the modern Celebrity from the heroes of the past, when fame was the by-product of greatness, the recognition of achievement. Taking Boorstin's own terminology—"well-knownness"—at face value and following his argument to its cynical conclusion, if fame was formerly the recognition of achievement, then modern *celebrity* (the recognition of "well-knownness"), in contrast, must be based on something other than achievement. In fact, at the extreme end of Boorstin's proposition, achievement—greatness—and *celebrity* are inversely proportional and mutually exclusive.

However, to adopt Boorstin's position is to overlook the simple fact that for every Paris Hilton that has seemingly progressed from heiress to debutante to tabloid fixture without actually doing anything or possessing any recognizable talent whatsoever, there is a Celebrity that has risen to well-knownness through some performative act—the soaring feats of Michael Jordan, the amazing manual dexterity of Slash, the wholly engrossing roles portrayed by Denzel Washington—that cannot be explained away

Introduction

by Boorstin's proposition.[2] This suggests that celebrity, as a term, is multifaceted, and not easily reducible to a single maxim. Or, perhaps it suggests that *celebrity* and fame are not the same thing; they are interrelated, and occasionally coexistent, but not necessarily interchangeable terms.

If fame is the derivative of greatness or great acts and *celebrity* is something else (the propagation of that greatness, perhaps, or, at least, the propagation of the *appearance* of greatness), the difference is clear. However, where the two intersect — where the famous Celebrity, or the person who is well-known for his/her performative acts, is situated — is an interesting phenomenon indeed. Chris Rojek (2001) posits that there are three types of *celebrity* status: ascribed, attributed, and achieved. Ascribed *celebrity* is the *celebrity* of "biological descent"; the king is respected because he is the king (p. 17). Attributed *celebrity* is "the result of the concentrated representation of an individual as noteworthy or exceptional by cultural intermediaries" (p. 18). This is the "human pseudo-event" Boorstin described, *celebrity* as defined by media representation and public attention. Achieved *celebrity* is, under the rubric described earlier, that mysterious gray area which lies between fame and *celebrity*. Achieved *celebrity* is the *celebrity* of accomplishment; as Rojek states, "In the public realm, they are recognized as individuals who possess rare talents or skills" (p. 18).

It is this third type of *celebrity*— the *celebrity* of achievement — with which this book is primarily concerned (or, more specifically, it is the intersection of the second and third types of *celebrity*). While Boorstin's characterization may be perfectly true under particular circumstances, it is not the only manner in which *celebrity* operates. It is, however, one of a number of useful precepts that can be used to define the boundaries of *celebrity*. Rojek's theory also seems incomplete, as pure achieved *celebrity* does not take into account the attributing function of mass media. For example, few would argue with the assertion that it takes a tremendous amount of physical skill, talent, and knowledge to play professional football at the level which is represented by the National Football League. However, merely being drafted into the NFL doesn't guarantee all players an equal amount of (or even equal access to) *celebrity* (well-knownness). While there is some logic to the fact that a quarterback may receive more attention than, perhaps, an offensive lineman, for example, even within the quarterback position, not all players are treated equally. This is the difference

Introduction

between a quality player (*achieved celebrity*) and an iconic player (*achieved celebrity* + *attributed celebrity*). It is the difference between Super Bowl Champion Ben Roethlisberger and Super Bowl Champion Peyton Manning. Peyton Manning has hosted *Saturday Night Live*, has performed in national television commercials and has been the spokesman for a variety of products. Manning also is the son of former NFL quarterback Archie Manning, and brother of Eli, the starting quarterback for the New York Giants (and also a Super Bowl champion). Manning's *celebrity* status is not merely a result of his on-field achievements; Roethlisberger's, to a large extent, is (even though Roethlisberger is the NFL's highest paid player [Weisman 2008]; financial worth does not necessarily result in greater *celebrity* status). But neither can Manning's on-field achievements be ignored; he certainly fulfills the notion of *achieved celebrity*. It would appear that there is room to define a hybrid of achieved and attributed *celebrity* that is particularly tied to modern mass media.

In addition to the three types of *celebrity*, Rojek defines a separate category of Celebrity: the "celetoid."[3] According to Rojek:

> Celetoids are the accessories of cultures organized around mass communications and staged authenticity. Examples include lottery winners, one-hit wonders, stalkers, whistle-blowers, sports' arena streakers, have-a-go-heroes, mistresses of public figures and the various other social types who command media attention one day, and are forgotten the next [p. 20].

Graeme Turner (2006) expands on this, extrapolating from the rise of the celetoid to describe the current media context — that includes the internet and reality television — in which *celebrity* status is viewed almost as a birthright. Turner states:

> In relation to the broader culture within which the consumption of celebrity occurs ... trends have resulted in celebrity itself mutating: no longer a magical condition, some research suggests that it is fast becoming an almost reasonable expectation for us to have of our everyday lives. The opportunity of becoming a celebrity has spread beyond the various elites and into the expectations of the population in general [p. 156].

Turner here refers to what he terms "DIY celebrity," a "do it yourself" type of *celebrity* which is generated from either the internet or, more commonly, from reality television programs. Reality television programs are uniquely positioned to generate a continual stream of celetoids and DIY Celebrities;

Introduction

the very construction of such programs involves the "discovery" of "ordinary" people and, to one degree or another, the elevation of these people to temporary *celebrity* status. Turner asserts that, as society increases its consumption of *celebrity* in terms of gossip, images, and information about Celebrities, the celetoid has become a viable alternative to "genuine" Celebrity commodities (p. 156). Each episode or season of a reality television program brings a fresh batch of *celebrity* commodities to consume, of celetoids to be used today and forgotten tomorrow; so much so that Turner coined the term "the demotic turn" for the democratized process which has increased production of celetoids through the rise in reality television (Turner 2006).

Given this, it would seem that the greatest differences between celetoid and *celebrity* are longevity and purpose — Rojek states, "Evanescence is the irrevocable condition of celetoid status, though in exceptional cases a celetoid may acquire a degree of longevity" (p. 22), and goes on to state that "the purpose of celebrity ... is to add value to economy and culture" (p. 118). If the celetoid is defined as, according to Turner, "the individual with no particular talents which might give them expectations of work in the entertainment industry ... and an especially short lifecycle as a public figure" (p. 156), then the Celebrity must be something relatively opposite — that is, an individual with some particular talent and a comparatively longer lifecycle as a public figure.[4]

The Study of Celebrity

The study of *celebrity* is a wide and diverse field, encompassing theoretical perspectives from social psychology to political economy, and operating in a vast array of contexts, from religion (Maltby, et al. 2002) to body image (King, et al. 2000) to politics (Lahusen 1996). A good deal of research has focused on the potential of celebrity endorsement within the advertising realm (Kahle & Homer 1985; McCracken 1989; Agrawal & Kamakura 1995; Mathur, Mathur & Rangan 1997; Goldsmith, Lafferty & Newell 2000), suggesting that the link between *celebrity* and political economy has effects beyond the commodification process. Celebrity influence also has been studied in relationship to effects on social movements

Introduction

(Meyer 1995), on construction of identity (Boon & Lomore 2001), and even on suicide rates (Martin & Koo 1997).

All of these studies, however, deal with *celebrity* in *relation* to something else. While a legal definition of celebrity (public figure) was established by the Supreme Court in 1964 (*New York Times v. Sullivan 376 U.S. 254 (1964)*), Gamson (1994) notes that studies dealing directly with the nature of *celebrity*— what constitutes it, how it functions, how it is maintained — are much less common. He states:

> The territory as a whole, however — audience interpretations, in particular, but also the relationships between discourse, production, and audiences — has been tremendously underexamined [p. 3].

C. Wright Mills' *The Power Elite* (1956) and Boorstin's *The Image* (1962) are two of the earlier examinations of the nature of modern *celebrity;* both take a rather cynical view of the emerging Hollywood subculture. However, Mills' work is less about *celebrity* than it is about the economic elite, and Boorstin's work is more about the negative side of *celebrity* than it is about the entirety of the nature of *celebrity*. Braudy's (1986) study of the nature of *celebrity* is historical, focusing on the desire through the ages for renown. Gamson builds upon this work, and approaches celebrity from a political economic standpoint, stating that

> fame is artificially producible and produced, well-knownness a salable and sold commodity, achievement divorceable and divorced from renown. The separation of notoriety from greatness, however, is taken as an indicator not of decline-of-civilization dangers but of unmined commercial opportunities [p. 57].

Dyer & McDonald (1998) contradict this point of view, pointing out that there is more to *celebrity* than promotion and commodity. Marshall (1997) agrees, noting that celebrity "operates as a way of providing distinctions and definitions of success" in business, politics, and art, and points out the increased discursive power *celebrity* affords, giving celebrities "a voice above others, a voice that is channeled into the media systems as being legitimately significant" (p. x).

In this respect, *celebrity* is not merely a commodity or status, but an intricate system through which meaning is made and social relations constituted. But *celebrity* is, by definition, of a dual nature; there is the Celebrity (the human being upon whom has been conferred status) and

Introduction

there is *celebrity*, either as defined as said status or as the system by which that status is socially manifest. Clearly, there is a difference between a Celebrity as a physical, tangible human being, and *celebrity* as a social and economic concept. The two are intertwined but not interchangeable; they rely upon each other for subsistence, but are distinct entities. Tina Fey is a Celebrity; the aura surrounding Tina Fey is *celebrity*.

There is another body of theories that, while not strictly focused on (or even written with consideration of) *celebrity* which, nevertheless, might be useful in understanding the way modern *celebrity* is constructed and operates. For example, Theodor Adorno and Max Horkheimer (2002) argued that, in the age of modern mass production of culture, a few large corporations have overtaken the entire production and distribution apparatus of cultural products. Under this regime of multinational conglomerates, culture has become a tool not for mirroring society, but for actually shaping society by commodifying and standardizing cultural products within society. Instead of providing for society's needs, the culture industry works to manipulate society into needing/wanting what the culture industry produces. In essence, we like popular culture because we have been fooled by giant corporations into thinking what we are consuming is good and good for us. It's a distraction technique to keep us (the masses) from attempting to gain any real power, either economic or social. A cynical point of view, not wholly without merit, but one with which I will be taking issue with in Chapter I.

Reality television has brought yet another twist to the study of *celebrity*. Although the reality genre has been around in its modern form since *Candid Camera* in the 1950s, thorough study of the reality television genre did not begin in earnest until the early 1990s. The early studies of reality television generally centered on crime shows such as *Cops* and *America's Most Wanted* (Cavendar & Bond-Maupin 1993, Oliver 1994, Pitman 2002). The MTV program *The Real World* became a topic of scrutiny as it rose in popularity (Orbe 1998), and as scholars worried that viewing repeated anti-social acts that seem to meet with very little consequence could have negative influences on audience members' behavior (Potter, Warren, Vaughan, Howley, Land & Hagemeyer 1997). Subsequent attempts have been made to understand the psychological appeal of reality television programs (Nabi, Biely, Morgan & Stitt 2003).

Introduction

Annette Hill (2002) examined the program *Big Brother,* concerned with authenticity and what happens when people are "really" themselves in an unreal environment. Rose & Wood (2005) suggest that reality television actually creates a form of "self-referential hyperauthenticity" for viewers to consume. Nick Couldry (2002) proposes that *Big Brother*, in particular, has dubious claim to the term "reality," and is more ritual event than accurate representation of proceedings.

Mark Andrejevic (2002) posits that the surveillance aspect of reality television has dangerous societal implications, due to the fact that it is largely presented not as social control but as democratization of *celebrity*. DeRose, Fursich, and Haskins (2003) seem to echo this sentiment, as their study of the reality show *Blind Date* suggests that the program serves to maintain hegemony in terms of race, class, and sexuality as well as "punish deviance from dominant conceptions of aesthetics, class, social, and intellectual abilities" (DeRose, Fursich & Haskins, 171).

The Problem with American Idol

The literature to date provides a strong foundation for the study of *celebrity*; however, it would appear that each of the leading theorists (Rojek and Turner, chiefly) offer an incomplete picture of *celebrity*. Returning to Graeme Turner, there may be a flaw in his analysis, or, at least, an area which the analysis is ill-prepared to deal with: how does one account for DIY *celebrity* crossing over to what Fairchild (2007) calls "authentic" *celebrity*—those perceived to embody comforting and familiar ways of 'being yourself in public?' While reality television programs provide a steady steam of celetoids for the consuming public, the Fox Television program *American Idol* has also created some incredibly successful Celebrities: Kelly Clarkson was the first *American Idol* winner; her debut album went multi-platinum[5] in seven months back in 2003. In 2006, in the same amount of time, her third album had gone three times over platinum (eventually becoming a six times platinum hit). Carrie Underwood's debut album earned the Season 4 winner a five-times-multi-platinum honor. It is not even necessary to win *American Idol* to sell millions of records; Season 5's fourth place contestant, Chris Daughtry, has the fastest-selling

Introduction

debut rock album in history, according to Nielsen Soundscan ratings — faster than either Elvis or The Beatles ("Daughtry locks down" 2007).

There may be mechanisms that help an individual evolve from celetoid to *celebrity*. One manner in which this may take place is through public performative act; the *achievement* of *celebrity* in front of an audience. If this is the case, that there is a fourth type of celebrity which is neither wholly achieved nor wholly attributed but an amalgamation of both, then how does one move from one to the other — in particular, how does one move from achieved celebrity to this fourth hybrid category? How does one go from being a "reality show contestant" to "Carrie Underwood"? What is the final product that *American Idol* creates?

In order to investigate these questions, this book proposes to examine this one specific venue of *celebrity* and ask the question: How does *celebrity* function here? How is it being generated? Are the contestants evolving from celetoid to Celebrity? How?

So What?

On the surface, some may see an in-depth study of *American Idol* as unnecessary and superfluous, at best. "*American Idol*? It's just a reality television show!" However, as will be discussed in Chapter II, the study of *celebrity* is no less than the study of the history of Western society. In turn, the study of *American Idol* is the study of how *celebrity* is made; a vital area of understanding necessary for insight into numerous aspects of American society — politics and democratic processes in particular.

American Idol draws more than 25 million viewers per episode — a number of viewers equal to the entire populations of Missouri, Maryland, Wisconsin, Minnesota, and Colorado combined, and more than the entire population of Australia. It is the single most successful television program of the last ten years. Even with a drop in ratings over the last few seasons, on its worst night, *Idol*'s ratings crush the competition. Over one billion votes have been cast in *Idol*'s seven seasons, and more than $500 million in revenue has been generated by the program and its former contestants. In 2006, *American Idol* raised $60 million for eight different charities (including America's Second Harvest and The Global Fund to Fight AIDS) through *Idol Gives Back*; in 2007, that number increased to $70 million.

Introduction

The manner in which *Idol* has dominated the television and music ratings and sales charts (respectively), combined with the positioning of *celebrity* as the central tenet of American society through which all other social constructs now flow (more on this in Chapter II) makes the study of *Idol* not only important and necessary, but temporally imperative. The time for finding out what makes the *Idol* machine so successful at creating lasting *celebrity* is *now*.

How an American Idol *Season Unfolds*

While the first three seasons of *American Idol* were formatted slightly differently, the fourth through seventh seasons followed the same structure. *Idol*'s full-time cast includes four music industry professionals: host Ryan Seacrest (a radio disc jockey and host of E! network's *E! News Daily*), and judges Simon Cowell (an A&R executive), Randy Jackson (a record producer and former bassist for Journey), and Paula Abdul (former pop music star).

Idol debuts each season with a series of episodes (four to eight episodes each season in all) cataloguing the "best and worst" auditions as the show travels the country to find the season's cast of contestants. Typically, the auditions draw thousands of people, and the viewer is led to believe each of these contestants stands before the three judges and sings.[6] The judges either tell the auditioner s/he does not possess the talent to continue in the competition, or the contestant is given a "golden ticket" to the next round of auditions. These "Hollywood Week" auditions are broadcast over three or four episodes, and consist of: an opening round, where each contestant sings a song of their own choice; a group sing round, where the contestants are placed into groups of two to five people and given a song to sing together; another solo round, where the remaining contestants sing a song with the band and backup singers; and finally, another solo round, where the contestant performs *a cappella* a song of their choice. In each of these rounds, a contestant can be eliminated by the judges immediately for a poor performance. At the end of Hollywood Week, each remaining contestant is brought individually before the judges to sit in "the chair" and is either dismissed or invited to the top 24.

Introduction

In the top 24 stage, the competition is broadcast over the course of three nights in a single week. On one night, all 12 of the female singers perform with the full band; on the other night, all 12 of the male singers perform. Following each performance, the three judges critique the contestant, who must stand on the stage alone and receive the feedback. Each performance is preceded by a video package featuring the contestant, giving some background and insight into who the performer is, his/her personality, and so forth. During those performance shows, viewers can call in (as many times as they like) or text message a vote for their favorite contestant. On Thursday, the two men and two women with the lowest number of viewer votes are eliminated. This process continues for the next two weeks until the competition is down to the top 12. Typically during these preliminary rounds, contestants are allowed to sing any song they like, and the audience and studio are small and intimate.

Once the top 12 has been established, the show moves to a larger theater, reduces its air time to only two nights per week, and the "theme nights" begin. These theme nights are organized around genres ("country night"), particular style categories ("Motown night"), or the songs of select performers ("Elvis night," or "Queen night"). Each contestant in the top 12 chooses a song from the given theme, and performs with a much larger band, a much larger stage, a much larger audience, and far more lighting/production than in the early stages. The video packages are also much longer and more elaborate. Contestants are still critiqued after every performance, and voters call or text in their votes at the end of the show. On the next night, the contestant with the lowest number of votes is eliminated.

During these semi-final rounds, the "elimination night" program normally consists of a group performance by the remaining contestants, Seacrest individually revealing whether each contestant is safe or in the "bottom three," one or more performances by guest musicians, one or more video packages of the contestants as a group, and finally, the elimination of the week's lowest-scoring contestant. The top 10 contestants are invited to perform on the summer *American Idol* live tour. The performance/elimination format continues each week until the final two contestants are established. The finale episodes are lavish affairs, with vastly increased production value, an enlarged backing band that typically

Introduction

includes a string section and a full choir, and the revealing of the year's "winner's theme song." This song becomes the winner's first released commercial single.

The season elimination finale has become one of the most highly rated television episodes of the year; the Season 7 finale drew 31.7 million viewers (Collins 2008). This episode features group performances from the entire top 10, individual performances by top 10 contestants singing duets with established music Celebrities, special Celebrity guest stars, and finally, the coronation of the season's new American Idol.

For the first three seasons of *American Idol*, a top 36 was selected by the judges, and contestants competed in a series of smaller elimination rounds in order to establish the top 12. The 36 contestants were broken into groups of 12, and each group had a week in which to perform. On the night following the performances, the top three contestants in terms of viewer votes advanced to the top 12, for a total of nine contestants. Then, there was a "wild card" round, in which the judges brought back 12 contestants they felt had been overlooked by the audience. The contestants performed, and the judges each selected a contestant who s/he felt deserved to be in the top 12. From this point, the competition continued in the same manner as every other season.[7]

Description of Research

The research problem of this book — by what mechanisms does DIY *celebrity* cross over into authentic *celebrity*? (or, more succinctly, how does a celetoid become a celebrity?) — is a vast and multifaceted issue. This book is an attempt to explore but one avenue by which the ascribing function of media may operate in relation to *celebrity* (whether that *celebrity* can be defined as *achieved, attributed,* or some fusion of the two), and to delineate the commodification process inherent in the creation of *celebrity*. Conceptually, however, the book necessarily needs to begin by putting some borders around the term *celebrity*. It's a term that everybody uses, but it means different things in different contexts, and those distinctions are *important*. Putting some walls around *celebrity* entails situating the term historically and rhetorically to better define precisely what it is that

Introduction

characterizes *celebrity*. But in order to do that, first the concept of *celebrity* must be situated within the context of popular culture as a whole.

Once the concept has been located within the realm of popular culture and specific terminology established historically and rhetorically, we can explore the attributing function of media. This model of *celebrity* will be applied to one particular instance of media: *American Idol*. *American Idol* provides an excellent arena in which to investigate *celebrity* because, at least ostensibly, the program's stated goal is to take "ordinary" people and turn a few of them into music superstars.

In order to examine the attributing processes embedded in the text (and thereby examining the ways in which meaning is made in respect to *celebrity* in this particular media instance), seven seasons of *American Idol* were textually analyzed, rhetorically and thematically.[8] An illustrative sample was collected after initially viewing the entire series with respect to the research questions. Data was analyzed under the model proposed by Roland Barthes (1981):

> We are then going to take a narrative text, and we're going to read it, as slowly as necessary, stopping as often as we have to ... and try to locate and classify ... not all the meanings of the text (which would be impossible because the text is open to infinity: no reader, no subject, no science can arrest the text) but the forms and codes according to which meanings are possible.... Our aim is not to find *the* meaning ... of the text.... Our aim is to manage to conceive, to imagine, to live the plurality of the text, the opening of its "significance" [p. 135].

To paraphrase, the sample was read, deliberately and meticulously, to discover the forms and codes by which *celebrity* is defined, generated, nurtured, and intensified in this specific instance, within this specific artifact.

Of course, textual analysis, particularly in respect to the study of television, is a prime target for criticism. As Creeber (2001) states:

> If audiences can read a text in a number of ways, then what is the validity and relevance of one textual interpretation? A textual analyst may give their reading intellectual credibility through the application of a dense theoretical discourse (like semiotics or psychoanalysis), but it is still only one interpretation among many [p. 82].

The main way to combat this criticism is to be as clear and precise as possible at the outset: this book is not an attempt to universalize a

Introduction

definition of *celebrity*, or to generalize that the manner in which *celebrity* manifests within *American Idol* is prescriptive for any other text or situation. The findings of this book are but one of many possible reading positions and interpretive conclusions that can be drawn from this particular text. The goal of this work is to suggest a model for interpreting the particular genus of *celebrity* which is manifest on *American Idol*. However, the theoretical framework, conceptual model, and data collection/analysis put forth in this book contributes to the larger network of conversations surrounding the nature and behavior of the social phenomenon we call *celebrity*, and as such, should be a valuable contribution to the growing sub-field of mass communication research that Peter Carlson calls "the infant science of celebritology" (Rein, Kotler & Stoller 2005).

But first, we need to begin at the beginning. What is *celebrity*? In order to answer that surprisingly complex question, first we need to ask, "Why talk seriously about popular culture in the first place?"

I
Ideas and Cabbages

> *In many ways, it is irrelevant to the capitalist whether his capital is in the form of ideas or cabbages.*
> P. Nesbitt-Larking, 2007, page 107

Popular Culture

What is popular culture?

A simple question, on the surface. Popular culture is culture that is popular. But popular culture is a much, much deeper subject, with roots that extend into the very core of modern society. In order to properly explicate the connections between *celebrity*, commodity, and reality television, it is necessary to — as previously stated — begin at the beginning.

The word "popular" is a derivative of the Latin word *populus*, meaning people. Popular culture is the culture of the people (although, as will be pointed out later, there is quite a good deal of argument as to *which* people). Fishwick states, "As long as there have been people, they have had stories, struggles, and culture" (2002, p. 3), and those stories, struggles, and culture have served specific sociological purposes. While all forms of culture function as a historical record of the time in which they are created and contain some measure of aesthetic quality, these are ancillary roles. As Jhally (2006) describes, "All societies seek to reproduce their constitutive social relations over time. If they cannot accomplish this, then a new set of social relations will develop, and a new type of society will emerge" (p. 47). One of the main ways in which societies maintain and replicate their "constitutive social relations" is through cultural artifacts. Therefore, the study of popular culture is the study of the production of cultural objects, the content of the objects themselves, the reception of the objects and the meanings attributed to them by the general public (Lovell).

But popular culture is not only ideologically or socially oriented. There is an inescapable economic component to popular culture as well, especially in the modern Western world. One of the foundational aspects of a capitalistic society is the disparity between those who have and those who have not. This divide between the classes bleeds over into the production and consumption of cultural objects. As Western society moved from agricultural capitalism to industrial capitalism, there was (and continues to be) a concurrent battle over culture among the wealthy elite, the working class, and the poor; this battle must be the starting point for studying popular culture (Hall, p. 442).

Popular culture is an extension of the people from whom it springs and for whom it is created. However, as Hall just pointed out, those from whom popular culture springs and those for whom it is created are not always the same people. In fact, the ability to produce and disseminate popular culture largely determines which constitutive social relations are reproduced within society.

For Antonio Gramsci, the modern state was defined by repression and control. This control could take on a multitude of forms, but were essentially broken down into two distinct categories: forces that are coercive and forces that are not coercive (1978, p. 12). Non-coercive forces are relatively benign social groups, such as the family, the church, clubs, and so forth (p. 12). Coercive forces are much more direct and malevolent, and can take the form of either physical coercion (the police, military, and judicial system can physically make individuals do what they want those individuals to do) or social coercion, wherein ideological forces press in on individuals to force compliance (Gramsci, 1978). These combined forces form the basis of domination by the ruling class.

Ideological beliefs serve to reinforce and justify the interests of the dominant group in society, and are, in fact, more important than the physical forms of coercion (Gramsci, 1978). Gramsci explained that no dominant group can maintain its status through physical coercion alone. Eventually, that group is going to have to be legitimated by the people it dominates — popular support is the only way to stay in power (benevolent dictatorships are far more effective than those ruled with an iron fist)

I. Ideas and Cabbages

(Gramsci, 1978). This popular support is achieved by cleverly manipulating the attitudes, beliefs, and practices of society until the dominant group's way of thinking becomes the "natural" way of behaving. Once the dominant group's values are fully integrated into society as the "common sense" way of doing things, it becomes much more difficult for anyone to challenge the dominant group. This cornering of the ideological market is referred to by Gramsci as *hegemony* (Gramsci, 1978).

Popular culture certainly has to be implicated as a main force by which hegemonic structures are created and maintained. In a society that is dominated by semiotics and media culture (particularly visual culture), popular media occupy a prominent (some might say, dominant) position in the dissemination of hegemonic principles. There is no aspect of the modern technological society that is not, in some way, touched by the media. Nearly every communication between human beings in contemporary Western society is mediated in some way, whether it is communication between the government and its citizens, or between the rich and the poor, or between a Celebrity and her fans. The fact that all of these processes must go through the media means that just about any text in modern society is vulnerable to manipulation by hegemonic forces. Every time one picks up a magazine, or turns on the television, or switches the station on the radio in contemporary society, one is being shown how to think, believe, and behave. One of Pierre Bourdieu's (1977) fundamental principles is that all communicative acts in modern society are inherently power relations at work. Because society is dominated by symbols and semiotic structures, those symbols and structures have a great amount of power. Symbols always benefit certain groups more than they benefit others. Therefore, those with the means to transmit their symbols while repressing the transmission of others' symbols have vastly more power within society (Bourdieu, 1977). Hall reminds us that "we can be certain that other forces ... have a stake in defining 'the people'...: 'the people' who need to be disciplined more, ruled better, more effectively policed, whose way of life needs to be protected from 'alien cultures,' and so on" (p. 453). For example, corporate America owns the television stations, the production studios, the satellite transmission and reception equipment, the broadcast machinery, and so on. It is no wonder, then, that the ideology of consumerism dominates the American popular cultural landscape.

American Idolatry

There is an implicit assumption in the phrase "popular culture." That is, "popular culture" assumes there is culture of another kind. Fishwick challenges that assumption, pointing out:

> Popular culture is as old as humanity itself. Culture has always been "popular," thriving on formula, archetypes and stereotypes, fads and follies. It is cyclic, repetitive, and powerful. Here today and gone tomorrow; just wait, it will be back in the next year, next decade, or even the next millennium. We like to think of ourselves as inventing mass production. Yet the Sumerians were mass producing funeral effigies centuries ago; so were they Egyptians, Tibetans, and Chinese. Most "new" ideas are old [p. 4].

By definition, according to Fishwick, culture *is* popular. But culture is *not only* popular. There is another central distinction within popular culture, as Hall offers:

> What is essential to the definition of popular culture is the relations which define "popular culture" in a continuing tension (relationship, influence and antagonism) to the dominant culture ... it treats the domain of cultural forms and activities as a constantly changing field [p. 449].

While popular culture is cyclic and repetitive, it is also fundamentally, capriciously mutable. Everything in popular culture is a copy of something else, and yet, everything in popular culture is under a constant state of almost random change. As the ideology of the dominant culture shifts, and as the hegemonic structures progress, popular culture adjusts to meet the demands of the consuming public.

Therefore, popular culture must be taken seriously. Especially if, like so much of cultural studies does, one ascribes to Gramsci's theories regarding hegemony. If the hegemony of the dominant culture is to be reinforced and perpetuated (or overthrown and replaced), then popular culture is the key site where the battle must take place. Hall explains that popular culture is one of the key domains in which the power struggle between the powerful and the powerless takes place, and that the stakes in that battle are incredibly high (p. 239). Popular culture matters because it is one of the major places in Western society where hegemony is both distributed and protected (p. 239).

Popular culture stands at the convergence point of politics, economics, and social practice. Although Schulman (1993) is speaking specifically

I. Ideas and Cabbages

about England, his thoughts can be extrapolated to include all of cultural studies when he says:

> Cultural studies addresses itself intensively to investigating meanings in human experience as they are realized in language and other signifying practices as well as to systematically examining institutional practices, the structure of British society, and contemporary political movements. Centering on hegemony and ideology, as they are manifested in political and educational practices, subcultures, and popular media texts, British cultural studies has applied Marxist concepts to everything from media treatments of mugging to Thatcherism [p. 63].

Thus, cultural studies, in examining the relationship between political economy, social practices, and economic realities, dramatically changes the way popular cultural media texts are engaged; "Cultural studies believes that culture matters and that it cannot simply be treated (dismissed) as the transparent — at least to the critic — public face of dominative and manipulative capitalists. Cultural studies emphasizes the complexity and contradictions, not only within culture, but in the relations between people, culture, and power" (Grossberg, 1997, p. 12). In doing so, it recognizes that popular culture is a force that must be taken quite seriously, because it serves the function of both mirror and change agent in society.

Second, it emphatically and directly rejects previously held ideas, most notably those of the Frankfurt School, that in order to study popular culture, it meant adopting "a position against and opposed to it, to view it as in need of replacement by a culture of another kind, usually 'high culture'" (Gunster, p. 174). This rejection of the necessity to oppose popular culture, and the rebuffing of the very idea that there is a "high culture" to begin with, is immediately a more inclusive stance which not only accepts, but places importance on, the social practices and artistic productions of non-dominant groups. For the Frankfurt School, culture which is popular could not possibly also be "good," not in any meaningful aesthetic, or social, or political manner. Popular culture was necessarily debased. However, as Stuart Hall points out, people are not cultural dopes (Hall, p. 232); their participation in or rejection of popular culture is based upon a deeper inner logic of cultural values and practices that are not universal and that are transitory between different populations. An individual person likes or does not like a particular form of popular culture because of who s/he is, where s/he comes from, and what unique experiences s/he has had. There is no debasement in popular culture; there is only the relationship between social practice and the social and material realities of people. People are not simply lumps of flesh waiting around for the mass-produced pap of capitalistic consumerism to help them escape from the dreariness of their paltry existence; they actually have some agency, some say in the manner in which popular culture is created and interpreted.

This is the interesting paradox within the traditional study of popular culture. Of course, the study of popular culture is not a new phenomenon; innumerable scholars have been interested in the machinations of popular culture for years, and volumes have been written on the ways in which popular culture is created, distributed, and consumed. However, as Alan McKee (2007) states:

> The everyday consumption of popular culture involves the use of popular aesthetic systems. And yet — amazingly — the intellectuals whose job it is to understand and comment on the cultures in which they live continue to know very little about these systems [p. 2].

What McKee is alluding to here is the fact that traditionally, and with few exceptions, the study of popular culture is conducted from the vantage point of observer rather than participant. Often, the more commonplace usage of the term "popular" is overlooked by those attempting to investigate popular culture. Hall echoes McKee, stating, "Take the most common-sense meaning: the things which are said to be 'popular' because masses of people listen to them, buy them, read them, consume them, and seem to enjoy them to the full" (p. 446). Popular culture is popular because *somebody* likes it; a lot of somebodies, in truth. However, too often, studies in popular culture adopt a position that this popular culture is being foisted upon an unsuspecting public which secretly clamors for something "better." McCabe (1986) explains:

> The millions who daily watch television are discounted in their torpor and their sloth, their tastes held to be of no account, artificial creations of an even more total penetration of capitalist relations of production (the Frankfurt School provides the most elaborate statement of such a position) [p. 7].

McKee goes on to explain the reason for the traditional positioning of popular culture studies, and his disdain for those who engage in this type of research is palpable:

I. Ideas and Cabbages

> For most intellectuals, popular culture is simply not their culture, and they don't know very much about it. They may know a lot about what Theodor Adorno, Stuart Hall, or Harold Bloom say about popular culture — but very little about popular culture itself [p. 2].

For example, this book is written from the perspective of one immersed in popular culture, a fan and avid viewer of the artifact at hand, someone familiar with the aesthetic systems in question. In this regard, the work brings a different point of view, not only to the literature, but to the subject of study itself than more "traditional" popular culture studies. The artifact in question — *American Idol* — is being examined from where most people read it — from the position of a fan. In doing so, this book serves as scholarship from *within* the culture. It is an insider examination of a cultural phenomenon rather than the observations of an unfamiliar outsider. In short, one should be very wary of someone who says, "I hate reality television," but cannot state a single fact about a single reality television program. The people who shout loudest about the state of popular culture are often the people who have the least practical exposure to it.

Popular Culture and Capitalism

As stated earlier, popular culture is inextricably linked to the ideology of capitalism and consumerism in modern Western society. Popular culture is the site for the eternal struggle between the ideas and symbols of the dominant class and those of the subjected classes. Marx and Engels (1956) first articulated this, stating:

> The ideas of the ruling class are in every epoch the ruling ideas, i.e., the class which is the ruling material force of society, is at the same time its ruling intellectual force. The class which has the means of material production at its disposal, has control at the same time over the means of mental production, so that thereby, generally speaking, the ideas of those who lack the means of mental production are also subject to it [p. 64].

Those who have the means to produce their ideology and distribute it are the ones who get to determine what the dominant ideologies within a society are. One of the essential tenets of capitalism as a system of social organization is the steady decrease in the number of people who have those means. Jhally states, "Capitalism is characterized by power and rewards being increasingly concentrated in the hands of those who own the means of production at the expense of the much larger group of people who own only their own labor power, which they sell in exchange for wages" (p. 47). As more power and rewards fall to fewer and fewer entities, necessarily the number and diversity of those without said power and rewards increases dramatically. Popular culture then must also diversify in order to reach those varied communities,[1] as Jordan (2006) illustrates:

> By implementing a post–Fordist strategy of diversifying their products and their marketing in order to incorporate diverse locales, media conglomerates use their marketplace power to design television shows for both a global audience and national and local niche audiences [p. 79].

Of course, television is not the only form of popular culture, but in most respects, Jordan's comment can be applied to nearly all forms of popular culture, from music to film to comic books. The principles are the same: diversify the product to appeal to the widest number of people, but also be aware of commercial opportunities in niche communities. At every turn — global, national, and local — there are opportunities to find consumers.

Consumers of Popular Culture

According to Featherstone (2007), "One of the earliest uses of the term consume meant 'to destroy, to use up, to waste, to exhaust'" (p. 21). This decidedly negative connotation of consumption seems to permeate discussions about modern Western consumer culture — because ultimately, in a capitalistic society, popular culture is necessarily consumer culture — particularly with respect to much of the critical studies literature on the subject. But that definition of consumption is, by far, not the only one. Featherstone delineates three main perspectives on consumer culture:

> 1. The view that consumer culture is premised upon the expansion of capitalist commodity production which has given rise to a vast accumulation of material culture in the form of consumer goods and sites for purchase and consumption [p. 13].

That is to say, under this perspective, that the function of popular culture is to be bought and sold, and therefore embedded within the cultural

I. Ideas and Cabbages

objects themselves are directives to buy, buy, buy (however c/overt those directives may be). This ideological concept serves the dual function of naturalizing consumerism and reinforcing the interests of the dominant group, in this case, corporate America. The commodities themselves require an expansion of the venues in which those commodities are sold, and an increase in the number of ways consumers may purchase those commodities.

John Berger (1972) is one proponent of this perspective. Popular culture "steals" the viewer's love of him/herself as s/he is, and offers to sell it back to him/her at the price of whatever the product the advertiser is selling costs (Berger, 1972). According to Berger, the media's job is to make the viewer feel vaguely dissatisfied about his/her life, and to suggest that if the viewer buys whatever the media are offering, then his/her life will be a lot better (Berger, 1972). If a viewer is constantly bombarded with messages that make the viewer vaguely dissatisfied about his/her life, then it doesn't take very much to convince that viewer that if s/he owned this thing, moved to this place, ate at this restaurant, vacationed at this destination, s/he would be happier/better/cooler/more lovable than s/he is right now. Media, according to Berger, play on that fear that has been ideologically engrained in modern Western individuals since birth — fear that they will be nothing. And if they have nothing, certainly that means they are nothing. But, with consumer culture, it is always the vague promise of some future happiness. Right now, life is not happy. But it *could* be. Later. Consume the commodities and happiness will follow.

> 2. The satisfaction derived from goods relates to their socially structured access in a zero-sum game in which satisfaction and status depend upon displaying and sustaining differences within conditions of inflation (the ways in which people use goods in order to create social bonds or distinctions) [Featherstone, p. 13].

Ascribing to this perspective are those who believe the ultimate purpose of popular culture is to delineate social groups. According to Pierre Bourdieu, modern Western societies have constructed two discrete systems of social stratification. First, as earlier described, there are economic strata — social position and distribution of power and influence are established based on the accumulation of money and property — capital. Secondly, there is a system that is cultural or symbolic. Social hierarchy, under this secondary system, is established based on the amount of cultural or symbolic "capital" one can generate (Bourdieu, 1977). This symbolic capital is then used to differentiate one's self from everyone else. Popular culture, therefore, becomes a key instrument of domination — within society, there are those who assume the roles of cultural producers and arbiters of symbolic power — and allows those specialists to argue that taste, an acquired "cultural competence," legitimizes social differences. Bourdieu (1984) states:

> Taste classifies, and it classifies the classifier. Social subjects, classified by their classifications, distinguish themselves by the distinctions they make, between the beautiful and the ugly, the distinguished and the vulgar, in which their position in the objective classifications is expressed or betrayed [p. 6].

Taste, therefore, becomes the gatekeeper that enforces class boundaries.

> 3. The question of the emotional pleasures of consumption, the dreams and desires which become celebrated in consumer cultural imagery and particular sites of consumption which variously generate direct bodily excitement and aesthetic pleasures [Featherstone, p. 13].

Under this perspective, there is no great secret about popular culture; as Ted Magder (2004) points out, "The business of television begins with a simple observation: people like to watch" (p. 141). Popular culture's main purpose is to be enjoyed, in whatever form that enjoyment manifests. Television is an excellent example of this; television represents nearly half of all time North Americans invest in media and/or cultural events, and the average U.S. household consumes a little more than 1,600 hours of television every year (p. 141). However, aesthetic pleasure is not unique to television viewing, nor does this perspective necessarily attach any sort of relativity to the nature of the aesthetic pleasure. Richard Collins (1990) offers:

> If a group experiences aesthetic pleasure in a hockey game (probably using such honorific terms as "exciting," "fun," "entertaining"), their judgments and choice have a comparable status to that of another group designating its experience of viewing Rembrandt's *The Night Watch* (and using a different honorific vocabulary as aesthetic [p. 264].

Of course, there are those who wish to stratify and categorize aesthetic pleasure into "high" and "low" forms of culture; however, for purposes of this discussion, such distinctions are not entirely relevant. The main point is that this perspective sees popular culture as a source of gratification, whatever the supposed quality of that gratification may be.[2]

Like most theories which deal with popular culture, none of these three perspectives is (most likely) as accurate as the fusion of all three perspectives into a coherent whole. None of the three perspectives are mutually exclusive, and all encapsulate a facet of popular culture. Taken together, they provide a fairly accurate picture of modern popular culture: corporately- and privately-produced commodities provide enjoyment and pleasure to both mass and niche audiences, which, in turn, create and maintain class differences based on the relative consumption of those commodities.

Cultural Commodities

It has been established that popular culture is consumer culture, and because of this, popular culture is also unavoidably commodity culture. This means that the economic aspects of the production of cultural products have a direct impact on the aesthetic and symbolic components of those cultural products. Nesbitt-Larking (2007) states:

> It matters a great deal that the means of media production belong to a tiny handful of individuals and that ownership is considered an absolute and unquestioned right. The forces of media production must be upgraded and innovated in order that the media as businesses remain sufficiently profitable. This leads inexorably to a process of economic failure, takeovers, acquisitions, and consolidations [p. 106].

Those economic struggles lead corporate culture producers to weigh the financial concerns of profitability against the aesthetic and symbolic concerns of artistic production. Cultural products must not only resonate with the public, but they must also be economically competitive. Capitalism fundamentally requires the maximization of profits at the expense of other products. It requires a commodity to literally defeat all other products for the attention and capital of consumers. It is the fundamental dichotomy of capitalism: on one hand, in order to generate new profits, the capitalist has to find new markets for his products; however, the capitalist also has to eradicate all competition for his product, because competition represents a risky loss in profits (Jordan, p. 79). So even though competition drives change in the capitalist economic system, in truth, concentration is the safest capitalist strategy (p. 79).

The necessity to compete and to defeat rival commodities inevitably pushes commodity producers toward concentration. The best way to ensure dominance of one's commodity is to eliminate all other competition — acquisition of the competitor removes that competitor from the market, freeing up attention that might otherwise have been diverted. Jordan elaborates:

> A mode of production designed to multiply capital by ceaselessly cultivating new markets inevitably gravitates towards concentration of ownership because of its relentless drive for profit [p. 80].

This duality of purpose in cultural production — symbolic and economic — has a profound impact on the nature and composition of the *meaning* of popular cultural objects. Regardless of whether that meaning is intrinsic to the cultural object itself or formulated in the interpretation of that object, it is always rooted in class struggle; popular culture is merely another venue for fighting the economic struggle (McCabe, p. 4).

However, the duality of cultural production is not an equal enterprise, especially in contemporary America. As a culture which is entirely dependent upon capitalism for the constitution of social relations, there is a sort of gloomy inevitability about popular culture: eventually, all cultural production will be based on economics rather than on aesthetics. Jhally refers to this as "real subsumption," explaining:

> Real subsumption refers to a situation in which the media become not ideological institutions but primarily economic ones. That is, investment in media is not for the purpose of ideological control but is for the purpose of reaping the biggest return. Culture is produced first and foremost as commodity rather than as ideology [p. 52].

Aesthetic or symbolic quality is forced to take a back seat to economic and financial return. Producers (capitalists) simply cannot afford to take as many risks artistically when they are concerned about how well those commodities will be able to compete for economic capital. Bill Ryan (1991) asserts:

> Because of the uncertainty of the cultural marketplace, companies tend to overcompensate by the overproduction of new releases. This appears as the

I. Ideas and Cabbages

> "throw it up against the wall and see if it sticks" or the "buckshot" philosophy of product release. The difficulty confronting all cultural commodities are caught in the ebb and flow of fashion, with market demand constantly shifting under the impact of competition and the flood of new releases it generates. To stay ahead, companies are forced to release a range of releases covering several genres and/or stars in the hope that one will become a best seller [p. 59].

This is not necessarily the case for other types of products in other venues or spheres of society. It is fairly easy to determine if one kitchen knife is better than another; it may be sharper, or more durable, or more flexible than another kitchen knife. "Better" is always a problematic term when dealing with cultural production. This is an obstacle inherent in the commodity form; cultural artifacts are unique because they don't satisfy material needs, but psychological wants; Marx's commodity analysis was more concerned with the former (Lovell, p. 476).

There is no way to determine when such a want has been satiated by a product, other than to ask the consumer directly. The satisfaction is of an individual kind; each person brings with him his own rubric for determining when a cultural product has fulfilled his need. A brick has fulfilled its need for the consumer when it is used to build a house or a wall. When has a television show fulfilled its need for the consumer? There is no inherent connection between the utility of a cultural commodity and the commodity's physical form (Lovell, p. 477).

The value of, for example, a Public Enemy concert tour T-shirt is not necessarily in the fact that it covers one's body. Any T-shirt could fulfill that need. The usefulness to the consumer stems from what the T-shirt represents: a connection to a particular ideology, membership in a community (in this case, a community of those who are knowledgeable about old-school rap music), and a verification of having "been there." Featherstone explains, "The practices of consumption, the planning, purchase, and display of consumer goods and experiences in everyday life cannot be understood merely via conceptions of exchange value and instrumental rational calculation" (p. 84). There is more to the consumption of cultural products than the simple commodity form. Cultural objects *mean* something; they have inherent symbolic and cultural capital that extends beyond their economic situation.

American Idolatry

It is not as if cultural products are placed into circulation and are immediately gobbled up by an insatiable, indiscriminate public. The hegemonic position intrinsic in mass-produced cultural products is not hidden; consumers fully understand the products they are being sold as they purchase those objects. Hall notes that since people are not "cultural dopes," they are absolutely able to understand how their lives are restructured and remodeled by the way in which popular culture represents ("i.e., re-present[s]") them; it is one of the unique powers of the culture industries to choose, repeat, force, and embed characterizations of people that fall in line with the ideals of the preferred or dominant culture (p. 447).

Every cultural product radiates a particular ideology or connection to a particular set of ideas and values. Wearing that article of clothing or that brand of perfume or driving that kind of car says something about who a person is and what s/he believes in. Featherstone states:

> The modern individual within consumer culture is made conscious that he speaks not only with his clothes, but with his home, furnishings, interior decoration, car and other activities which are to be read and classified in terms of the presence and absence of taste [p. 84].

Returning to Bourdieu for a moment, this presence or absence of taste is used as an arbitrary border delineating particular social classes from others. So, not only do cultural products have an economic and symbolic value, there is also a social value to the consumption of certain products over others. This is a second-order definition fundamental to the understanding of modern consumption: "Consumption ... must not be understood as the consumption of use-values, a material utility, but primarily as the consumption of signs" (Featherstone, p. 83).

Because this particular brand of usefulness is not inherent in the physical form of the commodity (the usefulness could just as easily be contained in a button, a baseball cap, a concert poster), it is difficult to determine which commodity form would best satisfy the need of the consumer. This is doubly difficult for commodities which have no tangible commodity form, such as music or film. Yes, you can download an .mp3 or purchase a DVD and in a sense possess the cultural object, but possession is not necessarily ownership. You may possess an .mp3 of "99 Problems," but that is simply a replica of the cultural object, not the cultural object itself. Even if you were able to somehow go get Jay-Z, bring the

I. Ideas and Cabbages

artist into your home, and get him to perform "99 Problems," you still do not own the cultural object. The song is intangible; it is impossible to physically own.

This intangibility has its positive side, however. A song cannot be "used up." There is no way to "run out of" a film. The commodity form may become increasingly rare to find (The Beatles' *White Album* on vinyl, for example, or an original stock print of *Citizen Kane*), but the cultural object itself can be indefinitely replicated. Therefore, once the want is satisfied in the consumer, the cultural object is available again and again to satisfy that want whenever it may return. Lovell explains, "[Cultural wants] are unlike material wants, in that the commodities which satisfy them are not always used up when they are used to satisfy that want" (p. 476). Another added benefit is that, because the cultural object cannot be used up, it is available for distribution to a nearly infinite number of consumers. A television show, for example, is a "public good"; it has a fixed cost, and that cost is the same whether one person watches it (consumes the commodity) or a thousand people or three million people (Jordan, p. 87). The amount of available program doesn't decrease just because one person watches it — in fact, the more people that consume the commodity, the more cost-effective and profitable the program becomes (p. 87). It is easier to sell an advertiser on a program that is popular than one nobody watches.

The ability to sell a particular cultural product to numerous consumers simultaneously is the entire foundation of the modern American television programming system. Television stations package audiences into demographic groups and sell them to advertisers. Advertisers receive air time; networks receive capital. The inherent durability of the intangible cultural object works in the favor of the networks, because there is literally almost no limit to the number of viewers a network can conceivably deliver. Although Lovell is, here, discussing paintings and sculptures, his comments could just as easily be applied to television programs or feature films or Top 40 hit singles:

> Cultural artifacts vary in the extent to which their usefulness in satisfying wants which "spring from the fancy" is bound up with physical form. Such artifacts, such as paintings or sculptures, wear out over a very long time, and there is no direct connection between their use and their being used up. The

American Idolatry

> Mona Lisa does not wear out more quickly when viewed by a hundred people rather than one in the course of a day [p. 477].

There is an intrinsic consequence to intangible, infinitely reproducible cultural commodities, though. Because there is no real way to predict whether a particular cultural object will satisfy the needs of the consuming public, and because the producers of cultural objects are forced into a scattershot approach to production in the hopes that at least one of the products they produce will resonate with consumers, once one product succeeds, there is almost instantly a rush to copy that product. For example, a successful television show can basically be guaranteed that in the next season, there will be multiple shows attempting to use the same format to garner ratings. Following the resounding success of the first season of *Survivor*, no less than a dozen "clone" programs were slated for air in the following fall programming season (Raftery, 2000). This rush to capitalize on the success of others makes innovation in the cultural production industry a risky and rare event. Ryan explains that

> new releases must be made to impact on the market immediately upon release. Since familiarity undercuts the originality of a new cultural commodity and familiarity itself is a function of time, manufacturers must attempt to make the immediate rate of sales growth accelerate as fast as possible following product launch. All other things being equal, the faster the rate, the higher the peak before the inevitable downturn [p. 58].

Producers simply cannot always afford to take a risk on a product that may bomb with consumers; yes, there is the occasional surprise hit that generates a faithful fan base, but the television industry doesn't run on surprise hits. It runs on routine (Magder, 143). The evidence remains that new cultural objects that resemble/replicate old, successful cultural objects sell more reliably than new cultural objects that are actually new.

However, although producers want to exploit familiarity as much as possible, so too must they make the new product appear as fresh as it can. Because of this, there must be a constant stream of new products on the market. A cultural object cannot be allowed to sit on the shelves too long. If it is unsuccessful, it must be immediately removed and replaced with something else. This places artists in a sort of creative prison: be imaginative, but only within these parameters; make this new program look like this old program, but not *too* much like it. Ryan continues:

I. Ideas and Cabbages

> Companies must organize production to generate a constant flow of originals to the reproduction process: they are locked into recurrent cycles of production. This means constant cycles of reinvestment in artistic labor, an imperative which also interacts with the organizational irrationalities of creativity. Companies must sign a stable of artists to maintain a flow of originals and plan production to have originals constantly in development [p. 58].

The real subsumption of the creative process makes it difficult for artists to break free with anything that is truly aesthetically autonomous. The mode of production of cultural objects within a capitalistic consumer culture generally follows thus:

> Capitalist producers of ... products must make and sell commodities which embody ... use-values if they are to succeed in meeting the wants which they satisfy, and through doing so, generating surplus-value. The producer must "give the public what it wants..." [Lovell, p. 481].

However, at the core of that sentiment is the salability of the cultural object; if it happens to also have artistic merit, so much the better. Jhally states:

> The system of exchange value (worth) subordinates use value (meaning). Television programs look like they do, not because this is the best that the American artistic community can come up with, but because programs have a role to play in the production and exchange of audiences [p. 59].

As noted earlier, especially in the realm of television production, viewers are often seen only as a string of ratings numbers and demographics. Efficiency often takes precedence over artistic merit.[3] Magder affirms that

> it is wrong to say that TV in the United States gives people what they most want to watch, or that it responds to the demands, interest, and needs of viewers. Instead, given the interests of advertisers and the habits of TV viewing, television executives often try to produce or schedule shows that are only marginally better than the other offerings available at the same time. The goal of U.S. television is to give people programming that they are willing to watch or, at the very least, programming from which they will not turn away [p. 143].

In this respect, the "best" cultural product is the product which draws the most consumers for the least amount of cost and effort on the part of the producers. The down side of this is, of course, that many times, producers fail to produce that "from which consumers will not turn away," and the results are a dismal cultural landscape. This is not only true of television; in fact, most cultural objects, from film to comic books to music, could be similarly categorized. As Jhally relates:

> The popular music industry is commodified through and through. It produces and sells records, and the survival of musicians and artists is dependent on whether they can produce profit for record companies. This is dependent upon their success within the commodity marketplace, not just on the quality of their performances [p. 57].

Ultimately, cultural objects must sell. And, as Jordan offers, "...the media marketplace is prone to failure because the constant drive for profit that defines the logic of capital results in a restricted range of media output" (p. 80).

Popular Culture and Political Economy

In the real subsumption world of modern popular culture, you should be disabused of any notions you may have about the "marketplace of ideas." As pointed out by Magder earlier, when all cultural production becomes economic transaction, aesthetic autonomy is subjugated to financial concern. Not only that, but mass produced cultural objects serve the second (but not necessarily secondary) purpose of reproducing and legitimating hegemonic positions of dominance by certain segments of society. Jhally affirms:

> The media are vital institutions that, far from providing a free marketplace of ideas, work to legitimate the existing distribution of power by controlling the context within which people think and define social problems and their possible solutions [p. 47].

The media are not innocent bystanders in a system of social stratification and hegemonic authority. They are active, integral participants. As discussed earlier by Pierre Bourdieu, symbolic relations are always power relations. So, too, are economic relations always power relations; as Berger highlights, "The power to spend money is the power to live" (p. 143). These power relations permeate capitalism as a system of social organization. Nesbitt-Larking states, "Capitalism is an economic system but it is also a system of social relations and political power" (p. 103).

I. Ideas and Cabbages

Earlier it was discussed that no dominant class can ever maintain its position of authority and power by dominion alone. This is especially true in a capitalistic consumer society. Jhally explains:

> For societies, such as capitalism, that are characterized by a wide disparity in the distribution of wealth and power, the vital questions of reproduction concern how a minority but dominant social class (capitalists) can maintain power over the vast majority of the population. There are two ways in which this reproduction can be accomplished. First, by sheer force (the use of the police and military). Second, reproduction can be accomplished through the consent of the dominated, by convincing the majority to identify with and to support the present system of rewards and power rather than opposing it, in fact to live their own domination as freedom [p. 47].

This second form of reproduction/domination encapsulates the media's role in legitimating social power relations. In many respects, the media primarily exist to produce and circulate meaning as well as capital — a political economy as well as symbolic and financial economies. Bourdieu, by way of Marx and Engels, earlier demonstrated that whoever controls the resources of symbolic production and distribution controls which ideas and values will be dominant in society. Nicholas Garnham continues along these lines:

> A delimited social group, pursuing economic or political ends, determines which meanings circulate and which do not, which stories are told about what, which arguments are given prominence and what cultural resources are made available and to whom. The analysis of this process is vital to an understanding of the power relationships involved in culture and their relationship to wider structures of domination [as cited in Calabrese, 2004, p. 2].

However, there are two wrinkles, if you will, in what might seem to be a completely unchallengeable position of supremacy by the dominant social class. First, media production and distribution have been somewhat democratized with the advent of the personal digital camcorder and widespread access to distribution venues on the Internet. Literally any person with a camera and an Internet connection can be a media producer; every minute, ten hours of video footage is uploaded to YouTube ("You Tube Fact Sheet" n.d.). Second, media have an ability to be counter-hegemonic, due to the niche nature of the commodity market. The main goal for the producers of cultural commodities is to sell those objects. As the proliferation of T-shirts featuring the silhouette of Ché Guevara, the success of films like *Fahrenheit 9/11*, and the history of popularity of bands from The Kinks to Rage Against the Machine attests, counterculture also sells, and sells well. When the ultimate end is economic capital, it does not always matter whether the product affirms the dominant culture's positions; in fact, cultural commodities are apt to articulate a wide range of ideas, values, and emotions, and only some of those will be representative of the dominant ideology (Lovell, p. 482). Many will actually represent class objectives that are adverse or even hostile toward capitalism (p. 482). Ryan agrees: "Understood in political-economic terms, there are different types of cultural commodities, each requiring specific systems of circulation" (p. 61). Cultural commodities which are produced by/for niche markets outside of the ideological reach of the dominant class require specialized distribution venues. (A corner vinyl shop in an urban environment usually bears little resemblance to a massive chain outlet like Virgin Records; comic book stores continue to cater to a certain type of collector despite avenues of distribution such as Barnes and Noble. The type of goods sold in these smaller niche outlets is also often significantly different than those sold in the larger chain venues.) However, as might be inferred from the terms "counter-hegemonic" and "counterculture," this type of product with originations in the subjected classes are the exception rather than the rule of cultural objects. In general, it could be said that this is the point of exploring a political economy of cultural objects. As Calabrese states, "A political economy of culture can claim to know which meanings do or do not circulate, which stories are told, and which arguments are most prominent as a result of inequality in the social relations of production" (p. 9). A political economy of (popular) culture must always keep in mind that there *are* alternative voices and alternative points of view, and that those alternatives *are* being distributed and consumed — just not to the extent of the cultural objects which serve as hegemonic devices.

But why is this important? What difference does a political economy of culture make? The answer is complicated. First, a political economy of culture challenges the notion that popular culture is foisted upon an unsuspecting public who then has no choice but to consume it. Second, it also challenges the idea that all popular culture is created equal, and that consumers cannot (or do not want to) tell the difference between cultural objects. Third, as will be discussed in a moment, examining a political economy of popular culture challenges the long-held view of some that popular culture cannot possibly contain anything of real value. McKee (2007) argues that

> the assumption that consumers of popular culture are indiscriminate seems to rest on the following chain of reasoning: these people consume trash; it is not possible that anybody could make an informed decision to choose trash rather than high culture; therefore they are not making informed decisions. But this syllogism doesn't follow. It assumes that it is not possible for aesthetic systems to exist against whose criteria trash might be judged as "good" culture. And this is wrong [p. 8].

The consumption of popular culture necessarily involves the use of aesthetic systems to determine which products will be consumed and which will be disregarded and discarded. The most important thing to remember about popular culture and political economy is that the consumption of popular culture begins with *choice*, and that choice involves informed decision-making. It is very easy to look in from outside a particular social group and pass judgment on their cultural object choices. However, to do so does disservice to the intellectual and aesthetic agency of those consumers. McKee (2007) continues:

> The consumers of popular culture already have aesthetic systems in place, which play a part in the intellectual work involved in making decisions about which trashy magazines to buy, which vulgar television programs to view, which dirty websites to visit. We may not approve of everything that they consume — but we can't leap from that fact to a claim that therefore there is no discrimination involved in their choices [p. 11].

In essence, it is clear that *someone* is watching, for example, *American Idol* — a lot of someones — and judging from the sales of CDs and other merchandise released by the contestants, someone is making a determination that those products are pretty good. From a political economy standpoint, in many respects, whether or not those outside of that consumer community agree about the quality of those products is largely irrelevant.

Commodity Culture: Reality Television

Annette Hill (2005) writes, "Popular series such as *American Idol* in the USA ... have attracted up to and over 50 percent of the market share, which means more than half the population of television viewers tuned into these programs" (p. 2). In some respects, Adorno portended the advent of reality television. Reality television is a sort of triumph of the culture industry: completely manufactured, often banal, and not always requiring full cognitive participation, reality television is concerned with capital first and aesthetics after. Murray & Ouellette (2004) write:

> We define reality TV as an unabashedly commercial genre united less by aesthetic rules or certainties than by the fusion of popular entertainment with a self-conscious claim to the discourse of the real [p. 2].

Note the use of the terms "often," and, "not always." Not all reality television is created equal. However, that doesn't stop critics of the genre from pretending as though every reality program is the same as all other reality programs. As Hill explains, "Since the early days of reality programming, critics have consistently attacked the genre for being voyeuristic, cheap, sensational television" (p. 7). In fact, according to Hill,

> In a UK report for the Campaign for Quality Television in 2003, reality TV was singled out by Michael Tracey of the University of Colorado as the "stuff of the vulgate," encouraging "moral and intellectual impoverishment in contemporary life." Robert Thompson of Syracuse University suggests that reality TV is popular because it is "stupid and moronic." Broadcaster Nick Clarke argues in his book *The Shadow of a Nation* that the popularity of reality TV has led to a dangerous blurring of boundaries between fact and fiction, and as a result reality TV has had a negative effect on modern society [p. 7].

In short, reality television is awful; it is "stupid" and "moronic," and only an idiot would find pleasure in it.

However, this point of view is problematic. As Hill points out, "To say that all reality TV is stupid and moronic is to ignore the development of the genre over the past decade" (p. 7). Yes, there are reality television programs that could easily be classified as the "stuff of the vulgate," but the same could be said for segments of any cultural medium. Even if one chooses to accept the premise of the high/low culture debate (a premise which, quite frankly, is patently ludicrous in its utter elitism and disregard for the aesthetic codes and practices of the "subclass"), there are examples of reality television that are far from stupid.

For instance, the television program *So You Think You Can Dance,*

I. Ideas and Cabbages

while couched in the trappings of, and inextricably linked to, the tropes and ideology of competitive reality television as a whole and Fremantle Entertainment's particular construction of competitive reality television in particular, has made a particular point of exposing its audience to both formal, traditional forms of dance and cutting edge, *avant garde* modern dance. Yes, the audience is pulled into a battle for affection in which its voting loyalties are bartered for among a group of attractive young dancers. However, while this is taking place, so too is the *paso doble,* the fox trot, and the Viennese and smooth waltz, all decidedly "*serious* culture" in the taxonomy of dance. But, for cultural critics like Theodor Adorno, for example, also note that content is not necessarily the marker of seriousness; intellectual engagement is.

With *So You Think You Can Dance*, choreographers like Wade Robson are concurrently taking modern dance to its most progressive and recondite places. Robson's affinity for aesthetic dissonance, taking those attractive dancers to a place of deliberate ugliness in costuming, makeup, music, and movement, is as challenging visually and artistically as any company in the world is currently performing. Viewers tuning in to participate in a relatively low-confrontation experience, such as a program like *Dancing With the Stars* presents,[4] are instead shocked into a more exigent space in which green-painted, seaweed-covered daemons cavort about in bizarre, awkward movements to Tom Waits' *2:19.* This is dance which rejects the standard societal notions of beauty, instead finding its own criterion for aesthetic pleasure in that which society deems disturbing. Theodor Adorno wrote:

> The countless agencies of mass production and its culture impress standardized behavior on the individual as the only natural, decent, and rational one... Everything which is different, from the idea to criminality, is exposed to the force of the collective [Horkheimer & Adorno, p. 22].

In distinction, pieces on *So You Think You Can Dance* from Wade Robson, Shane Sparks, Tyce D'Orio, and Mia Michaels stand in stark contrast, using standardized, rational conceptions of beauty in movement and appearance not as the foundation of their dances, but as the Other against which the dances are distinguished. The collective is jarringly forced from its comfort zone — one of the classic indicators of artistic merit. Ray notes:

True, the culture industry can simulate art's autonomy and invoke the pretence of its promise of happiness. But the fact that the art institutions are still here and still produce a functional, if enfeebled, autonomy suggests that what the culture industry offers is not a good enough substitute to really fool anybody. Mere entertainment distracts but falls short of the more challenging and effective compensations offered by art under capitalism, even if it has become more difficult to determine where one ends and the other begins [p. 243].

Programs such as *So You Think You Can Dance* take this theory one step farther, in that this product with origination within the culture industry offers more than "mere entertainment" (a problematic phrase in and of itself, as it presupposes entertainment somehow has no cultural value), with a level of challenge and effective compensation beyond traditional television fare. It operates both inside and outside of "art under capitalism," with one foot in the art world and one foot in the culture industry. Adorno wrote that:

> Amusement congeals into boredom, since, to be amusement, it must cost no effort ... the product prescribes each reaction, not through any actual coherence — which collapses once exposed to thought — but through signals. Any logical connection presupposing mental capacity is scrupulously avoided [Horkheimer & Adorno, p. 109].

So You Think You Can Dance patently rejects this notion, and is not only designed to encourage attention instead of boredom, but requires — demands — mental presence and aesthetic acumen in order to fully understand its merits. In short, you can put the show on while you do the dishes if you want to, but if you want to actually understand what's going on, you have to watch it. Carefully.

The important thing to remember here is that reality television programs cannot be lumped into one group; there are subgenres within the larger category of "reality television" that can be broken up into a typology of eight different "reality archetypes":

Sports and Sports Entertainment: Traditional sporting events fall under this category, including football, basketball, soccer, and so forth. Sports Entertainment covers professional wrestling, martial arts exhibitions, and the like.

News Magazine and Crime: The News Magazine and/or Crime cate-

I. Ideas and Cabbages

gory includes standard news magazine format programs such as *20/20* and *48 Hours*, but also contains pseudo-documentaries like *Cops* and *America's Most Wanted*.

Game Shows: Traditional game shows such as *Jeopardy!* and *Wheel of Fortune*, as well as new-breed game shows like *Who Wants to be a Millionaire?* and *Deal or No Deal* make up this category.

Instructional/DIY: Do-it-yourself and instructional shows range from home-improvement programs, such as *This Old House* and *Trading Spaces*, to cooking shows, like *30 Minute Meals* or *Essence of Emeril*, to a wide variety of other programs which provide step-by-step instruction.

Dating: Dating shows follow a variety of formats, but generally involve the formation of romantic relationships. Shows such as *The Bachelor*, *Next*, and even *Flavor of Love* are examples of this archetype.

Situational Living: The long-time staple of reality television, situation living shows such as *The Real World* simply place cameras in a house or apartment, and voyeuristically broadcast the happenings within.

Observatory Competition: Observatory Competition shows entail a variety of competitions in which the audience may only watch the events unfold without any direct influence. *Survivor* and *The Amazing Race* are examples.

Participatory Competition: American Idol, Dancing with the Stars, American Inventor, and other programs where the audience has a direct effect on the outcome of the competition (through telephone or online voting) make up this category.

The remainder of this book will focus on competitive reality television programs, and participatory competitive reality television programs in specific. Why participatory competitive reality television programs? Participatory competitive reality television programs embody Daniel Boorstin's definition of the "pseudo-event," and as Boorstin's theory is one of the seminal theories upon which the study of modern celebrity is founded, it seems a good place to begin. Boorstin defines a "pseudo-event" through four criteria: the event occurs, not through natural happenstance, but because it has been arranged, instigated, or planned by someone to occur; the event is instigated to be "reported or reproduced ... its success is measured by how widely it is reported ... time relations in it are commonly fictitious" (p. 11); a discussion of the event almost certainly contains an element of "whether it really happened" (p. 11); and the event is designed to be a "self-fulfilling prophecy" (p. 12). Participatory competitive reality television programs normally fulfill all four requirements. For example, let's consider *American Idol*.

American Idol

Cecile Frot-Coutaz, executive producer of *Idol*, has said, "It's a very simple show.... It's about, it's trying to find the next kind of great singer, and it's about the American dream. It's about taking people who live a normal life in some remote part of the country, but have an amazing talent, discovering that talent and making the dream come true. I think there's something very powerful about that" (Huff, p. 124). A lot of people over the years have apparently agreed. *American Idol* has been a ratings juggernaut since its beginning. As Hill (2005) reports:

> In 2002, the finale of the reality talent show *American Idol* attracted 23 million viewers, and a market share of 30 percent, with almost half the country's teenage female viewers tuning in to watch the show. In January 2003, *American Idol* drew nearly 25 million viewers two nights running, making it "the most watched non-sports show in the network's history" [p. 3].

American Idol's lineage began in the United Kingdom. On October 5, 2001, the British television station ITV1 debuted a radical new television program called *Pop Idol*. The idea was simple: a nationwide talent show in which viewers would select the next big new singer in the United Kingdom. Created by music producer Simon Fuller in 1998, his company, 19 Entertainment, launched *Pop Idol* to high ratings in the UK, and quickly moved to export the show overseas.

American Idol debuted on Fox Network on June 11, 2002, to 9.9 million viewers. That number increased by the season finale to more than 23 million viewers ("The Nielson Company" 2008). On January 16, 2007, *American Idol* debuted to 41.84 million viewers — more than seven times the number of viewers of its closest competitor, *Law and Order: Criminal Intent* (Berman 2007).

Kelly Clarkson was the first *American Idol* winner; her debut album

I. Ideas and Cabbages

went multi-platinum in seven months back in 2003. In 2006, in the same amount of time, her third album had sold three million copies, eventually becoming a six times multi-platinum hit. Carrie Underwood's debut album netted the Season 4 winner a five times multi-platinum honor. It is not even necessary to win *American Idol* to sell millions of records; Season 5's fourth-place contestant, Chris Daughtry, has the fastest-selling debut rock album in history, according to Nielsen Soundscan ratings ("Daughtry Once Again" 2007).

American Idol is a ratings powerhouse to be certain. Carter (2007) describes competing network executives in much the same manner as a fan of horror novelist Stephen King might describe his latest novel:

> Once a year an unrelenting monster invades a town, and all the townspeople, cowed by years of being crushed under its massive claws, have to pay it fealty or run off and hide until it goes back into a six-month hibernation [para. 1].

In fact, other networks have even taken to programming away from *Idol*, since even well-established series have had difficulty competing. Carter goes on to report that ABC moved one of its flagship programs, *Lost*, from 9 P.M. on Wednesday to 10 P.M. in order to avoid direct competition with *Idol* (para. 19). In fact, on condition of anonymity (due to the network's wishes not to publicly admit *Idol*'s dominance), one senior network executive "said the shadow *American Idol* casts was so formidable that 'we have *Idol* strategy sessions'" (para. 19).

In terms of ratings, *American Idol* is the 500-pound gorilla of television — all other programs simply try to stay out of its way and avoid the destruction it can cause.

Of course, all of this success in the ratings translates to dollars through advertising revenue. For the 2007 spring television season, purchasing a 30-second advertising spot during *American Idol* cost more than $600,000 ("American Idol Highest" 2007), meaning each episode generated more than $9 million of revenue per half hour. Given that *Idol* airs three times a week for at least one hour per episode (often, especially during the audition and early competition episodes, two hours at a time), *Idol* is generating enormous income for Fox. In fact, the season finale of Season 5, in which Taylor Hicks competed against Katherine McPhee for the crown, drew $1.3 million for a 30-second advertising spot ("American Idol Highest" 2007).

American Idolatry

American Idol represents a particular convergence between political, symbolic, and capital economies. First, to become a top twenty contestant on *Idol*, one very literally has to sell him/herself completely to Fremantle/19 Entertainment. Huff writes:

> As part of their deals to appear on *American Idol*, the winner's first album is produced by and released by record companies associated with the producers. The show producers control what songs and the direction they'll take early on. Anyone making it into the top 10 of *American Idol* is signed to a deal for future work [p. 124].

American Idol winners are contractually obligated to sing the songs *Idol*'s companion companies want them to sing and release the albums *Idol*'s companion companies want them to release. The producer of *American Idol* owns one of these companion companies. Morgan Summerfield (2006) reports:

> Winners of *American Idol* competitions receive a recording contract from 19 Entertainment, owned by founder of the *American Idol* show Simon Fuller. Simon Cowell, one of the judges for the show, stated in an interview with Copley News Service in February of 2004, "I own the recording rights — the winners and other contestants sign with my label" [para. 4].

However, the control of 19 Entertainment does not stop at recording opportunities; "19 Entertainment not only controls their recording contracts, but every other aspect of their careers including merchandising touring, sponsorship and movie deals" (Summerfield, para. 4). Contestants have very little free will under the terms of the contract they sign with 19 Entertainment. For example, just prior to the anniversary of September 11, the *New York Times* wrote that Kelly Clarkson wanted to back out of singing the national anthem at the Lincoln Memorial because she had been criticized by friends and media outlets for turning the national day of mourning into a publicity stunt (Olsen 2002). Clarkson responded, "I think it is a bad idea.... If anybody thinks I'm trying to market anything, well, that's awful ... I am not going to do it" (quoted in Olsen 2002). Later in the same *Times* article, 19 Entertainment's Tom Ennis assured everyone he would "allay Ms. Clarkson's concerns and that she would sing the anthem on Sept. 11" (quoted in Olsen 2002)—and sing she did.

Participants are also locked into a long and labyrinthine confidentiality agreement which states that disclosing anything about the inner work-

I. Ideas and Cabbages

ings of *American Idol* or about the contract *Idol* made them sign could result in damages of upwards of five million dollars (Olsen 2002). In addition, the recording company, the management company, and the merchandising company are all owned and operated by 19 Group, which Olsen calls a "fundamental conflict of interest" to anyone who understands the way the music industry operates (Olsen 2002). Contestants must also sign away their right to negotiate the contract with 19 Entertainment and BMG Music. However, contestants sign away far more than their rights to negotiation. An actual excerpt from the contract reads:

> I hereby grant the Producer the unconditional right throughout the universe in perpetuity to use, simulate, or portray my name, likeness, voice, singing voice, personality, personal identification or personal experiences, my life story, biographical data, incidents, situations, events which heretofore occurred or hereafter occur...

Essentially, 19 Entertainment owns not only the contestant's participatory footage from the show, but the rights to portrayal of the contestant in any way producers see fit, forever. Of particular note is the word "simulate," producers can, in effect, digitally reproduce the voice or likeness of any contestant and make that reproduction say or do anything the producers see fit, whether the actual contestant wants it to happen or not. Additionally, the contract contains language to the effect that contestants understand they are agreeing to a "relinquishing of the soul," and, beyond that, the contract also gives explicit permission to the promoters to fabricate information about the contestant—in other words, to *lie* (Summerfield, para.7). The contract states:

> "Other parties ... may reveal and/or relate information about me of personal, private, intimate, surprising, defamatory, disparaging, embarrassing or unfavorable nature that may be factual and/or fictional" [quoted in Summerfield, para. 7].

In short, if the producers can't legitimately promote the contestant, they are legally allowed to just invent information about the contestant—without consulting the contestant in any way first. And, as earlier showed, the contestant is also not allowed to refute what is said about him/her—to the tune of five million dollars, if s/he does.

19 Entertainment quite literally owns every contestant: voice, body,

and, apparently, "soul." 19 Entertainment has the right to release any sort of story they wish about a particular contestant, and the contestant can do nothing to counteract the story without violating his/her agreement and incurring a more than five-million dollar liability. Chapter II of this book explores more in-depth the return to a history of exploitation and pseudo-slavery the 19 Entertainment contract represents. The contract is so Draconian that many lawyers believe it might not even be enforceable. Olsen states:

> L.A. music attorney Kenneth Freundlich ... is ... highly critical of the contract and its ramifications. He notes that the contract omits a routine provision: the advice to consult your own lawyer or forever waive your right to complain later that you didn't. "Perhaps this was left out so as not to suggest to a contestant something she might not otherwise have thought of," he says. He wonders whether the absence of this provision might make the *American Idol* contract ultimately unenforceable [para. 38].

Predictably, *American Idol*'s producers are unapologetic about the nature of the contractual burden they have placed on contestants. As Simon Cowell once publicly stated:

> "None of them, when they win, are going to turn and give the money to charity," Cowell said. "This is a get rich quick scheme for somebody. And if you don't like it, don't play" [Huff, 125].

There have been a limited number of academic studies on *American Idol*. Simon Cowell (2003) (no relation to the judge on *American Idol*) questioned the identity narratives of the contestants on *Idol*, and suggested that the program is a "fantasy of participatory democracy" (para. 15), a "fiction of a stronger and more effective democracy" (para. 15) than the one actually present in American society. Su Holmes raises questions surrounding the narrative of stardom and the politics of interactivity in the British version of *American Idol, Pop Idol*. Liesbet van Zoonen (2004) argues that fan communities surrounding programs like *Idol* and those comprising political constituencies around candidates exhibit high degrees of similarity, in terms of characteristics such as knowledge, discussion, and emotional investment. Juliet Williams (2005) calls participatory programs like *Idol* a "shadow realm" to the political public sphere in which "anxieties and tensions produced by the practice of democracy are given free play" (p. 637). Jungmin Lee (2006) examined the tendency of audience

I. Ideas and Cabbages

members to vote for contestants of the same race as the voter. Nightingale and Dwyer (2006) argue that participatory reality television programs such as *Idol* attempt to erase the distinction between citizen and consumer.

Perhaps the most thorough study of the relationship between *American Idol* and the struggle among capital, political, and symbolic economies is Charles Fairchild's 2007 piece, "Building the Authentic Celebrity: The 'Idol' Phenomenon in the Attention Economy." Fairchild argues that *Idol* is specifically designed to create, perpetuate, and maintain a consumer relationship based on generating discreet brands which build affective investment in the contestants (and, by extension, the show itself and subsequent merchandise) (2007). Fairchild states:

> The contestants [are] catalysts for the establishment of very particular kinds of relationships and enter into an expressive context that [is] carefully designed to capitalize on the relationships they [are] expected to establish with various segments of the audience [p. 358].

According to Fairchild, the primary goal of the *Idol* franchise is to create a particular type of celebrity product which reinforces the credibility of the entire context of the program, or, as Fairchild states, demonstrate "the producers' credibility to craft a context in which authentic musical celebrities can emerge" (p. 358). However, this credibility is under constant assault; Paula Abdul's S7 gaffe in which she critiqued a contestant's singing performance that had not yet occurred (prompting speculation that the judges either pre-formulate their "live" commentary during rehearsals or are handed commentary to dole out by the producers) is but one *Idol* situation which has generated a great deal of controversy (BBC News, 2008, Dickey, 2008, Hibbard, 2008, Wyatt, 2008). Fairchild states, "The competition appears to be so carefully controlled and scripted as to be rigged" (p. 360). Whether this can be stated categorically remains to be seen.

Summary

Popular culture exists to replicate the constitutive social relations of a given society through the production and distribution of cultural objects. Popular culture is an extension of the people from (and for) whom it is created. The ideological beliefs transmitted by popular culture reinforce and justify the interests of the dominant group in society, and popular culture is one of the main mechanisms by which hegemonic force operates, particularly in Western society. With every turn of the television channel, radio station, or magazine page, one is being told how to look, believe, and behave — and those messages being transmitted work to the benefit of certain groups at the expense of other groups. This is because those who have the means by which to produce and distribute their ideology are in a position to determine what symbols and ideas are included in popular culture and which are excluded.

There are three main perspectives on consumer culture. The first is that popular culture exists to be bought and sold, and are therefore embedded with directives to consume. The second is that popular culture's essential purpose is to stratify social groups via economic and symbolic capital, with "taste" as the arbiter of social class. Third, and perhaps most intuitive, is that popular culture's main purpose is to be consumed and enjoyed — to provide aesthetic pleasure. Inherent in all three perspectives is the notion that cultural products must not only connect with the public, but must be economically competitive as well. Due to the nature of capitalism as the central tenet of Western society, popular culture is subject to an increasing amount of "real subsumption"; that is, all cultural production seems to be based upon economics rather than aesthetic quality. However, it should be remembered that cultural objects always *mean* something; they have symbolic and cultural capital that extends beyond economic interest. Every cultural object exudes ideology and a connection to a particular set of ideas and values.

For this reason, a focus on the political economy of popular culture is valuable in its study. A political economy of popular culture not only challenges the notion that gullible consumers have cultural objects imposed upon them, but returns agency in aesthetic decision-making to the consumer and rejects the notion that popular culture cannot contain real value.

II
Dude! I Met Elway!

Fame has been the bane of my life, and I would gladly have given it up.
I have been forced to live a false life, and all the people I know,
with the exception of a handful, have been affected by my being famous.
People don't relate to you but to the myth they think you are,
and the myth is always wrong.
— Marlon Brando (Brando & Lindsey, 1994)

Celebrity Is as Celebrity Does

I recently attended a concert with my wife. This is not an uncommon occurrence; we both love music, and although we are significantly busier than we were a few years ago (when concert-going was a nearly biweekly event), we still make time to catch our favorite artists when they come to town.

At this particular event, in the box office lobby, my wife noticed a large, blond man standing in a shaded corner and nudged me. She whispered, "I think that's Elway." Indeed, it was the former Denver Broncos quarterback and his companion. They were attempting to be unobtrusive and blend in, but Elway is a rather large man, and quite possibly more famous than any other person in the history of Denver.

We approached the box office ticket window, and, upon receiving our tickets, happened to make eye contact. He smiled, and we spoke briefly, ending with a handshake and going on about our concert-attending business. The next day, when relaying the events of the previous evening to some colleagues, I absently ended the tale with, "Oh, and, guess what? I met Elway!"[1]

Such tales of celebrity run-ins are told all over the world every day.

American Idolatry

There is something about meeting a celebrity which transcends the ordinary experiences of daily life, and merits special attention. It is not simply the brush with fame; as David Giles (2000) points out, "The terms 'fame' and 'celebrity' are not strictly interchangeable" (p. 3). To be certain, having met Elway is a celebrity encounter. The difference is distinct; John Elway's fame is a product of his *celebrity* status; Giles reminds that "the defining characteristic of celebrity is that it is essentially a media production" (p. 3). Elway is a Celebrity because he has been carefully packaged as such by a media machine. In this respect, John Elway is as much a commodity as the Denver Broncos license plate holder on my car or the orange and blue beer stein I drink from each Sunday in autumn. The roots of contemporary *celebrity* are planted deep in the past; P. David Marshall (1997) states:

> Much like the concept of individualism, the use of the term celebrity in its contemporary (ambiguous) form developed in the nineteenth century. Studying examples of prior usage, one can see the transformation of its sense from an affinity with piety and religion to some modern sense of false value. The two faces of capitalism — that of defaced value and prized commodity value — are contained within these transforming definitions. The term celebrity has come to embody the ambiguity of the public forms of subjectivity under capitalism [p. 4].

The undertone in Marshall's words is clear: contemporary *celebrity* is a product, a commodified construct with economic value. However, clearly, there is a difference between a Celebrity as a physical, tangible human being, and *celebrity* as a social and economic concept. The two are intertwined but not interchangeable; they rely upon each other for subsistence, but are distinct entities. Elway is a Celebrity; the aura surrounding Elway is *celebrity*.

Celebrity status is not necessarily positive; in many cases, it is seen as the underbelly of fame. This, too, has its roots in the nineteenth century. Marshall states:

> An interesting ... example from the mid–nineteenth century gives evidence that the term celebrity was [not] a moniker of solemnity but rather a term of some derogation: "They [Spinoza's successors] had celebrity, Spinoza has fame." In this case, celebrity describes a more fleeting, ephemeral connotation of fame [p. 5].

II. Dude! I Met Elway!

Celebrity, then, is a particular kind of fame — one which is generated and sustained by media production. To be certain, there is a process of reification and commodification at work. However, it would be inaccurate to categorize *celebrity* and Celebrities merely as commodities. There are other processes at work as well which lend to the place that Celebrities occupy in contemporary society.

The study of *celebrity* is as much about society writ large as it is about Celebrities themselves; it is truly "an especially striking and challenging case study in the production and reception of culture" (Gamson, 1994, p. 5). In studying the role of the modern Celebrity, one is also considering the role of the individual in contemporary society and the inevitable culmination of consumer society in the reification and commodification of personalities — of people. The Celebrity not only defines who we, as a society, are, but more importantly, who we are not. Flora (2008) writes:

> Celebrities are fascinating because they live in a parallel universe — one that looks and feels just like ours yet is light-years beyond our reach. Stars cry to Diane Sawyer about their problems — failed marriages, hardscrabble upbringings, bad career decisions — and we can relate. The paparazzi catch them in wet hair and a stained t-shirt, and we're thrilled. They're ordinary folks, just like us. And yet... [p. 33].

Celebrity has become the modern prism through which all mainstream measures of success have been filtered: what it means to "make it," what it means to be "glamorous," "beautiful," or "desirable," and what it means to be "fashionable" are all reflected through the prism of *celebrity*. In many ways, Su Holmes (2006) is correct when she states that, "fame can be argued to be a 'new' dominant discursive formation that shapes subjectivity, identity and belonging, and which 'speaks' in articulating frameworks about relations of power and the merits of individual success" (Holmes, 35). Ultimately, this is the central illusion of contemporary *celebrity*. It reinforces the ideological fallacy that "anyone can make it" if only s/he can be "discovered." It is a "myth of success ... grounded in the belief that the class system, the old-boy network, does not apply to America. However, one of the myth's ambiguities is whether success is possible for anyone, regardless of talent or application" (Dyer, 2006, p. 157). That is to say, all Celebrities are not created equal, and, just as in other avenues of American society, not every individual is guaranteed equal access to the bootstraps by which to pull one's self up. This "success myth" is the cornerstone of *celebrity* (and, indeed, one of the central tenets of American society as a whole). However, the success myth has several elements which are not only contradictory, but inherently mutually exclusive. There are, according to Richard Dyer, four fundamental claims of the success myth: "(i) that ordinariness is the hallmark of the star; (ii) that the system rewards talent and 'specialness'; (iii) that luck, 'breaks,' which may happen to anyone typify the career of the star; and (iv) that hard work and professionalism are necessary for stardom" (p. 157). What makes a Celebrity unique is that, under other circumstances, the individual would be "just another guy" if it weren't for the enormous amount of talent the individual possesses (and if it weren't for the fortunate "break" of someone having discovered that talent). Through training and hard work, a little talent, and being in the right place at the right time, any one of us could play in the NBA, or sing on Broadway, or star in a major motion picture.

And who wouldn't want to be a Celebrity? The perks of contemporary *celebrity* are on display through a constant stream of media representations of power, glamour, and financial independence. In short, "the desire for fame, stardom, or celebrification stems from a need to be wanted in a society where being famous appears to offer enormous material, economic, social and psychic rewards" (Holmes, p. 2). No matter the field, the drive for being well known is palpable, whether it is the temporary fame of the Employee of the Month, the validation that comes with academic publication, or the adulation of a nation that an Olympic gold medal brings. Because *celebrity* itself is now a commodity, it is no longer enough, for many Americans, to simply be good at a job; for many, "fame is no longer a perk of success but a necessary ingredient, whether as a socialite, chef, scholar, or skateboarder" (Chaudbry, p. 159). In a society oriented toward the individual rather than the collective—an "I" society—the modern self is pushed toward a psyche that is extremely conceited and self-involved; these qualities are then reflected in much of Celebrity culture (Holmes, p. 2). It's no wonder that the Celebrity occupies so much discursive space and carries such vast cultural, economic, and social capital. In fact, the rise of the Celebrity and the centralization of fame in contemporary Western society is so extensive and pervasive in

II. Dude! I Met Elway!

day-to-day life that it occupies its own central space as fame culture (Holmes, p. 36).

Who is responsible for the situation and positioning of *celebrity* as the prism through which individual success is now filtered? There may be a reflexive tendency to immediately implicate "The Media," as "The Media" is[2] a ready scapegoat for all of society's ills. To be fair, the media do contribute to, as Holmes asserts, quite a bit of fear and uncertainty about who to be and how to behave in a society in which identity is both flexible and, often, manufactured (p. 2). The media obviously have their part to play; as noted in Chapter I, since they are one of the primary ways in which the ideology of the dominant class is disseminated. The success myth, as an essential precept of capitalism, figures heavily in media representations. It makes sense, therefore, that the media would share some of the culpability in *celebrity*'s central positioning. As Chaudbry writes, "Our preoccupation with fame is at least partly explained by our immersion in a media-saturated world that constantly tells us ... we should be famous if we possibly can, because it is the best, perhaps the only, way to be" (p. 159).

However, to lay the blame solely at the feet of the media absolves the rest of society of their participation in the celebrity system. Celebrities are not created in a vacuum; someone is watching the films, buying the CDs, reading the tabloid magazines and tuning in to the celebrity gossip programs. Flora offers, "It's easy to blame the media for [our] cognitive whiplash. But the real celebrity spinmeister is our own mind, which tricks us into believing the stars are our lovers and our social intimates" (p. 33). These illusions — these "little fictions," as Walter Lippmann categorized them[3] — that we tell ourselves are legion. Sarah Chalke would really be quite infatuated with me if I only could meet her. (And believe me, Sarah, you would be.) It would not be a complete embarrassment if I were to play one-on-one with LeBron James. (I drain threes like no man's business.) will.i.am would love to hear my demo CD (which sounds eerily like Dave Chappelle's *8 Mile* parody, in which he just keeps shouting, "Spaghetti! Spaghetti! Spaghetti-Os!"). The essential dichotomy of the Celebrity is that they are like us, but not like us. They are the romanticized version of us — us at our best. Celebrities offer comfort and redemption in a confusing and increasingly isolating world of text messages, computer chats, and virtual reality; as society becomes more atomized and individuals become more and more anomic, they look for connection with romanticized Celebrities in a "self-directed healing process" (Holmes, p. 3). In a society where face-to-face interactions with real people is decreasing, fandom provides a sense of contact — an "illusion of intimacy"— that tries to make up for that increasing isolation (p. 3).

The Celebrity, therefore, serves not only the ideological purposes of perpetuating the success myth and the economic purpose of selling products (often themselves, as will be discussed later), but also serves as a doorway for connecting people to each other (Holmes, p. 3). The exchange, not just of information regarding Celebrities but of validation of interest in Celebrities, serves as a sort of social capital in and of itself. Instead of trade in goods and services, the currency is knowledge. McDonald (2000) affirms:

> It would be worth adding to Dyer's notion of star image the relevance of gossip, for informal talk about well-known performers is one of the clearest examples of how stars enter into popular culture and everyday life [p. 6].

Ask a stranger his feelings about thermodynamic nuclear fission, and he may return, at best, a blank stare. Ask his feelings about the emotional breakdown of Britney Spears, and even if he has no passionate feelings on the subject, he is likely to, at least, a) know who Britney Spears is; and b) know she underwent recent emotional turmoil. Celebrity gossip is a pervasive force in American media; one is likely to encounter it at some point, like it or not. In that, it becomes a universalizing agent — an entrée to conversation when other avenues are unavailable.[4]

Derakhshani (2008) refers to the obsessive nature of the American Celebrity gossip machine as "not some aberration, but an intrinsic aspect of the central economic, social, and political force in Western life: consumerism" (p. 29). For what is a Celebrity if not another product to be purchased, consumed, and discarded? And what is the gossip about a Celebrity — who s/he is marrying, what "feud" in which s/he is engaged, what raging drug/alcohol problem s/he is dealing with — if not a consumer report? Derakhshani argues:

> Celebrity culture reflects consumerism by flattening distinctions; if all cultural products — from video games to poems, from roller sneakers to religious

II. Dude! I Met Elway!

beliefs — are reduced to commodities, then the only thing that matters is buying and selling. A Rembrandt and a Lil' Abner comic strip are basically the same thing as long as they entertain me or make me a profit. Celeb culture has helped bring about the commodification of human life [p. 29].

The Celebrity, as stated earlier, is no different than a license plate holder or a beer mug; s/he exists for consumption, and is constructed through an amalgamation of power dynamics and economic forces. Marshall (1997) points out:

> The term celebrity has a metaphor for value in modern society. More specifically, it describes a type of value that can be articulated through an individual and celebrated publicly as important and significant. The term is linked to past power structures (i.e., the church) and now has connotations that link it to modern power structures (i.e., capitalism) [p. 7].

Celebrity and Celebrities exist as a commodity, in the classic, Marxist sense of the term. Carefully packaged, surrounded by teams of publicists and personal managers, the Celebrity is certainly "an object outside us, a thing that by its properties satisfies human wants of some sort or another" (Marx, p. 303). The Celebrity is a product of labor (both the labor of the Celebrity him/herself, and that of the team of people surrounding him/her), and, for Marx, "that which determines the magnitude of the value of any article is the amount of labour socially necessary, or the labour time socially necessary for its production" (p. 306).

In the case of the Celebrity, the value of the Celebrity is determined by the amount of time necessary to cultivate and promote the Celebrity's "fame." Since the 1950s, Hollywood has been in the business of churning out the Celebrity commodity. Mendelson (2007) writes that the actors of the 1920s were "studio owned and operated commodities" that were "manufactured, tested, and refined" as film studios began to recognize that the star of a film was more of an audience draw than the film's title. By 1915, the focus of presenting actors had changed from presenting the actor's work to presenting the actor's image as "larger than life" (Mendelson, 2007). Fan magazines such as *Photoplay* were produced by the studios, giving them complete control over the actor's image while presenting audiences with a "real, inside" look at the star (Mendelson, 2007). Not until the studio system collapse of the 1950s would actors be considered "self-owned commodities" with a measure of control over their own image (Mendelson, 2007). More on this later in this chapter.

The Historical Origins of Modern Celebrity

How does *celebrity* accomplish its work? As earlier stated, *celebrity* is a multi-faceted and slippery concept, existing not just on a commodity level, but also on an ideological level, a legal level, and a symbolic level. Each of these aspects of *celebrity* has its own form and function. To most accurately describe how *celebrity* functions, it may be helpful to first explore how *celebrity*, in its modern form, evolved.

David Giles (2000) writes, "The history of fame is about nothing less than the history of Western civilization. It is also about the history of the individual" (p. 12). One of the hallmarks of contemporary society is a focus away from the collective and toward the individual — the transition from a "we" society to a "me" society. Every major cultural, political, and social development of the past 3,000 years has been tracked through the accomplishments of the individual: from religious (Jesus, Mohammed, and the Virgin Mary) to political (the democratic revolution of the United States with George Washington and Thomas Jefferson at the forefront; the Roman empire with its succession of Caesers) to military (Genghis Khan to Napoleon Bonaparte to General Norman Schwarzkopf) (Giles, p. 12). No area of modern societal development has escaped framing through individual achievement.[5] As Giles states, "Even revolutionary attempts to overthrow an individual-oriented economic system with a collective one have had individuals at the helm, be they Lenin or Trotsky. The reason we cannot imagine history without individuals is because it has always been written this way" (p. 12).

Alexander the Great has been recognized as the "first famous person" (Giles, p. 14), although the concept of fame is much older than that. However, the Roman era brought a distinct change to the way in which fame was conceptualized, as words like *fama* and *celibritas* became common terms in everyday vocabulary; also, for really the first time, there was an acknowledgment that civic honors could be bestowed upon even those who were not born into nobility (Giles, p. 15). Later in the Roman empire,

II. Dude! I Met Elway!

it was Augustus who introduced two major modern features of *celebrity* that survive to this day: the widespread use of his image to publicize (having his face inscribed on coins with the slogan *aequitas Augusti*—"the fairness of Augustus") and popularization of particular styles of clothing (the toga) (Giles, p. 15). The important thing to remember about these early conceptions of fame is that they existed "as the province of the top layer of a natural hierarchy"; (Giles, p. 17) Alexander the Great and Augustus both enjoyed the "divine right of kings." While one did not need to have been necessarily born into nobility to achieve *fama* or *celebritas*, some other "natural" ability was thought to have catapulted an individual to the upper echelon: military judgment, physical prowess, mental acumen, or the like. Fame was tied to heroic virtue,[7] as Gamson illustrates:

> Before we had celebrities we had heroes... Now, what those hero types all share, of course, are admirable qualities—qualities that somehow set them apart from the rest of us. They have done things, acted in the world: written, thought, understood, led [p. 10].

As Western society further progressed, belief in concepts like the divine right of kingship and the secularization of society inherently led to a reconceptualization of the notion of fame. This shift, however, came with a cost. With what Chris Rojek (2001) refers to as "the death of God" (p. 13) and a rejection of monarchal systems of societal organization to more democratic ones, the notion of fame morphed from "an affinity with piety and religion to some modern sense of false value" (Marshall, p. 4). That is to say, especially in America, that fame began to gain distance from the idea of natural hierarchy. Rojek argues that the American Revolution "sought to overthrow not merely the institutions of colonialism but the ideology of monarchical power too. It replaced them with an alternate ideology, in some ways no less flawed and fantastic: the ideology of the common man" (p. 13).

Two factors led to the wide acceptance of the focus on the agency of the "common man" to rise to fame. First, beginning in the 16th century, copper engraving and the printing press enabled extensive dissemination of images, particularly those of the individual face (Gamson, p. 17). Second, leading writers began to promote the concept. In America, Benjamin Franklin "promoted the image of 'self-made man,' emphasizing the individual's ability to navigate his or her own course to fame," while in Europe, Jean-Jacques Rousseau "sought fame for naturalness, a fame for inner qualities, for what one is without the overlay of social forms" (Giles, p. 18). The discourse changed from the notion of innate possession of fame (or the qualities/virtues necessary to be worthy of fame) as birthright to a more egalitarian version of fame in which any person could rise to fame through hard work and determination. This conceptualization of fame reached its zenith in what R.W.B. Lewis termed the "American Adam," "a figure of innocence and promise who was, as Emerson defined him, 'the simple genuine self against the whole world'" (Henderson, p. 6). This Adamic hero was a product of self-reliance, perseverance and achievement, and "would become the central figure in the quest for national legitimacy" (Henderson, p. 7). The Adamic hero represented America itself, a nation determined to pick itself up by its collective bootstraps and make its way in the world on the merits of its own plucky spirit. In doing so, the Adamic hero also reformulated the manner in which fame was received by the rest of society. As Marshall (1997) writes:

> The celebrity ... is not distant but attainable — touchable by the multitude. The greatness of the celebrity is something that can be shared and, in essence, celebrated loudly and with a touch of vulgar pride. It is the ideal representation of the triumph of the masses [p. 6].

Instead of the Adamic hero belonging to the kingship, the nobility, the upper echelon of some widely recognized yet vaguely arbitrary hierarchy, the Adamic hero belonged to everyone. He was of the people, by the people, for the people. The Adamic hero was every one of us, if we only kept at it long enough and tempered our successes with a reinvestment in hard work. The success myth was born.

When Western society experienced what Boorstin referred to as the "Graphic Revolution," the face of fame changed again. The reproduction of images and the relative speed at which information could be disseminated brought with it major transformation in the nature and extent of *celebrity*. Henderson writes:

> The emergence of photography and chromolithography in post–Civil War America led to an explosive growth in such mass publications as newspapers and magazines ... the circulation of daily papers increased 400% between

II. Dude! I Met Elway!

1870 and 1900, partly as a result of technology and partly because of rising literacy rates and the growth of leisure time [p. 7].

In addition to the boom in literacy and the advancement of technology, the United States experienced rampant growth through immigration. Between 1890 and 1920, over 23 million new immigrants entered the United States, and with them came new markets for distribution of the success myth — and new publications, such as *McClure's*, with which to disseminate that myth (Henderson, p. 8). The very fabric of American society changed dramatically between 1890 and 1920 with the arrival of so many immigrants; by 1920, the United States was a completely different country than it had been pre–Civil War. For example, in the 1920s, Gilbert Seldes began to write about the "lively arts": "jazz, musicals, radio, and motion pictures that were creating an 'American' culture to match the country's new immigrant, urban personality" (Henderson, p. 8).

With this new American culture came a paradigm shift away from the traditional subjects of magazine and newspaper features and toward the entertainers which were beginning to define the culture. Lowenthal writes, "From 1901 to 1914, 74% of subjects in *The Saturday Evening Post* and *Colliers* were about politics, business, etc. From 1922 to 1941, over half came from entertainment (sports and movies)" (as cited in Henderson, p. 9). This last category — movie entertainers — rapidly became a focal point of national magazine coverage. The celebrity system was born during this period of rapid attention reallocation and the shifting of the cultural tectonic plates.

As described in Chapter I, film (like music and television) is an intangible medium — there is nothing to physically own when the product is consumed. The problem with this was recognized by producers from the early days of the film industry, as studios "needed product differentiation to stabilize demand and price, especially crucial given the intangibility of the film product" (Gamson, p. 25). It was possible to sell tickets to a film based on the title or subject matter of a film alone, but this method failed to take advantage of the briskly expanding asset also seeing a dramatic rise at the time: the American press. The press during the rise of the cinematic celebrity was starving for sensationalist news, and film producers quickly realized that the easiest way to publicize their films was to promote the stars of the films as "personalities" (Giles, p. 21).

American Idolatry

Film was the ideal incubator for the American celebrity system.[8] The production of a film is an inherently fragmented construction process, with each task precisely specialized and compartmentalized (McDonald, p. 24). Directors direct, editors edit, lighting technicians hang the lights and camera operators operate the cameras. Because each of those tasks requires specific knowledge or technical skills that most of the other people within the production team do not possess, it was easy to confer the same sort of professional awe to the art of acting. Also, narrative structures changed with the development of sound technology and shot composition changed with advancement in cinematographic techniques (McDonald, p. 24). Preferencing of the subject within the screen space and the ability to engender emotion through music and dialogue fundamentally changed the relationship between actor and audience. Finally, studios began to actively disseminate information about the performers to the general public (McDonald, p. 24). For the first time, actors were known not only for their work on screen, but also for their character in their real lives (McDonald, p. 32). The press began making distinction between performers' reel lives and their real lives. The Hollywood industry turned performers into household names, literally, in an attempt to create "commercial and legal entities" which could, in turn, be used as "a means of promotion in the public domain" (McDonald, p. 39).

The constructed identity became the new paradigm in Hollywood, as the American celebrity system further developed. Teams of trainers and coaches would take raw materials — "undiscovered talent" — and turn them into polished celebrity products. The process was extensive and intrusive, as McDonald describes:

> Once signed to the studio, new talent would undergo an apprenticeship, during which time the studio would begin to mould the images of contract players. Apprentices would receive tuition from the studio's own speech and diction coaches, together with acting classes with the drama coach and, in some cases, singing and dancing lessons. Other optional lessons were offered in etiquette, movement, fencing, horseback riding, swimming, boxing, and languages. Advice on fashion, make-up, and skin care were also available [p. 44].

Because of the work involved in creating, cultivating, and packaging celebrity products, studios wanted to maintain iron grips on their invest-

II. Dude! I Met Elway!

ments. The contracts studios placed actors under in the 1930s and 1940s were, by all accounts, Draconian — in many ways, they amounted to indentured servitude. A studio would hire an actor with a contract that was valid for up to seven years, during which time, the studio had the exclusive rights to that actor's services (McDonald, p. 62). The studio could terminate this contract at any time; however, the actor signed away his/her legal right to do so (McDonald, p. 62). The studio had complete control over how much the actor was paid, in which productions the actor would appear, how many roles the actor could take in a given year, and the ability to suspend an actor without pay if s/he complained about a role or refused to play a particular part (McDonald, p. 63). The studio could even "loan" the actor to another studio (without the actor's consent), and often included so-called "morality clauses": if a performer behaved in such a way as to bring disrepute to the studio or "discontinuity to [their] image," the actor could be shelved without pay (McDonald, p. 63). In this case, because the actor was under contract, s/he could not pursue alternate avenues of theatrical employment, but would not be paid by the studio, either. It was an effective tool for punishment of a disobedient or defiant Celebrity. Basically, "film performers were ... studio-owned-and-operated commodities" (Gamson, p. 25).

It was imperative to the studios' continued success in marketing Celebrities that their on-screen roles and their off-screen personalities became linked — so much so that studios would deploy "exploitation crews" of up to 100 employees to construct and direct the Celebrity's image under an organizational scheme not all that different from a newspaper city room (Gamson, p. 27). In order to boost ticket sales at the box office, these crews created images for their Celebrities that often had little to do with the actual person they were representing (Gamson, p. 38). The main stock in trade for these exploitation crews was glamour. The marketing of the Hollywood mystique was big business in the early days of the American celebrity system, and the vehicle for advertising the Hollywood mystique was the movie Celebrity. Henderson writes:

> Movie celebrities came to represent the visual quintessence of glamour. Stars such as Marlene Dietrich, Joan Crawford, and Greta Garbo glowed with glamour — draped in diamonds and wrapped in silk, feathers, and fur, they were silvered beings worshipped by what Norma Desmond in

American Idolatry

Sunset Boulevard would call "all those little people out there in the dark" [p. 9].

The early age of the American celebrity system was characterized by this focus on glamour, on mystique. But, to be clear, there was already (even at this fledgling stage) structures in place that would come to define the American celebrity system for the rest of its history: a centrality of visual media as "the prime arbiters of celebrity and the bestowers of honor," the existence of professional image managers, and a "tightly controlled production system mass producing entertainment celebrities for a widely consuming audience" (Gamson, p. 28). These characteristics would be the paradigmatic structures that would define *celebrity* in America in the years to come.

The American celebrity system was fundamentally and permanently transformed by the advent of the television. Before the television became a household staple, Celebrities were people who were both distant and special—one had to leave the house and go to the theater to see Celebrities "in the flesh" (Gamson, p. 24). Television brought the Celebrity into individual living rooms, particularly after the decline in audience at the close of World War II (McDonald, p. 113). Television also brought a rampant increase in the number and diversity of Celebrities. Giles writes, "As media outlets (newspapers, magazines, TV channels) increase in number there is a concurrent increase in the number of 'special people' who provide so much of their material" (Giles, p. 25). Not only this, but as the number of channels rose (especially with the advent of cable), the amount of 24/7 coverage also increased, and this combination of factors has completely changed contemporary celebrity culture. Formerly, "celebrity was broadly encompassing, encouraging general agreement at least in mainstream culture;" now, "contemporary celebrity is carefully niched, appealing not to wide swaths of society but to minute slivers" (Henderson, p. 11). As pointed out in Chapter I, cultural commodities are increasingly narrowcast at specific segments of the consuming public; it did not take long for *celebrity* to follow suit.

There have always been small pockets of resistance to the dominant archetype of the American Celebrity. Take, for example, the case of baseball legend Ted Williams:

II. Dude! I Met Elway!

What Ted Williams wanted to be famous for was his hitting. He wanted everyone who cared about baseball to know that he was — as he believed and may well have been — the greatest hitter who ever lived; what he didn't want to do was take on any of the effort off the baseball field involved in making this known. As an active player, Williams gave no interviews, signed no baseballs or photographs, chose not to be obliging in any way to journalists or fans. A rebarbative character, not to mention a slightly menacing s.o.b., Williams, if you had asked him, would have said that it was enough that he was the last man to hit .400; he did it on the field, and therefore didn't have to sell himself off the field [Epstein, 2005, 13].

While it would seem this resistance exemplifies a backlash against the state of *celebrity*—perpetuated by a series of media recluses from J.D. Salinger to Johnny Depp—in actuality, the fact that Williams was an anomaly—the exception rather than the rule—reaffirms the default position for *celebrity*. *Celebrity* is not innate; it is created, primarily through media production. Williams did not want to have any active part in the publicizing of his own accomplishments. In essence, Williams wanted to be *famous*, but did not want to be a Celebrity. It is this performative aspect of *celebrity* that distinguishes it from fame. With fame, one's deeds stand heroically for themselves. With *celebrity*, one's deeds must be actively advertised. While it appears that there are still some who "clearly [lament] the old, 'good' fame, deriding the 'fame of the moment' brought about by 'immediate communication,' and the importance of both performance and the body, for fame in the twentieth century" (Giles, p. 18), in many ways, Holmes may be more accurate when she claims that once fame is described in terms of visibility instead of achievement, differentiating between "good" fame and "bad" fame is irrelevant (p. 298).

An Aside Regarding Celebrity *as Property Right*

One tenet beginning to emerge in this discussion regarding *celebrity* is the distinctive split between *celebrity* and Celebrity. That is to say that the actual human being and the "well-knownness" s/he generates are separate entities. Holmes confirms:

> In a society where merit is no longer the sole deciding factor in fame, recognition and self-exposure are now believed to be absolute goods in themselves:

fame promises acceptability, even if one commits the most heinous crime, because thereby people will finally know who you are, and you will be saved from the living death of being unknown [p. 298].

This recognition or exposure is a commodity in and of itself. As such, it makes sense that a tradition has developed of seeing publicity rights as property rights, particularly when applied to Celebrities. Fundamentally, all people in the public eye have publicity rights, and those rights "allow them to control the manner in which others use their image" (Halbert & Wood, 2003, p. 37). Especially in the United States, where the cultural world is characterized by privately-owned cultural symbols from which people appropriate to construct their distinctive personalities, it is no surprise that media entities attempt to assert ownership over the public persona of people, given that those media entities largely created the core cultural content (Halbert & Wood, p. 38). Halbert & Wood argue:

> As public space becomes increasingly subject to surveillance by video camera and webcams, as private information is mined for data to help sell products, and as culture itself is privatized and owned by large corporate interests, the autonomy that each person assumes when establishing both a public and private persona is put at risk [p. 38].

This attempt to corporatize and commodify every aspect of individual existence is marked by the rise in the number and variety of venues for publication of intimate details of a Celebrity's life and the paparazzi to uncover the dirt. Holmes elaborates, reminding that because of the Internet, every single knowable fact, verified or unsubstantiated, allegation or confirmation, can be dissected by both the media and by fans — every inch of Celebrity skin is on display, and Celebrities are increasingly forced through a gauntlet of reporters prying into what is presented as an "unmediated" view of the Celebrity's life (p. 35).

People are increasingly viewed, due in large part to a societal focus on property rights and an increase in the amount and type of surveillance under which Americans increasingly live, as a divided "bundle of rights"— many of which are alienable, making it easier to separate the individual from the right (Halbert & Wood, p. 38).

The first case to establish publicity rights was *Haelan Laboratories,*

II. Dude! I Met Elway!

Inc. v. Topps Chewing Gum, Inc. in 1953, which recognized the value of a baseball player's name and likeness on baseball cards, and legal scholars and the Supreme Court have further defined those rights in the years since (Halbert & Wood, p. 39). Legal precedent has established "personalities" as property by asserting that it takes labor to create a public image, and that people have a right to assign publicity, licensing use of their public persona (including their names and likenesses) commercially as they choose (Halbert & Wood, p. 39). That public persona is not only the Celebrity's name and likeness, but "his or her films ... the promotion of those films and of the star through pin-ups, public appearances, studio hand-outs and so on, as well as interviews, biographies and coverage in the press of the star's doings and 'private' life" (Dyer, p. 2).

The accordance of property rights to public persona is an application of Locke's labor theory of property. The rationale goes like this:

> Since the celebrity spends time, money, and energy in developing a commercially lucrative persona, that persona is the fruit of the celebrity's labor and entitles her to its rewards. Moreover, in line with the labor theory of property, it is often argued that advertisers who appropriate celebrity personas without permission, much like "pirates" or "free riders," improperly reap what others have sown [Halbert & Wood, p. 39].

In fact, so sacred has an individual's image been held — "too precious to be crassly commercialized, especially without consent" — that even as far back as 1905, the Supreme Court of Georgia likened the misappropriation of identity for the intent of advertising similar to slavery (Halbert & Wood, p. 48). Of course, crassly commercializing one's *own* image is perfectly acceptable, and invoking one's publicity rights can prevent others from using the Celebrity's persona to sell merchandise with which the Celebrity does not wish to be associated. The right to publicity covers "a person's nickname, signature, physical pose, characterizations, singing style, vocal characteristic, [or] body parts; so long as these are distinctive and the public identifies them with the holder of the right" (Halbert & Wood, p. 40). A person's public persona and image are that person's property. Furthermore, Jacoby & Zimmerman (2002) have argued that publicity rights to a persona constitute a commodity to such a degree that they could be seized and exploited by unpaid creditors.

Recent trends in celebrity culture have created new legal issues for the appropriation of publicity rights. First, there is the issue of what to do about "hybrid" personas — fictional characters which share close properties with the non-fictional personas who portray them. For example, the situation comedy *Seinfeld* involved a main character named Jerry Seinfeld — a character played by comedian Jerry Seinfeld. Where the fictional character ends and the human persona begins can be complicated to establish; "because this hybrid persona contains both the actor's human persona and the character's fictional persona, determining whether works displaying such persona exploit a human persona or a fictional persona is very difficult" (Halbert & Wood, p. 41).

Secondly, reality television has created issues in the application of publicity rights. Most reality television contestants sign away their right to publicity to the company which produces the reality show — these contestants no longer own their own public personas, nor can they control use of those personas (Halbert & Wood, p. 42). The contracts that these contestants sign, as described in Chapter I, "go beyond protecting [the producers'] interests in a fictional character to their interest in owning the public persona for the person upon which this character was based (if indeed there is a difference between the person and the character)" (Halbert & Wood, p. 42). In order to understand the kind of "aggressive extension of property rights — the corporate takeover of an individual's ability to control their image" (Halbert & Wood, p. 45) these reality show contracts represent, one need only buy into one simple precept: "...one must assume that a [reality show] cast member has no public personality but the one constructed by [the network]" (Halbert & Wood, p. 48). This raises a specific problem, though. The "cast member" is also a "real person," and (especially in the case of the *American Idol* contract) where the factual part of the person's identity diverges from the fictional part is difficult to determine (Halbert & Wood, p. 48). This leaves many, such as Halbert & Wood, to wonder, "If [the producers] own the public persona of an individual, what is left for the individual to own? Is any public display of identity 'real?' Is there any private 'self' behind these images?" (Halbert & Wood, p. 48).

II. Dude! I Met Elway!
A Rhetorical Consideration of Celebrity

Celebrity is, at its core, an act of persuasion. We may not always recognize it as such; Flora points out, "The brain simply doesn't recognize that it's being fooled by TV and movies ... hundreds of thousands of years ago, it was impossible for someone not to know you if you knew them. And if they didn't kill you, they were probably your friend" (Flora, p. 35). This is no longer the case. It is very possible, and in many cases *probable*, that there are a great number of people who know each of us that we have never met. In that one-way interaction lies the persuasive element — more on this later in this section.

As has been discussed earlier, the modern definition of *celebrity* is inherently linked to the secularization of society. The term itself derives from the Latin *celebrem*, meaning both "fame" and "being thronged" (Rojek, p. 9). Also deriving from the Latin *celebrem* is the French *célèbre*, or "well known in public" (Rojek, p. 9). In both cases, *celebrity* is intrinsically tied to a public, and "acknowledges the fickle, temporary nature of the market in human sentiments" (Rojek, p. 9).

Celebrity, as a rhetorical concept, has it roots as far back as the beginning of rhetoric; all the way back to Georgias and Protagoras. Billig (1987) refers to Protagoras as the first real show business personality, likening the Greek debating circles to boxing rings. If the academic lecture circuit was the boxing ring, then Protagoras was its Floyd Mayweather, pound for pound the greatest fighter in the world. While Aristotle and Socrates shunned these competitive contests, Protagoras turned them into lucrative business, becoming the first person to charge for lectures (Billig, 1987).

Georgias took this agonistic aspect one step further. While Protagoras was a firm believer that there were two sides to every issue (or, more specifically, that every logos has an anti-logos), Georgias needed no such logic. For Georgias, rhetoric was a simple behavioral process. If the speech was convincing enough, given with enough passion and enough appearance of truth, then it did not matter what the content was (Billig, 1987). Georgias was not concerned whether this power was "good" or "bad." It was a simple matter of stimulus and response. If Protagoras was the first "media celebrity," then Georgias was the first "spin doctor."

In order for the symbolic functions of *celebrity* to work, there needs to be a connection forged between the Celebrity and the audience member. This connection functions on a number of rhetorical levels, beginning with identification. It is not enough for a contestant on a participatory competitive reality television show or a Celebrity on a talk show to perform well. The television personality is also carefully creating an image of him/herself for the viewer. In participatory competitive reality television, the contestant is attempting to ingratiate him/herself and persuade the audience member to call in and vote for him/her. According to Kenneth Burke, for the contestant to get the audience member to pick up the phone, the contestant must convince the audience member that they share ideas, beliefs, and values, or that the contestant's success is also somehow a success for the audience member (Billig, 1987). (Of course, those successes are not all that shared; viewers do not receive checks from *American Idol* contestants for the album sales and concert tour revenue they helped the contestant generate by voting for him/her dozens of times.)

There are multiple ways this identification can be established. Hans Robert Jauss delineates five types of identification that may come into play between Celebrity and audience. First, there is associative identification, in which "the barriers between audience and actors are broken, and there is a celebration of active participation" (quoted in Marshall, p. 69). This is the identification between, for example, a band on stage and the fan in the audience at a concert. Secondly, there is admiring identification, wherein "the actions of the hero are exemplary for a particular community — the perfect hero" (Marshall, p. 69). Sports figures are the first celebrity type to come to mind when thinking of admiring identification, but political leaders, musicians, artists, and others are certainly admired as exemplars for their audiences. Thirdly, Jauss points to sympathetic identification, in which "there is a solidarity with the character or suffering personality. We place ourselves in the position of the hero" (Marshall, p. 69). The relationship between the fan at home and the contestant on a participatory competitive reality television program could intuitively be characterized this way. There is also cathartic identification, which "represents an abstraction or an aestheticized relation to the hero. In this way a moral or judgment can be drawn from the aesthetic experience and the reader feels a sense of emancipation through his or her involvement with the character" (Marshall, p. 69). This type of identification occurs most

II. Dude! I Met Elway!

often between an audience member and a fictional character, such as the identification between a fan and Luke Skywalker, wherein the fan learns life lessons through the Jedi Code. Finally, there is ironic modality, which entails "a consistent denial of any expected form of identification [with] the text of the character. There is maintenance of the interaction with the audience without a sense of the closure of character identification" (Marshall, p. 69). This type of identification is one of the hallmarks of modernist fiction and postmodern criticism (Marshall, p. 69) — the expectation that there will be no meaningful identification between the reader and the character/Celebrity text at all.

The ideological construct of the success myth also helps structure the identification between the contestant and the audience member (or all Celebrities and their fans, in truth). This contestant is a person who has a chance to "make it" — to finally reach for and grab that brass ring — if only you, at home, will help make it a reality. In the case of participatory competitive reality television, it is repeatedly stressed that these are "regular Joes" who have been "discovered" in auditions from around the country; potential diamonds in the rough. As delineated in Chapter I, the dominant ideology of the United States encourages buy-in to the success myth. Celebrity is almost a birth-right.[10] This helps facilitate audience identification with the contestants; if someone would only discover that viewer at home, s/he has enough talent that s/he could be successful, too. S/he can live vicariously through the chosen contestant; by helping to ensure the fulfillment of the contestant's success myth, it leaves the door open to the possibility that the viewer's might not be all that far behind.

In many ways, this is simply a reflection of Emerson's (1876) "representative man" theory. Emerson posited that some people rise to fame and celebrity because they embody qualities or ideals that we want to believe live inside of us, too (Emerson, 1876). We seek out and recognize these traits in other people, and then celebrate them (Emerson, 1876). However, we are not celebrating these "representative men" in and of themselves. Emerson is very careful to end each of his essays in *Representative Men* with a list of the faults of each of the heroes he describes. The point of this is that we should not be worshipping people for who they are, but for the potential each of them makes us see in ourselves. Emerson's argument is essentially, "'Praise me because I am unique ... but praise me as well because my uniqueness is only a more intense version of your own'" (Gamson, p. 18). In participatory competitive reality television, it is not the talent of the contestant we are rewarding, but the way in which the transformation of this ordinary citizen speaks to our own potential triumphs.

Celebrity also finds its foundation in the Aristotelian concept of *ethos*. Originally, Aristotle described *ethos* as the character of the speaker. This was tied directly to trustworthiness, as *ethos* could be strengthened through artful oratory. This is not the same thing as fame, which, as discussed earlier, springs from heroism, or *celebrity*, which is somewhat manufactured. Though fame and *celebrity* are two different things, both spring intrinsically from *ethos*. *Ethos* is not something that can be produced; it can be augmented, but a rhetor either has *ethos* or s/he does not. Under Aristotle, there are three ways that a rhetor can display *ethos:* through *phronesis*, or practical wisdom/skills, through *arête*, or virtue/excellence, or through *eunoia*, or goodwill toward the audience. Since *ethos* cannot be created (only enhanced), it is a sort of innate characteristic of the rhetor. It could be a natural charisma, or a commanding presence, or any one of a number of other factors which comprise this innate *ethos*, but it is obvious that some Celebrities have more *ethos* than others.[11]

James Monaco delineates three types of celebrity, differentiating the hero ("a famous person who has actually done something in an active sense") from the star (which is "not, as popularly conceived, an actor. Whereas the actor assumes roles, the star works on playing him- or herself") and the lowest form of celebrity, the "quasar" (someone who "has virtually no control over his or her image") (quoted in Marshall, p. 16). Boorstin (1961) echoes this separation of the heroic from the celebrity; overall, he has a fairly pessimistic view toward celebrity culture. He believes that in the far past, when someone was labeled a "great man," he was believed to have been imbued with some special talent or power from God that was used to overcome tremendous obstacles (Boorstin, 1961). Now, he says, we still have the idea that "well-knownness" comes from "greatness," but that there is no actual "greatness" in today's celebrities (Boorstin, 1961). They are not "famous," as they are not heroes. They are celebrities, because they are being celebrated not for their deeds, but because they are well known. Boorstin offers that when a great man appeared in the past,

II. Dude! I Met Elway!

we used to attribute it to God; now we can attribute it to a good publicist (Boorstin, 1961).

There appears to be a philosophical split in the literature regarding fame as to whether or not fame can be "good" or "bad." Epstein writes:

> Oliver Goldsmith, in his poem "The Deserted Villages," refers to "good fame," which implies that there is also a bad or false fame. Bad fame is sometimes thought to be fame in the present, or fame on earth, while good fame is that bestowed by posterity... Not false but wretched fame is covered by the word "infamy" ... while the lower, or pejorative, order of celebrity is covered by the word "notoriety" [Epstein, p. 14].

William Hazlitt, writing in the early 1800s, also speculated on whether "the nature of the celebrity involved discerning whether or not the individual was pursuing the highest of ends, unfettered by the desire for personal glory" (Marshall, p. 7). However, scholarship would seem to suggest that, in fact, by linking fame and heroism there is no such thing as bad fame — just as it suggests by linking *celebrity* and false praise there is no such thing as good *celebrity*.

In all cases, however, there is one constant: "Celebrity suggests ephemerality, while fame has a shot at reaching the happy shores of posterity" (Epstein, 2005, p. 14). Also, throughout the literature, there is a tinge, however slight, of accusation in the discussion of *celebrity*. Epstein (2005) makes the strongest outright indictment (although, by no means, is he alone in his assessment):

> [Celebrities] should all be judged guilty until proven innocent. Guilty of what, precisely? I'd say of fraudulence (however minor); of inflating their brilliance, accomplishments, worth; of passing themselves off as something they aren't, or at least are not quite. If fraudulence is the crime, publicity is the means by which the caper has been brought off [p. 15].

Under this logic, the mere act of possessing or using *celebrity* is essentially deceptive, although following Goffman's (1959) theory of presentation of self, all people are actors who perform on the "stage," selecting appropriate costumes and props as necessary, and retreat to the "backstage," where one can "be himself" (Goffman, 1959). One does not have to be a Celebrity to engage in this duality of self; "The public presentation of self is always a staged activity, in which the human actor presents a 'front' or 'face' to others while keeping a significant portion of the self in reserve" (Rojek, p. 11). So, while "celebrity status always implies a split between a private self and a public self" (Rojek, p. 11), it is not only Celebrities who engage in this duality. There is a heightened sense of "really" at work with the Celebrity that does not, intuitively, seem to function the same way with the people who surround us every day — "The private/public, individual/society dichotomy can be embodied by stars in various ways; the emphasis can fall at either end of the spectrum... Mostly too there is a sense of 'really' in play — people/stars are really themselves in private or perhaps in public but at any rate somewhere" (Dyer, p. 13). However, there does seem to be much more interest when it is a Celebrity that the speculation is about, as "social distance is the precondition of ... celebrity" (Rojek, p. 12). That is to say, wondering what one's neighbors are up to behind their closed door is neither as interesting nor as fantastical as what a Celebrity might be doing behind hers.

Celebrity, as discussed earlier, has become the defining prism through which American culture is now filtered. Holmes argues that fame is a mechanism for allowing alienated and anomic citizens to feel like a part of something — a material culture in which they can invest (p. 35). It is the "glue that holds the cultural center together" (p. 35).

Even within the realm of academics, *celebrity* has become an integral measure of success. Epstein (2005) suggests, "The most celebrated intellectuals of our day have been those most skillful at gaining publicity for their writing and their pronouncements" (p. 21). He argues that there are now academic Celebrities who, not on the power of scholarship and intelligence or classroom effectiveness, but on the power of exposure in the right journals and at the right conferences and through the right guest appearances in the *New York Times* and on National Public Radio, have elevated themselves to prominent positions in the academic community (p. 20). Epstein illustrates:

> The academic star, who is really the academic celebrity, is now a fairly common figure in what the world, that ignorant ninny, reckons the Great American Universities... By measure of pure celebrity, Cornel West is, at the moment, the star of all academic stars... He records rap CDs and appears at benefits with movie stars and famous athletes. When the president of Harvard spoke critically to West about his work not constituting serious scholarship ... it made front page news in the *New York Times*. West left, as we now know, and was instantly welcomed by Princeton [p. 19].

II. Dude! I Met Elway!

Time and time again, there is the recurrent theme of *celebrity* scholarship and discussion that intrinsic to the concept of *celebrity* is a falsehood or undeserved nature. West makes for an appropriate exemplar: putting aside the claims of so-called "serious scholarship," by virtue of the fact that West has chosen to appear in venues outside of the traditional academic circles, it is viewed by some within the academy as undeserved recognition. The word "celebrity," as used here, is certainly pejorative. It is as if the critics of *celebrity* wish to simply reduce it "to an admittedly rather crude equation: celebrity = impact on public consciousness" (Chaudbry, p. 10). However, this ignores the multi-faceted nature of *celebrity* and the extent to which it has come to define social relations within Western culture.

Summary

The terms "fame" and "celebrity" are interlinked but not necessarily interchangeable. There is a distinct difference between the physical, tangible human being Celebrity represents and the social and economic concepts that constitute *celebrity* as a cultural construct. *Celebrity* has become the prism through which mainstream measures of success are filtered in Western society—at the core of modern measures of accomplishment is the "success myth." The success myth rises out of the notion that any one of us could be a Celebrity with the right amount of talent, luck, and opportunity.

Celebrity is also a universalizing agent within Western society; even if one has no particular feelings about a certain Celebrity, chances are s/he can recognize the Celebrity and may even know a few bits of gossip about the Celebrity. Celebrities serve as a form of social cement, binding strangers together through casual knowledge and offering entrée routes into conversation. The stories of Celebrities are the stories of the history of the modern world; every major cultural, political, and social development of the past 3,000 years is traced through the individual—from Jesus to George Washington.

Celebrity and Celebrities exist as commodity forms in modern society, but this was not always the case historically. In the Roman era, civic honors were reserved for those who were either born into nobility or

American Idolatry

possessed some sort of innate military, philosophical, or artistic gift. Later in the Roman era, Augustus began widespread use of his own image as publicity, and the popularization of his particular clothing style — two aspects of *celebrity* that survive to this day. In the 16th century, modern printing capabilities expanded the reach of *celebrity*, and writers such as Benjamin Franklin began promoting the idea of the "self-made man." This concept of the Adamic hero — the hero of the people, for the people, by the people — dominated *celebrity* discourse throughout the 17th and 18th centuries. The Graphic Revolution again changed the face of *celebrity*, as an increase in literacy and advancements in printing and distribution technologies vastly amplified the scope of *celebrity*.

Film became the primary venue for the evolution of the *celebrity* in the early 20th century. Film production companies were able to create both glamour and mystique by exacting Draconian control over the Celebrities under their contracts. The advent of television permanently transformed the American celebrity system. Celebrities were no longer distant; the Celebrity could now enter the individual living room and the audience could apprehend the Celebrity in a more intimate environment. Other aspects of *celebrity* include the fundamental property rights inherent in the publicity of one's image, and the Aristotelian concept of *ethos*, or character.

3

Jay-Z Is One of Us, Only Not

You aren't famous until my mother has heard of you.
— Jay Leno

Celebrity and Symbolism

As has been discussed in Chapter I, the dominant culture's ideologies and priorities enjoy a favored position within media—logically, this also means that those who are most successful within these ideologies and in line with these priorities have the best chance of becoming Celebrities. Celebrities, in turn, benefit from a particular type of power that is, as Marshall notes, anchored in two distinct loci: "the realm of individual identity and the realm of the supporting group of followers" (Marshall, p. 25). The power of the Celebrity is unique in that it is a suggestive power rather than an authoritative power; the Celebrity can persuade but cannot demand. Alberoni (1962) argues, "The star is not endowed with authoritative power and ... his decisions are not collectively felt to have any influence on the life and the future of members of the collectivity" (Alberoni, 110). Because the Celebrity has *influence* rather than *control*, s/he is uniquely situated to fulfill three symbolic functions: First, Celebrities model appropriate cultural behavior — they are "the ultimate sellers. They sell us things. And because of the intimacy and kinship we feel for them, they humanize the process" (Derakhshani, p. 30). It is important to note that what Celebrities sell is not just product but ideology as well.[1] Secondly, they are the personification of consumption — they know what to buy, what is "in," where to buy it and how to flaunt it. Celebrities are "ideal consumers, always buying more. Luxurious lifestyles make celebs symbols for consumption itself" (Derakhshani, p. 30). Thirdly, as has been repeatedly pointed out, they themselves are commodities. There is a vast selection of Celebrity commodities for audiences to enjoy, and "as consumer goods whose lives are laid out for us to enjoy, celebs are (nothing but?) objects to be bought and sold — and eventually discarded" (Derakhshani, 30).

The first of these three symbolic functions — Celebrities as cultural behavioral models — may be the most important of all. The Celebrity represents what it means to be an individual in our consumerist society — what it means to be a person, what it means to be a consumer (Holmes, p. 9).

Because, as discussed in the previous chapter, all of American society is foundationally driven by ideas of individuality and individual success (particularly economic success), it makes perfect sense that Celebrities, who have achieved levels of individual success and wealth to which most Americans will never come close, would stand as models for "typical ways of behaving, feeling, and thinking in contemporary society, ways that have been socially, culturally, historically constructed" (Dyer, p. 15). The flip side of the coin, however, is the fact that "individual success" is a term that can only be loosely utilized when discussing the Celebrity. As will be discussed later in this chapter, a Celebrity is the product of labor — not just his/her own labor, but the labor of dozens of others as well. In this manner, "they are not straightforward affirmations of individualism. On the contrary, they articulate both the promise and the difficulty that the notion of individuality presents for all of us who live by it" (Dyer, p. 7). The totemic nature of Celebrity also does not open up the meaning of those Celebrities entirely to subjective interpretation. As McDonald writes:

> The images of stars are open to a range of meanings and readings but that range is inevitably limited. At one level, the meaning of star image is constrained by the content of star texts. Jack Nicholson smiles in a particular way. He speaks with a certain rhythm. Opinions may differ over whether Jack Nicholson is charming or vulgar, menacing or sexy, but it seems unlikely that his image will be read as conveying innocence and moral purity [McDonald, p. 7].

III. Jay-Z Is One of Us, Only Not

According to Flora, "Celebrities tap into powerful motivational systems designed to foster romantic love and to urge us to find a mate. Stars summon our most human yearnings: to love, admire, copy, and, of course, to gossip and to jeer" (Flora, p. 34). Their standing as cultural prototypes (archetypes?) provide society with valuable communizing potential — as society incessantly subdivides into smaller and smaller segments and finer and finer niches, people are far less apt to collectively come across the same cultural experiences (read the same books, watch the same films, and so on) (Keats, p. 155). Celebrities provide cultural touchstones at the same time they serve as cultural totems for how (or how not) to behave. We may not all *care* when Brad Pitt and Angelina Jolie produce (or, more likely, adopt) a new child, but almost all of us *know* that it happened. We all "know when Lindsay Lohan is in rehab. And for an instant, we could all recognize the father of Anna Nicole Smith's baby" (Keats, p. 155).

Celebrities are also uniquely positioned to suggest ways in which we can all be "good capitalist consumers" because of their totemic nature. Part of what makes a Celebrity a Celebrity is his/her ability to function in multiple arenas in a variety of contexts; Marshall argues that the "viability of a celebrity can be translated as the celebrity's capacity to appeal to an audience through a specific array of commodities or services" (Marshall, p. 186). Michael Jordan was, perhaps, the greatest basketball player ever to play the game; however, his influence was felt most through the enormous endorsement power his name and likeness could generate. Jordan sold jerseys, shoes, Gatorade, breakfast cereal, as well as having his own Saturday morning cartoon and his own professional golf tournament. It is well documented that Jordan was, at the height of his career, the highest-paid single athlete in the history of professional team sports, even though, at the time, his salary from the Chicago Bulls was a relatively paltry $3.2 million dollars a year (Vancil 1991). (Consider that in 2008, the lowest paid player in the top 40 salaries in the NBA made $11 million ["NBA Salaries" n.d.].) Celebrities that can sell goods as well as ideology are Celebrities with staying power.

The second symbolic function — that Celebrities represent the ideal consumer — is an offshoot of the first symbolic function. That is to say, according to Rojek, "We will not understand the peculiar hold that celebrities exert over us today unless we recognize that celebrity culture is irrevocably bound up with commodity culture" (Rojek, 14). Celebrities do not just sell things; Celebrities buy things. Lots of things. Britney Spears spends over $240,000 per month—the average American household spends just over $48,000 a *year* (Hau 2007). Supermodel Rachel Hunter once spent $15,000 on a custom-made Mediterranean-style house for her dog; Tom Cruise and Katie Holmes bought a $200,000 Sonogram machine for their home for daily baby checks while Holmes was pregnant ("The Fabulous Life" n.d.).

But it is not only the extravagant purchases that make Celebrities models for consumption. Celebrities dictate what is fashionable. According to one study, 55 percent of people 16–24 years of age look to Celebrities for fashion direction ("Fashion's Red Carpet" 2006). Brand names get boosts from Celebrities being seen in public wearing particular clothes; designers fight tooth and nail over which Celebrities will be wearing which clothes on the red carpet at awards shows. During the late 1990s, Jennifer Aniston's hairstyle was one of the most requested hairstyles at salons around the world (just as "Farrah hair" dominated the 1970s and, most recently, Victoria Beckham's "Posh bob" has gained enormous popularity) ("Name That Do!" 2008). It is not only fashion in which Celebrities help dictate trends. The entire function of the website "Coolspotters" is to catalogue the products which Celebrities are using in their daily lives and exhorting visitors to the website to use the same products as their favorite Celebrity. Megan Fox uses a Blackberry 8820; so should you ("Megan Fox" n.d.). George Clooney frequents the restaurant Madeo in Los Angeles; do you ("George Clooney" n.d.)? What Celebrities buy shows society what to buy—but more importantly, it shows society that they *should* buy. Buy something. Buy anything. In this regard, Celebrities, "in this fluid construction of identity through consumption, represent flags, markers, or buoys for the clustering of cultural significance through patterns of consumption" (Marshall, p. 245).

Likewise, Celebrities, through their conspicuous consumption and trend-setting, represent exemplars of their fan communities in a symbiotic relationship. Crooks & Castles clothing is popular partly because Celebrities such as Jay Z wear it in public; conversely, Jay Z chooses to wear Crooks & Castles as opposed to other brands precisely because it is the type of clothing to which his fans can connect. In this regard, Jay Z's

III. Jay-Z Is One of Us, Only Not

"formative power rests with the people as an expression of popular culture and social will" (Marshall, p. 56). Through his consumption choices, Jay Z becomes "one of us," even when, clearly, he no longer is. However, "for the subordinate cultures, the celebrity articulates an avenue for the expression of their own notions of freedom, fantasy, and needs" (Marshall, p. 56). Jay Z is the kind of person we would be if we had Jay Z's money. He buys what we *would* buy, wears what we *would* wear, eats at the restaurants we *would* frequent.

The third symbolic function of Celebrities — to be commodities themselves — is a complex phenomenon, borne of the rooting of all Western media in capitalist principles. By virtue of the organizational structure of society under a capitalist matrix, consumers are driven to accumulate, and the markets dictate that proper accumulation is founded upon constantly changing wants on the part of the consumer (Rojek, p. 14). This consumer restiveness "in industrial culture partly derives from the capitalist requirement to initiate perpetual commodity and brand innovation" (Rojek, p. 14). When new products are introduced in relentless perpetuity, "desire is alienable, transferable, since wants must be perpetually switched in response to market developments. The market inevitably turned the public face of the celebrity into a commodity" (Rojek, 14). Old, reliable Celebrities continue to draw market share, but there are new Celebrities entering the marketplace all the time, competing for attention and resources.

In this, Celebrities are, in many ways, disposable commodities, both for the consumer and for the producer. For the consumer, "although they clearly want a celebrity with demonstrated attention-getting capacity, entertainment buyers do not necessarily need one with the demonstrated capacity of audience loyalty" (Gamson, p. 83). In fact, there is some measure of social capital to be gained by "discovering" a new band, a new book, a new film that one's acquaintances have not yet experienced. The "trendsetter" label is certainly one worth acquiring in an individualistically-based society. On the other hand, for producers, new Celebrities are more easily exploitable in terms of investment to profit ratio; a Celebrity "who is hot and recognizable but not established is easier to come by and less expensive to employ than a major star" (Gamson, p. 83). While there is great potential benefit in terms of box office receipts in paying the salary that a star like Tom Hanks commands, often, it is safer to cast a less well-known actor in that role, invest less capital in the production, and take the chance that the actor can rise to the occasion.

Both Celebrity and *celebrity* are constructed through an amalgamation of power dynamics and economic forces. Marshall (1997) points out that:

> The term celebrity has a metaphor for value in modern society. More specifically, it describes a type of value that can be articulated through an individual and celebrated publicly as important and significant. The term is linked to past power structures (i.e., the church) and now has connotations that link it to modern power structures (i.e., capitalism) [p. 7].

Celebrity and Celebrities exist as a commodity, in the classic, Marxist sense of the term. Carefully packaged, surrounded by teams of publicists and personal managers, the Celebrity is certainly "an object outside us, a thing that by its properties satisfies human wants of some sort or another" (Marx, p. 303). The Celebrity is a product of labor (both the labor of the Celebrity him/herself, and that of the team of people surrounding him/her), and, for Marx, "that which determines the magnitude of the value of any article is the amount of labour socially necessary, or the labour time socially necessary for its production" (p. 306). In the case of the Celebrity, the value of the Celebrity is determined by the amount of time necessary to cultivate and promote the Celebrity's fame. However, the Celebrity is most often divorced from the labor required to create him/her. Dyer writes, "Stars are involved in making themselves into commodities; they are both labour and the thing that labour produces. They do not produce themselves alone" (p. 5). Reese Witherspoon, for example, is recognized as being highly paid because she is a "big star," not because she has a dedicated team of lawyers, managers, publicists, and advisors all dedicated to the goal of earning her more money. Mendelson states:

> To create and manage this consistent image, a celebrity must surround him- or herself with an army of assistants; what Rojek calls "cultural intermediaries." These include agents, publicists, fashion and beauty consultants, talent coaches and security staff... The image of a celebrity is an institutional edifice, maintained and protected by armies of press agents, makeup artists, and bodyguards. It usually falls to the publicist to ensure the consistency and control of the celebrity's image and to find the means to get that image into the public [p. 175].

III. Jay-Z Is One of Us, Only Not

This is labor in production of a commodity, in a very literal sense. These cultural intermediaries are employed to do work on an assembly line, and the end product is *celebrity*. But this labor involved in creating the "big star" is pushed to the background. Witherspoon exists, in Marx's terms, as a fetishized commodity. The labor necessary to produce the commodity is masked by the commodity itself. If Celebrity and *celebrity* are taken to be two distinct entities, where "attention-getting capacity" is the function of *celebrity* and securing and maintenance of that capacity is the function of a Celebrity, then Gamson is correct when he states:

> Celebrity is clearly ... an established commercial enterprise, made up of highly developed and institutionally linked professions and subindustries such as public relations, entertainment law, celebrity journalism and photography, grooming and training, managing and agenting, novelty sales. As carriers of the central commodity (attention-getting capacity), celebrity performers are themselves products [p. 64].

The subindustries are not readily apparent in the product itself, hence the labor has been masked or relegated to the background, fetishizing the commodity. The Celebrity is even more detached from the labor necessary to produce him or her because his/her fame exists intertextually across a wide range of discourses. We recognize a Celebrity, such as Witherspoon, not simply from her films, but also from television appearances on talk shows, magazine interviews, newspaper stories, paparazzi photographs, and a variety of other sources. The diversity of labor necessary to produce the commodity puts additional distance between the commodity and the labor.

This intertextuality reveals another facet of the Celebrity commodity — the necessity for the commodity to be both accessible and unattainable to the consumer. In this respect, the private and public spheres of the Celebrity's life must have a certain amount of openness, because *celebrity* is not simply about the work of making movies or walking the red carpet. *Celebrity* functions all the time, 24 hours a day. In this respect, I will give Boorstin his due: it is quite accurate to say that, in many ways in this context, the famous are famous for being famous. Lee Barron (2006), for example, in his remarkably in-depth study of Elizabeth Hurley, remarked that she exemplifies the distinction between actor and celebrity because her appeal is multifarious; she gains (wanted or otherwise) media attention often simply by appearing in public, no matter how mundane the activity or how glamorous. For example, one recent magazine cover featured a photograph of her shopping with the subsequent headlines claiming to reveal what she "really eats" [p. 530].

Hurley garnered headlines regarding her condition leading up to a confirmation of her pregnancy, and continued to make news through the birth of her son and the subsequent paternity suit involving the child's father (p. 530). These headlines were not regarding Hurley's occupation as an actress or a model, but regarding Hurley's private status as a citizen. In 2002, Hurley was a news staple for being Elizabeth Hurley.

Like all commodities, the Celebrity has both a use value and an exchange value. The use value is determined by the ability of a commodity to fill some sort of need. If a commodity is not desirable, or does not serve some function, then it has no use value. Marx states, "Use values become a reality only by use or consumption: they also constitute the substance of all wealth, whatever may be the social form of that wealth" (p. 303). In the case of the Celebrity, the social form of that wealth is the construct of fame. Fame is ostensibly determined by use value; the more talented (or, at the least, media savvy) a performer is, the more their services will be desired, and the higher use value they possess.

Marx states, "Exchange value ... presents itself as a quantitative relation, as the proportion in which values in use of one sort are exchanged for those of another sort, a relation constantly changing with time and place" (p. 304). Exchange value does not necessarily correlate with use value. While use value is inherent in the commodity, exchange value is based on how much of another commodity one is willing to exchange for the product. The ratio of use value to exchange value is, at least in Hollywood, mercurial at best. As Marshall writes, "The convertibility of value, a value that emphasizes inherent 'exchange value' over 'use value,' is the persistent reality" (p. 11).

One major issue, though, with determining "use value" is that the argument assumes that use value is limited to the work of a Celebrity at his or her chosen occupational niche. *Celebrity* does work beyond this. A Celebrity is not simply an actor, a musician, a basketball player. The

III. Jay-Z Is One of Us, Only Not

Celebrity is also required to maintain *celebrity* in "real life"; she must appear on the red carpet, selling glamour, ethereality, and Versace. She must grant magazine interviews and talk about her dog and her children. Her work does not end when the director yells, "Cut!" This maintenance of intertextual identity is crucial in the continued success of the *celebrity* commodity as well as the Celebrity commodity. It is what makes each Celebrity a unique product. Choi & Rifon (2007) point out:

> Although celebrities share some common characteristics, including recognition, status, and popularity, each celebrity embodies his or her own unique image in the media. While one celebrity may be considered an appropriate endorser for one brand, she or he may be completely wrong for another based on the public's perception of her/his distinctive image [p. 305].

The intertextual identity of a Celebrity is also important because of the third work function of *celebrity*: perpetuation of the Celebrity commodity. *Celebrity* does not merely exist to sell films and the intertextual identity. It must also replicate itself, propagating *celebrity* status as long as it can. It is not enough to simply entice fans into idolizing the Celebrity — not when a new Celebrity commodity will inevitably enter the marketplace in such a way that it is in direct competition for audience attention. There is an economic imperative in even this function of *celebrity*.

> Engle & Kasser (2005) posit that Celebrity idolization is performed through acquisition and possession of merchandise adorned with the Celebrity's image, such as DVDs, CDs, clothes, key chains, and the like [Engle & Kasser, p. 268]. Those objects that were formerly owned by the Celebrity or are autographed by the Celebrity are often very valuable to fans and sell for extremely high prices [p. 268]. Many fan web sites link out to other sites which also sell the Celebrity's merchandise, concert tickets, and so on [p. 268]. Engle & Kasser directly correlate materialism and idolization.

So the work of *celebrity* is not limited only to the Celebrity's occupational niche, nor is it limited to the Celebrity's cultivated image. Jennifer Love Hewitt does not only act and sing, nor does she only walk the red carpet and give magazine interviews — she also acts as de facto spokeswoman for an entire range of Jennifer Love Hewitt merchandise, from posters to calendars to desktop screen savers. It is a third form of work the *celebrity* commodity is called upon to perform. This work also extends to the use of *celebrity* to endorse other, non-*celebrity* products, such as everything from cars to shoes to pharmaceuticals (Batra & Homer 2004, Moynihan 2004, Kripalani 2006, L'Etang 2006), as the first and second symbolic functions of Celebrities earlier suggested.

The mechanisms of commodity capitalism itself are the driving force behind this third work function of *celebrity*. The marketability of a Celebrity's ancillary merchandise is fundamental; hence, the need for stars to continually "reinvent themselves" in order to stay one step ahead of the consumer's attention span. Rojek states:

> Capitalism requires consumers to develop an abstract desire for commodities. Desire is necessarily an abstract compulsion under capitalism, because the logic of economic accumulation means that it must be transferred in response to commodity and brand innovation. This abstract quality renders desire alienable from consumers, since they are routinely required to replace strong commodity wants with new ones. The compulsion of abstract desire under capitalism transforms the individual from a desiring object into a calculating object of desire. Consumers do not simply nourish wants for the commodity; they routinely construct the façade of embodiment in order to be desired by the abstracted mass. Fashion and taste cultures intensify and mirror this tendency. Celebrity culture is therefore partly the expression of a cultural axis organized around abstract desire [p. 187].

Society, as discussed in Chapter II, is conditioned to move from one product to another as a function of style, trend, "keeping up with the Joneses." This extends to the entertainment industry as well; attend a movie, and the first thing one sees is a trailer for another movie. It is routine for television stations to overlay graphics (sometimes as large as 50 percent of the screen) for other upcoming television programs. One cannot even finish consuming the current product before advertising for the next product begins. This is the commodity culture in which *celebrity* must compete. Rojek reminds, "Consumers under capitalism do not experience unifying fulfillment when desire is matched with possession. For the abstract quality of desire means that wants are never satisfied by possessing a particular commodity" (p. 187). I want Alyssa Milano, but only until I have her. Once I have her, have apprehended her in some way (on film, on television, in a magazine, on the Internet), I am satiated but not satisfied. In a few days (hours, minutes, seconds), I am hungry again and wondering what (who) is next? In some ways, the answer is irrelevant; any commodity will do when the end goal is wanting, not having—not to

III. Jay-Z Is One of Us, Only Not

savor, but to simply consume.² This is the wall *celebrity* is up against. It must, in order to continue to exist, not only reify its tangible asset (i.e., the Celebrity), but relay a transitory quality to that asset — the asset can be "new," "different," "fresh." Once that product is dated it is through, unless a "comeback" can be staged. The product, the Celebrity, has to be wanted, desired, in order for it to continue to exist as a commodity. Otherwise it is, as stated earlier, completely disposable. Rojek points out:

> Capitalism demands that consumers consume, but it also requires them to be conscious of the built-in obsolescence of the commodity. All forms of consumption, then, have a provisional quality, which again reinforces the split between having and wanting in the consumer. Celebrity culture is one of the most important mechanisms for mobilizing abstract desire. It embodies desire in an animate object, which allows for deeper levels of attachment and identification than with inanimate commodities. Celebrities can be reinvented to renew desire, and because of this they are extremely efficient resources in the mobilization of global desire. In a word, they humanize desire [p. 189].

In point of fact, *celebrity* is so dependent upon the reification of the Celebrity — and so adept at it — that the commodity is often able to live on, even after death (Cooper, 2005). People still swear they have seen Tupac, years after his death. John Lennon continues to be a topic of conversation among music aficionados. And, still, few Celebrities enjoy the popularity and relevance that Elvis Presley maintains, though he has been deceased for over thirty years. This is proof that while the Celebrity and *celebrity* inhabit the same space, it is a parasitic rather than symbiotic relationship. The Celebrity needs *celebrity*, not the other way around. *Celebrity*, as a commodity, has the potential to endure far beyond the mortal shell which once embodied it.

The disposable nature of *celebrity* cannot be discounted, however. The ultimate in disposable Celebrity commodity is what Rojek refers to as the "celetoid." Rojek writes: "I propose celetoid as the term for any form of compressed, concentrated attributed celebrity. I distinguish celetoids from celebrities because, generally, the latter enjoy a more durable career with the public" (p. 20). The celetoid's rise to their moment of fame is meteoric, as is the rate at which s/he disappears from the public consciousness (p. 21). Reality television has a particular advantage in the generation of celetoids as limited-run Celebrities, as the celetoid is in the public eye for a finite amount of time (the length of time of a season) and is quickly and easily replaced with the next season's new batch of celetoids. Even on a popular program such as *Survivor*, very few of the contestants from the early seasons continue to be household names (if they ever were to begin with). This, Rojek says, is the "irrevocable condition of celetoid status"—evanescence—although he does concede that "in exceptional cases a celetoid may acquire a degree of longevity" (p. 22). For example, *Survivor*'s first winner, Richard Hatch, remained in the public eye long after his season of *Survivor* ended, largely on the basis of his legal battles over his *Survivor* winnings and taxes ("Prison Agony" 2008). This, however, is the exception rather than the rule. Most celetoids, by definition, are here today and forgotten tomorrow.

While reality television may seem like a democratization of *celebrity*, at least to the point of celetoid status, not every scholar agrees with this categorization. Holmes, for example, argues that although it is fashionable to believe, thanks to reality TV, that anyone can become a Celebrity, the truth is that the participant's success is completely constrained by the context of the program—s/he can only journey where the "reality space" allows him/her (p. 46). That is to say that the democratization analogy can only be taken so far. In engineering "Celebrities" (celetoids) for public consumption, producers are attempting to fundamentally alter the constitution of the Celebrity commodity, often with mixed results. Marshall (2006) argues:

> These programs themselves are very controlled and contrived constructions of celebrity discourse in and of themselves. Television, through these programs, has dispensed with the originary text that defines and makes the star and has begun constructing "celebrities" through its narratives of the intimate via a plethora of strategically placed cameras and microphones. It should also be noted here that this construction of celebrities of the moment by television has demanded the development of contracts that resemble the old film studio era in their control of their talent [p. 643].

This last assertion is important: a Celebrity is a product of the processing of raw materials—and raw materials are capital investments. Therefore, as McDonald states, "Star contracts must deal with stars as both labour and capital, defining relationships over not only the star as a

III. Jay-Z Is One of Us, Only Not

particular category of worker but also the star as a property and a product that can be exploited for commercial purposes in image markets" (p. 12). The producers must, as evidenced in Chapters I and II, take explicit and often Draconian control over their capital investment, as a celetoid is much less likely to produce continued economic returns than an "actual" Celebrity.

Externally, it appears to the viewer as if ordinary people are being provided a space in which to reveal that they are secretly extraordinary — that they could be an amazing dancer or singer or comedian if just given an opportunity to show the world (Holmes, p. 29). Shows like *Idol* present themselves to auditioners as searching for "raw talent" that is "waiting to be discovered" (p. 29).

Internally, however, the contracts those "would-be" hopefuls are made to sign reveal what is truly at stake: capital returns. While it is apparent that the manner in which a celetoid is produced is similar to the way in which a Celebrity is produced, clearly the two processes are not the same. If the "fame hierarchy" begins with the hero at the top, and the Celebrity next, then the celetoid's place is at or near the bottom. Reality television contestants can be thought of in one of two ways: either as the embodiment of manufactured *celebrity*, or as the lowest level of disposable/renewable Celebrity (p. 7).

Symbolically, the Celebrity serves three distinct functions. First, the Celebrity is a model for "how to be" in society. The Celebrity is:

> the independent individual par excellence; he or she represents the meaning of freedom and accessibility in a culture. The close scrutiny that is given to celebrities is to accentuate the possibility and potential for individuals to shape themselves unfettered by the constraints of a hierarchical society [Marshall, 1997, p. 246].

The system of societal organization (capitalism) uses Celebrities to "promote individualism and illusions of democracy (the 'anyone can do it' myth)" (Giles, p. 19), and popular media are used to substantiate the success myth by inculcating audience members with a desire (and often step-by-step plans) to harness a modicum of star-like quality through style and behavior (Holmes, p. 30). Secondly, the Celebrity promulgates conspicuous consumption through trendsetting and openly lavish lifestyle. The Celebrity encourages individuals to be good consumers by publicly consuming. Finally, the Celebrity him/herself is a commodity, an "'investment'—like all raw materials, they often require a good deal of processing before they are marketable—and that investment 'must be protected'" (Gamson, p. 45). The Celebrity is the product of labor and deliberate construction by a wide range of subindustries solely dedicated to the *celebrity* commodity. This leads to a dichotomy in the way in which Celebrities are thought of by society: "On the one hand, we adore celebrities as representing success and achievement; on the other, we ridicule them for representing 'false' values of commodity and exchange" (Giles, p. 19).

Even with all of this in mind, it is difficult to categorize *celebrity* and Celebrities as mere commodities. To do so ignores the very real dynamics of social exchange—"celebrity" is a social construct as well as an economic construct. Rojek points out, "In the strongest versions of the culture industry thesis, celebrity is explained as the triumph of the manipulative influence of entertainment moguls, PR specialists and image makers. The knowledge, desire, and judgment of the audience are sidelined" (p. 43). There is an element of human social exchange that is undeniable in the character of *celebrity* which involves systematic making of meaning.

Theoretical Approaches to the Social Construction of Celebrity

Rojek delineates the three main theoretical approaches to the study of modern *celebrity*. Each approach has influenced the discourse surrounding *celebrity*, and each brings a unique perspective on the phenomenon.

Subjectivist approaches to *celebrity* begin from a position that *celebrity* is the "reflection of innate talent" (Rojek, p. 29). This is an extension of the early history of fame, during which time, as explained earlier in this chapter, fame was seen as either divinely imparted or tied to a "specialness" in the individual. The subjectivist approach assumes talent to be a "unique, ultimately inexplicable phenomenon" (Rojek, p. 29) that cannot be learned or replicated. Under the subjectivist perspective, Celebrities arise because of their "authentic, gifted self" rather than from public action

III. Jay-Z Is One of Us, Only Not

or public virtue (Gamson, p. 31). This meritocratic view of fame is extended into modern *celebrity* through what Gamson calls

> the new, consumerist language: the celebrity rises, selected for his personality (revealed through his lifestyle choices), an irrational, but nonetheless organic, "folk" phenomenon. The theme of the discovery of greatness, earlier termed a greatness of character, was translated into the discovery of a combination of "talent," "star quality," and "personality" [p. 31].

In essence, a Celebrity becomes a Celebrity because s/he was born to do so. S/he was destined for greatness. It is a sort of circular logic which comprises a self-fulfilling prophecy: "Greatness is built in, it is who you are. If one works at it, or gets a lucky break, it may be discovered. If it is discovered, one becomes celebrated for it, which is evidence that one had it to begin with" (Gamson, p. 32). From a commodity standpoint, the Celebrity

> might be thought of as tapping the surplus material and symbolic value that is inherent in the economic and moral frameworks governing everyday life. On this reckoning, celebrity is, so to speak, the embodiment of surplus, since it radiates greater material and symbolic power than non-celebrity [Rojek, p. 31].

One example of a subjectivist approach to *celebrity* is found in the work of Max Weber. Some of the social construction of *celebrity* can be explained by returning to Weber's (1978) seminal essay, *The Types of Legitimate Domination*. In it, Weber defines "charisma" as "a certain quality of an individual personality by virtue of which he is considered extraordinary and treated as endowed with supernatural, superhuman, or at least specifically exceptional powers or qualities" (p. 241). Marshall points out that "Weber identifies charisma as a 'gift' from the grace of God" (p. 20). Weber is speaking, of course, of religious leaders, kings, and so on, who can affect significant social revolution through the power of personality. However, as Gertrud Koch (1999) points out, Weber's theory of charismatic authority can very easily be read in terms of mediated communication:

> Charismatic authority would have to do with influence being exercised over the masses for a limited period of time that relies primarily on the communications media and makes use especially of speech. In the age of advanced technologies of dissemination, at their most effective in the way they reduce

time differences, wielding charismatic influence becomes an automatic by-product of the star system [p. 212].

A Celebrity enjoys a certain measure of power over dissemination of information, not because s/he is an expert on any one particular subject, but because s/he has accumulated enough *celebrity* in his/her own field to command use of the media for alternate purposes (p. 212).

So the Celebrity is not merely a commodity which can be exchanged on the economic market, but also a human being that is granted a certain amount of exceptionality by virtue of *celebrity* which can be used in a variety of ways, from speaking out against a war to mobilizing the population to recycle.

Because this sort of exceptionality relies upon an ascribing of "extraordinary" status to the Celebrity, it is imperative that encounters between the Celebrity and the "common folk" take place in specific and proscribed, ritualized ways. These performative mechanisms are actually part and parcel of the continued production of charisma; one does not simply walk up to the palace gates and demand to meet the king. The king has his job to do: he must appear to be extraordinary, exceptional, superhuman. Rojek delineates the parallel to *celebrity*:

> [Weber] argued that charismatic authority is, by definition, inspirational. It depends on apparently miraculous or semi-miraculous occurrences, such as prophesies that come true, battles that are always won, powers of healing that never falter, artistic performances that succeed time and again. All of these features have overtones in the modern concept of celebrity [p. 32].

At the same time, however, it is also essential that the Celebrity appear to be "one of us." S/he cannot be too far removed from the population at large, otherwise, the economic potential of *celebrity* could be jeopardized. We must be able to see a little bit of ourselves in the Celebrity; it is how the commodification and reification of the Celebrity is masked. Marshall (1997) states:

> The star is meant to epitomize the potential of everyone in American society. We are psychically drawn to identify with the stars as ourselves. This, however, is only appearance. The dialectical reality is that the star is part of a system of false promise in the system of capital, which offers the reward of stardom to a random few in order to perpetuate the myth of potential universal success [p. 9].

III. Jay-Z Is One of Us, Only Not

Identification keeps the Celebrity accessible; this is especially true for actors, whose ability to portray characters as "real" is key in their perception as adept at their craft. Again, as pointed out earlier, there is a reason Celebrities go out of their way to appear on talk shows and in magazine interviews. The illusion that the Celebrity can somehow be apprehended in a tangible sense must be maintained. One is (probably) never going to meet Natalie Portman, but theoretically, one could, and if s/he did, s/he might be shocked to find out that Portman behaved "like a regular person."

This is a fairly universal desire of contemporary society — to get beyond the reified Celebrity commodity and discover a "real" person. This is revealed in a multitude of ways, from societal fascination with celebrity weddings to the proliferation of paparazzi to the seemingly endless parade of nude photographs of Celebrities on the Internet. Dyer (1986) explains that

> the audience is obsessively and incessantly searching the star persona for the real and the authentic. We are aware that stars are appearances, yet the whole media construction of stars encourages us to think in terms of "really." What is Marilyn Monroe "really" like? Is Paul Newman "really" the same as he appears in his films? [p. 17].

There are several drives at play here; there is an intense desire by both fans (consumers) and by media to circumvent the constructed (manufactured) façade of the Celebrity and expose the "real" person beneath (Holmes and Redmond, p. 4). It is one of the primary ways in which modern fame is distributed and understood (p. 4). And, at its very most basic, this desire centers on the physical body of the Celebrity; the Celebrity's flesh is his/her most basic "truth." Holmes and Redmond explain:

> If one can see the famous person stripped of all their finery, then one is supposedly getting unrestricted and unfiltered access to gaze at, and be intimate with, their primal state. If one gets to see the star or celebrity body as flawed (fat, spotty, wrinkled), then one is supposedly getting a more natural or unmediated picture of them [p. 4].

The naked Celebrity is either a confirmation that underneath the glamour, s/he is either truly attractive (enviable), or (maybe just like us) disappointing — s/he is either worthy of being idealized or, like us, imperfect

American Idolatry

(mortal) (p. 4). In apprehending the Celebrity in this fashion, we provide ourselves with a convenient illusion that we have somehow cheated the system — that we have outmaneuvered the *celebrity* machine and seen the truth behind the reified commodity. We have pulled back the curtain and seen the old man working the levers of the Wizard. However, this is not necessarily the case. We are simply acting out the roles and rituals ingrained in us since we were young. Society teaches each of us how to behave in the presence of the king. As Kerry Ferris (2004) states, we might be spellbound when we see a Celebrity on the subway or in the mall, but it can also be extremely awkward:

> We are conditioned to look for and find pleasure in the knowledge that the extraordinary star experiences ordinary trials, and celebrity stories are usually constructed to reveal that fame and fortune do not necessarily smooth over the problems of everyday life. But we are also disturbed by the collision of the ideal with the real: when celebrities undergo the mundane ordeals of real life, fans must reevaluate their idealized image of celebrity life [p. 241].

When these two frames of reference slam into each other, there is a consequential avalanche of emotion: anticipation, disillusionment, delight, superciliousness, and embarrassment, all of which are experienced internally because of the situational constraints of the venue (p. 241).

Even in these supposedly "real" encounters with *celebrity*, the commodity consumption process is at work. So while it is clear that Celebrity and *celebrity* are not completely and wholly defined by the culture industry perspective, neither is it safe to say that Celebrity and *celebrity* are totally social exchange processes. The functioning of *celebrity* in contemporary society lies somewhere in the middle. That does not preclude "much of the popular biographical literature on celebrity [from being] based upon Subjectivist assumptions" (Rojek, p. 32). It is a common refrain in *celebrity* literature: There will never be another John Lennon (Marilyn Monroe, Audrey Hepburn, Kurt Cobain, etc.).

Structuralist approaches to *celebrity* take an entirely different route to explaining the phenomenon. Rather than *celebrity* being some reflection of innate, inherent talent or "gifts" on the part of the Celebrity, *celebrity* is "investigated as the expression of universal structural rules embedded in society" (Rojek, p. 33). That is to say, *celebrity* is a natural part of the hegemonic socialization process that was bound to emerge as part and

III. Jay-Z Is One of Us, Only Not

parcel of the rise of the culture industry. *Celebrity* surfaces as another form of social control within organized entertainment. Rojek writes:

> [The culture industry's] ultimate aim is to reinforce and extend the rule of capital. Celebrities are conceptualized as one of the means through which capitalism achieves its ends of subduing and exploiting the masses. They express an ideology of heroic individualism, upward mobility and choice in social conditions wherein standardization, monotony and routine prevail. Thus the identification of the masses with celebrity is always false consciousness, since celebrities are not regarded as reflections of reality, but fabrications designed to enhance the rule of capital [p. 33].

As explained by the second symbolic function of *celebrity*, and echoed by Guy Debord, "The purpose of celebrity culture is to shepherd the populace into imitative consumption" (quoted in Rojek, p. 34). This is not only a practical function (direct endorsement), but a political function as well (imparting the ideology of consumerism). Consumerism is not the only ideological construct that Celebrities are responsible for perpetuating under a Structuralist approach. Marshall (1997) argues:

> The star is meant to epitomize the potential of everyone in American society. We are psychically drawn to identify with stars as ourselves. This, however, is only appearance. The dialectical reality is that the star is part of a system of false promise in the system of capital, which offers the reward of stardom to a random few in order to perpetuate the myth of potential universal success [p. 9].

The success myth, as argued earlier, is one of the primary ideological constructs of late modern capitalism and one of the primary hegemonic devices of modern culture industries. In perpetuating the myth that "anyone can be famous" through a combination of hard work, perseverance, and luck, Celebrities keep "the masses" working hard (toward capitalist ends), persevering, and invested. Rojek writes:

> Celebrities are attempts to contain the mass. They do so principally by symbolic means. That is, they present preferred models of subjectivity with which audiences are encouraged to identify. They are, so to speak, "the star police" of modern democracies. In other words, they radiate glamour and attraction, and, in their achieved form, they automatically demonstrate that the system rewards talent and cherishes upward mobility [p. 38].

The Celebrity, then, is an ideal type of hero that arises out of the masses (Marshall, p. 8). However, in the Celebrity's achievement, his/her very existence is used to propagate the notion that s/he could be any one of us. The Celebrity "operates to articulate, and legitimate, various forms of subjectivity that enhance the value of individuality and personality. Through these means, order and compliance are reproduced" (Rojek, p. 37). After all, how can one achieve this level of greatness unless one plays by the rules and stays out of trouble? In many ways, Edgar Morin is correct in describing Celebrities as "akin to transformers, accumulating and enlarging the dehumanized desires of the audience, and momentarily rehumanizing them through dramatized public representation and release" (quoted in Rojek, p. 35). Everyone within society is socialized from birth to (rather abstractly) desire to "be somebody"; ours is a history of the triumph of the individual, and Celebrities are the outward manifestation of those "dehumanized desires."

As early as the 1960s, scholars like Lowenthal began to recognize the gradual shift toward Celebrities, these "popular (Populist?) heroes," in media representation. The former "idols of production (i.e., business leaders, politicians, captains of industry)," were being replaced with "idols of consumption" (Marshall, p. 10). Orin Klapp thought this was a natural result of social groups formulating character types to operate as role models of leadership (Rojek, p. 19).

Ultimately, under a Structuralist approach, there are three main premises from which discourse evolves. First, a Celebrity is "the epitome of the individual for identification and idealization in society" (Rojek, p. 19). That is, the Celebrity is a hero of the masses, for the masses. Secondly, a Celebrity is "not wholly determined by the culture industries and is therefore somewhat created and constructed by the audience's reading of dominant cultural representations" (Rojek, p. 19). The Celebrity is an integral function of the culture industries and of the hegemonic structures of the dominant class, but must appeal to (and be able to be comprehended by) the subjective meaning-making of the audience at large. Third, the Celebrity "is a commodity, and therefore expresses a form of valorization of the individual and personality that is coherent with capitalism and the associated consumer culture" (Rojek, p. 19). The most successful Celebrities are those who can skillfully articulate the benefits of conspicuous consumption and capitalistic principles without alienating the very audience they have been sent to distract.

III. Jay-Z Is One of Us, Only Not

The Post-Structuralist approach to Celebrities tends to ignore the creation of Celebrities entirely in favor of concentrating on "the omnipresent celebrity image and the codes of representation through which this image is reproduced, developed, and consumed" (Rojek, p, 44). That is, in a Post-Structuralist approach, study is less about the Celebrity and more about the distribution of the Celebrity's *celebrity*. Yes, as Dyer asserts, "stars represent typical ways of behaving, feeling, and thinking in contemporary society," but more importantly, "star images are inflected and modified by the mass media and the productive assimilation of the audience" (Rojek, 44). While Celebrities are suggesting particular ways to live, they are constrained by the ability of the media to alter or distort their image and by the ability of the audience to produce selective readings of those media texts.

For example, there is a long-standing hierarchical division between film stars and television stars. Actor Lance Henriksen once turned down a role on *X-Files* (at the height of the program's popularity) because he does not "do television" (Elias 1996). Connor MacLeod, the hero of the *Highlander* films, had to be recast when the films were adapted for television because Christopher Lambert refused to allow his likeness to be used on the television series past the pilot episode ("There Can Be" 2006). For some film actors, television is "beneath" them. There is a perception of a lesser status associated with television. Marshall explains some of the stigma, stating, "Because of the obvious and omnipresent advertising function of television, the celebrity who arises from television programming is associated more directly than the film celebrity with the industrial nature of entertainment" (p. 121). Television is seen more as direct sales, and the actor on a television program has less control over his/her image due to the pervasive presence of straightforward advertising. Marshall continues, "The television personality is surrounded by other messages that are unconnected to the narrative focus of his or her program" (p. 121). This ubiquity of advertising "cheapens" the Celebrity's image, which in turn changes the audience's "productive assimilation" of the Celebrity image.

The Post-Structuralist approach stands in direct contrast to the Subjectivist approach. Rojek argues that "by addressing celebrity as a field of production, representation, and consumption, [Post-Structuralists] move away from Subjectivist accounts that prioritize the meaning of celebrity in the character, talent, and embodiment of the subject" (p. 44). Privileging intrinsic talent or strength of character overlooks the fact that there are skills that can be learned and techniques that can be perfected which produce results, regardless of natural talent. Dyer (1986) writes:

> First, the person is a body, a psychology, a set of skills that have to be mined and worked up into a star image. This work, of fashioning the star out of the raw material of the person, varies in the degree to which it respects what artists sometimes refer to as the inherent qualities of the material; makeup, coiffure, clothing, dieting and body-building can all make more or less of the body features they start with, and personality is no less malleable, skills no less learnable [p. 5].

Some measure of innate talent is helpful, but not necessary. Post-Structuralism circumvents the single-focused perspective of the Subjectivist movement and the "monolithic, static analysis frequently associated with Structuralism" by "pursuing celebrity as the emerging property of interactions in a determinate field of interest" (Rojek, p. 45). Essentially, the celebrity image—*celebrity*—becomes, "like machinery, an example of what Karl Marx calls 'congealed labour': something that is used with further labour (scripting, acting, directing, managing, filming, editing) to produce another commodity, a film" (Dyer, p. 5). The image, which is, by definition, a "fundamentally intertextual sign," (Marshall, 58) is more important than the human who embodies it. The person is, in fact, almost interchangeable with any other person. Rojek writes that. "celebrity culture is, in fact, overwhelmingly a culture of surface relations" (p. 46), a mechanical operation in which people are turned into objects which take on a centrality that eventually eclipses the original person. The ultimate display of this operation is the staged Celebrity display, such as the Academy Awards. Gamson illustrates:

> Film premieres and award shows are perhaps the clearest example of the industrial nature of celebrity at work. They are precisely Boorstin's "pseudo-events." For most participants, they are not events to be experienced but parts of their job. Staged and stage managed by entertainment organizations, they are routinely, habitually covered by news organizations. They are consciously and carefully organized to facilitate the capture and dissemination of standardized celebrity images in magazines and on television. These are true assembly lines, small parts in the more elaborate manufacture of fame: publicist brings person to media, person pauses, photographer shoots, person

III. Jay-Z Is One of Us, Only Not

becomes image, image is disseminated. Labor is divided. Media workers, eager for celebrity images for sales purposes, shoot the same standard pose photos and ask simple questions that receive standardized answers. Entertainment industry publicists and celebrities, eager for coverage for promotional purposes, provide easy but controlled access to celebrity images. The operation is mechanical, designed, routine [p. 61].

The mechanizing reification of Celebrity commodities under Post-Structuralism results in "desire in an animate object, which allows for deeper levels of attachment and identification than with inanimate commodities" (Rojek, p. 189). Essentially, desiring a Celebrity teaches individuals to desire other commodities with the same fervor. The actual Celebrity, as discussed earlier in this chapter, is fairly interchangeable, because it is the wanting that is important, not the having. An individual "responds to celebrity through abstract desire. This desire is alienable in as much as it switches in response to commodity and brand innovation" (Rojek, p. 47). Wanting one Celebrity does not preclude one from wanting other, newer Celebrities (or old favorite Celebrities in new incarnations).

Another effect of positioning *celebrity* from a Post-Structuralist viewpoint that focuses more on image than personal qualities or social organization is that it exposes the "celebrification" processes at work within society. That is to say, there is a "general tendency to frame social encounters in mediagenic filters that both reflect and reinforce the compulsion of abstract desire" (Rojek, p. 187). By "mediagenic," Rojek is referring to "elements and styles that are compatible with the conventions of self-projection and interaction, fashioned and refined by the mass media" (p. 187). This celebrification can be applied to almost any object in society: the iPod, Perez Hilton, Ugg boots, abstractions such as "sex, drugs, and rock and roll"— any commodity which augments an individual's image in the eyes of those around him/her. It is a sort of "radiated glory" which is reflected off of the individual, increasing the abstract desire of others for that individual.

But the important factor to remember in this celebrification process is that the *appearance* of "cool" is much, much more important than actually *being* "cool," from a Post-Structuralist point of view. Image trumps, and, as stated earlier, wanting is more essential than having. Because of the unique structure of capitalism, "consumers under capitalism do not experience unifying fulfillment when desire is matched with possession. For the abstract quality of desire means that wants are never satisfied by possessing a particular commodity" (Rojek, p. 187).

A Theoretical Toolbox for Analyzing Celebrity

The goal of this book thus far was to construct an historical, rhetorical, and theoretical framework for the study of *celebrity* and to develop from it a set of tools with which to analyze Celebrities. As was discussed throughout chapters II and III, *celebrity* and Celebrities occupy similar but separate spaces within society. The two are products not only of the economic, capital forces of the culture industry, but a precise construction of social exchange. As Marshall (1997) states:

> The celebrity is simultaneously a construction of the dominant culture and a construction of the subordinate audiences of the culture. It embodies two forms of rationalization of the culture that are elements of the working hegemony. For members of the dominant culture, the segment of society that controls most of the forms of cultural production, the celebrity rationalizes both their production (by providing a clear embodiment of cultural power) and their conceptions of their audience. For members of the subordinate classes, who constitute the audience of the celebrity, the celebrity rationalizes their comprehension of the general culture by providing a bridge between the powerless and the powerful. These conceptions of the celebrity, those rising from below (the audience) and emerging from above (the cultural and political producers), never entirely merge into one coherent form of celebrity identity. They do converge — in a very material sense — on the person who is the celebrity. He or she represents therefore a site for processes of hegemony. To use a New Age formulation, the celebrity is a "channeling" device for the negotiation of cultural space and position for the entire culture [p. 48].

Thus, when I meet Elway at a concert, it is not a capital exchange that takes place; to some extent, culture has an autonomy from strategic use. *Celebrity* is a commodity, to be certain, but it is also a system for making meaning which intersects with commodity, but cannot be reduced to it. Then again, it would be myopic to insist that some sort of exchange is not taking place. Elway is giving me that which he produces (his *celebrity*);

III. Jay-Z Is One of Us, Only Not

I am giving him that which he needs to subsist (recognition). A commodity exchange has taken place. It is dual processes happening simultaneously, and, as in any sort of exchange, there are risks and rewards. As Ferris points out:

> When the extraordinary and the ordinary intersect in everyday life, as they do in celebrity sightings, the stakes are high and so are the potential rewards. If the seer comports herself properly, she comes away with at least an exciting story to tell about her encounter with fame and at most a picture or autograph as a trophy of that encounter. But if the seer falters or fails to behave properly, he may have only the embarrassment of rejection to show for his serendipitous brush with greatness. The dynamics of celebrity sightings feature a moral order laden with risk and reward, and the accounts of the seers reveal a clear orientation toward reaping rewards while reducing risks [p. 260].

Such is the nature of *celebrity* in contemporary society — both as a site of commodity exchange and of meaning making. It is not simply a matter of, as Gamson contends, "Silly amusement, contrived distraction, and endless hype [becoming] the foremost means of social control" (Gamson, p. 7). The Celebrity is a much more complex product than that.

With that in mind, I propose the following "toolbox" for the analysis of *celebrity*— a set of considerations to explore when examining *celebrity* discourse. These tools are modified from Marshall's original set of considerations, updated in light of the information contained in this chapter and the last. Marshall's considerations — the things to look for when analyzing a celebrity text that not only define it *as* a celebrity text but also define *how much* of a celebrity text it is — are as follows:

1. collective/audience conceptualizations of *celebrity*
2. the categorical types of individuality that are expressed through the Celebrity
3. the cultural industries' construction of the Celebrity
4. the relative commodity status of the Celebrity
5. the form of cultural legitimation that the Celebrity, singly or as part of an entire system, may represent; and
6. the unstable nature of the meaning of the Celebrity — the processual and dynamic changeability of the individual celebrity and the entire system of celebrity (Marshall, 1997, p. 51).

Added to this list of consideration are the following:

7. the perceived virtuosity/performative excellence of the Celebrity that augments *arête;* and
8. the Celebrity's relative advocacy/endorsement of other commodities

There are multiple reasons for these two additions to Marshall's original six considerations. First, as explained earlier in this book, I reject the notion that *celebrity* can be generated in a vacuum. Celebrities cannot achieve a level of "well-knownness" that would mark them as a Celebrity without doing *something*. Boorstin's claim that *celebrity* is the state of being well-known for being well-known does not practically align with the modern *celebrity* experience. Thus, I believe an examination of the perceived virtuosity and/or performative excellence of the individual in question is not only appropriate, but necessary. This performative excellence can be read as specific to the occupational locus of the individual, or taken as global to all intertextual incarnations of the individual. For example, one could evaluate the virtuosity of a professional athlete based solely on athletic performance (i.e., How well does Peyton Manning play football, and how does his relative skill contribute to his "star power?"), or one could evaluate his performative excellence more in totality (i.e., How well does Peyton Manning play football, perform in commercial endorsements, participate on *Saturday Night Live*, and so on, and how does his ability to "be Peyton Manning" in public contribute to his "star power?"). Both would seem to be equally valid considerations.

Secondly, it has been established that one of the main functions of *celebrity* is to provide examples for the general public of how to consume, what to consume, and, in general, to promote consumption as a positive and natural experience. An individual who is not engaged in this praxis doesn't really qualify as a Celebrity, per se. It is one of the defining characteristics of *celebrity*. Therefore, considering the relative volume of the individual's endorsements of specific consumer products or of consumption as a natural practice and the efficacy of those appeals also would seem to be relevant and appropriate.

This "toolbox" provides eight specific yet interlinking spheres that can be used to triangulate the relative positioning of an individual in the

III. Jay-Z Is One of Us, Only Not

public eye on the continuum between celetoid and *celebrity*. At the extreme ends of the spectrum, much like ultraviolet and infrared in the color spectrum, are the private citizen (or non-*celebrity*) and the "superstar" (or mega-*celebrity*). At the lowest end of the spectrum, the non-*celebrity* does not exist in the public consciousness at all; s/he may be well-known in some small, local way, but does not have a *mediated* existence. At the highest end of the *celebrity* spectrum, the superstar lives almost an entirely mediated existence — the public knows almost his/her every move, personal information, relationship status, and so on. These individuals could be termed "the Celebrity's Celebrity," in that even other Celebrities revere them — Elvis Presley, Madonna, Prince, Meryl Streep, and Jack Nicholson all come to mind.

Using Marshall's updated "toolbox," the rest of this book attempts to address the following research questions. The question with which I began, which sparked the desire to study the relationship between this particular cultural artifact and *celebrity* in the first place, was:

RQ1: What is the final product that *American Idol* creates?

That is to say, I am not surprised that I can name all of the former *American Idol* winners off the top of my head; I can also name all of the winners of a variety of other competitive reality television shows without assistance, too — *Survivor, So You Think You Can Dance?, America's Next Top Model, Dancing with the Stars,* and so on. However, I am an admitted "reality junkie"; I spend a great deal of time watching and studying competitive reality television. I am not your normal, average viewer — I am somewhat of a crazy person when it comes to reality television. What began to be increasingly interesting to me is that other people around me knew former *American Idol* contestants as well — and not only the winners. People who would say they do not regularly watch *American Idol* or who have never even seen the show — my mother, for example — still recognize the fact that this artist or that artist got their start on *Idol*. The same does not, anecdotally, appear to be true for other competitive reality programs. The contestants do not seem to enjoy the same sort of cultural cachet.[3]

Therefore, it would appear that *American Idol* produces contestants who do not conform to the norms of unscripted competitive television programs — many of the contestants do not simply fade away from public consciousness at the end of the season. If this is the case, then what is it that *American Idol* creates? Is it celetoid? *Celebrity*? Something in-between? This led me to a second research question:

> RQ2: What does the triangulation provided by Marshall's "toolbox" tell us about the contestants on *American Idol*?

Perhaps, using Marshall's "toolbox," it would be demonstrated that *American Idol's* contestants are not all that different from other competitive reality show contestants after all. Or, perhaps it would reveal that the contestants are, in fact, undergoing a public commodification into *celebrity* products. It could be that the answer lies somewhere in the middle.

Summary

Celebrities serve symbolic functions as well as commercial/commodity functions: they model appropriate consumer behavior, personify consumption, and serve as commodities themselves. They are disposable, intertextual, and fetishized commodities, and represent both social and economic capital exchange.

There are three main approaches to the study of *celebrity*. Subjectivist approaches assume that a Celebrity becomes a Celebrity because that is what s/he was born to do — *celebrity* is the individual's destiny. Structuralist approaches see *celebrity* as part of the hegemonic socialization process, and view the most successful Celebrities as those who can articulate the benefits of capitalist consumption without alienating the audience. Post-Structuralist approaches argue that the celebrification process is more important than the actual Celebrity, and that the process is a mechanical operation that turns people into objects.

IV

When Someone's Down on the Floor, Kick Them

> "I would like to be famous because I can't cook,
> I can't clean, and I can't walk my own dog."
> — Mikalah Gordon, S4E24*

Collective/Audience Conceptualizations of Celebrity

American Idol presents representations of collective conceptualizations of *Celebrity*—what society says it means to "be" a Celebrity—in four very specific ways. First, it presents the contestants in situations where they are encouraged to "act like" a Celebrity and given opportunities to encounter the types of experiences that Celebrities are subjected to/have access to. Secondly, *Idol*'s mainstay cast members (particularly Ryan Seacrest) continually reference ways in which the contestants represent common generalizations about *celebrity* status. Thirdly, *Idol* often shows contestants acquiring the material components of *celebrity* in terms of possessions that display an increase in wealth. Finally, Idol reinforces the *celebrity* status of particular Celebrities as exemplars of *celebrity*hood as a whole. These people are given legendary status, as if granted such standing by public fiat. In both instances, *celebrity* is presented as a status level that is earned rather than constructed, and the commodity nature of

---

*Episodes of American Idol *in this book are annotated with a letter/number code indicating the season and the episode number. For example, S4E24 as used to cite the above quotation, refers to the 24th episode of season 4 of *American Idol.

101

celebrity is masked by the centralization of *arête* as the ultimate arbiter of *celebrity* significance.

From the very first season of *Idol*, the show has presented many of the attributes described in Chapter III as the natural, collectively accepted representation of how a Celebrity behaves. In S1E6, Kelly Clarkson leans out of a gleaming, spotless Ford Focus and exclaims, "Everyone wants to be me because I'm an American idol, baby!"[1] and over the course of the next six seasons of the show, we come to believe she may be absolutely correct. By S1E11, the contestants are "giving back" to the community through volunteer work with Habitat for Humanity, and Seacrest authenticates the *celebrity* nature of this volunteerism, declaring that the contestants will be living a celebrity life, receiving "fame and fortune," but before that, they want to (read: are contracted to) give back through Habitat for Humanity. The contestants are taken to south central Los Angeles and put to "work" building a house (how much actual work the contestants do on the house is never revealed).

The contestants here are simply taking a break from their normal daily routine of being Celebrities, despite the fact that a mere five weeks prior, they were "ordinary citizens." *Celebrity* moves at a rapid pace; it takes very little time for a person on *American Idol* to move along the continuum from "nobody" to Celebrity, as evidenced by Ryan Starr, who, while working on the Habitat for Humanity house, reports, "It's good for us to do this kind of stuff because it makes you realize you're a regular person just like everybody else" (S1E11). The verb Starr chooses is significant; note that she says, "realize you're a regular person," not "remember you're a regular person" or something to that effect. In less than a month, Starr has apparently all but forgotten what her life was like prior to *American Idol*; to such a degree that she is able to receive an epiphany while performing volunteer work.

As described in Chapter III, Celebrities are "supposed" to behave in particular ways in particular situations, and from the start, *Idol* provides the contestants with opportunities to show the audience that they are now Celebrities, and can too behave in the ways that are expected of them. For example, in a skit designed to showcase *Idol* sponsor Ford's automobiles (S1E18), Justin Guarini and Kelly Clarkson are shown walking and discussing the fact that famous people have to become accustomed to having

IV. When Someone's Down on the Floor, Kick Them

fans. Clarkson says that some of the fans can be "animals," and Guarini responds that he is not afraid of them. Suddenly, Guarini is grabbed from off-screen and yanked around the corner of a building. Fabric from his shirt and smoke comes flying/pouring from around the corner, and then Guarini rushes back into view. He is harried and disheveled, with torn clothing and mussed hair. He scuttles into a car with the other contestants, and explains, "These women came out of nowhere. They grabbed me. They were tearing my clothes and kissing ... and it was absolutely fabulous!" Not only has Guarini behaved in the manner expected of him as a Celebrity (he enjoys the attention and adoration of his fans, even when it is presumably a little violent), but he has elicited the "appropriate" behavior in his fans as well. They are "supposed" to clamor for his attention, even if it means ripping at his clothes and hair and kissing him, and he is "supposed" to view this as the normal relationship between fan and Celebrity.

Learning the correct behavior of a Celebrity is a naturalization process, one in which the contestants are engaged throughout the length of the *Idol* season in preparation for their eventual graduation into the larger *celebrity* universe. Being a Celebrity is a great deal of work, as explained in Chapter III. If it were simply the preparation and performance of a song every week, the *Idol* contestants would be under far less stress and scrutiny. However, *celebrity* encompasses more than simple performance of a particular task — there is the work of "being," and the *Idol* contestants must learn to perform these functions as well. The audience is occasionally given a glimpse into the life of these newly-minted Celebrities; for example, in S4E30, the contestants explain a week in their life on *Idol*. On Thursdays, the contestants choose a song, then work with a vocal coach and a pianist to cut the length to around a minute and a half.[2] Traditionally, barring a schedule change on Fox, *American Idol* airs on Tuesday and Wednesday evenings. Thursday, it appears, is then given over to the work of performance preparation — the "actual" job of the *Idol* contestant.

As the segment continues, we learn Fridays are scheduled for interviews and shopping. The producers sit down with the contestants and put together their pre-performance interview packages, then they are taken shopping for performance night clothing. Vonzell Solomon here reveals that while the show provides a stylist, the contestant has ultimate control over what s/he is wearing on show night. Friday, then, is a celebrification day. The *Idol* contestants perform two distinct functions of *celebrity* simultaneously: not only are they preparing to "look like" a Celebrity is supposed to look, but they are, in the process, acquiring goods. They are displaying conspicuous consumption — recall, one of the primary purposes of *celebrity*.

Occasionally, Saturday is a day of rest/time off from the show. However, even when the contestants have the day off, Carrie Underwood discloses, their time off is organized and they tend to stay together as a group. In this particular segment, the contestants are all shown bowling together. These days off are rare, though. Normally, Saturday is a day for recording. According to this segment, *Idol* records at the Record Plant in Hollywood. The Record Plant studio, opened in Los Angeles in 1969, has hosted more Grammy-winning artists than any other studio in history ("Record Plant" n.d.). Music icons from Jimi Hendrix to Prince to R.E.M. have recorded at The Record Plant ("Record Plant" n.d.), and in procuring the studio for their contestants, *Idol* instantly lends a radiated credibility/legitimacy based upon the legacy of the artists in whose company the contestants find themselves.

Also of note is the fact that the contestants are kept under watch, even during their "off" times. There are very few situations in which this corralling of the contestants is lifted; S7 contestant Brooke White was even forced to miss her sister's wedding, which was scheduled well before White became a contestant, because it fell on a Saturday during the *Idol* season.

Sunday is a working day for the contestants, because it is the day that they film the Ford promotional commercial. Sundays, like Fridays, are given to the promotion of conspicuous consumption — in this case, using the *celebrity* status of the *Idol* contestants to promote one of the sponsors' automobiles. This is a secondary function of the *Idol* Celebrities (if we take as granted the first function of the *Idol* Celebrities is to make, promote, and sell music), but an important one nonetheless. The relationship between *American Idol* and its sponsors will be discussed in more detail later in this book.

On Monday, it is a return to the primary work of the *Idol* contestants — rehearsing with the studio band and preparing to perform on live television. This is the unglamorous part of the creation of a Celebrity,

IV. When Someone's Down on the Floor, Kick Them

much like the time a film actor spends working out in the gym with personal trainers, taking lessons from speech and diction coaches, and so forth. The *Idol* contestants spend Mondays being infused with the labor of others, as well as honing their own skills for the inevitable public consumption coming on Tuesdays and Wednesdays, as described in the next part of the segment.

Tuesday morning, the contestants engage in a final walk-through of the show for the purpose of arranging the cameras, and then they wait for show time. Tuesday is another day where the *Idol* contestants perform the rituals of *celebrity* as expected of them by the common conceptualization dictated by society. That is to say, the *Idol* contestants are primped and preened by a team of trained professional makeup artists, hair dressers, and stylists, then sent out under the hot lights in front of the studio audience to perform for their approval. This is what is expected of professional *celebrity* musicians.

Wednesday, then, is the denouement: come Wednesday, someone's immediate *Idol* experience comes to an end. However, as will be discussed later, this is hardly the end of *Idol celebrity* for some of the contestants.

Inherent in this brief view into the daily life of the *Idol* contestants is a subtext of celebrification/preparation for *celebrity* life. The expectations of a fan public are inculcated in the contestants on a daily basis: the Celebrity is expected to prepare and practice for public performance, to go to the places other Celebrities go and work in the same venues in which other Celebrities work, to buy the kind of products Celebrities buy and sell the kind of products other Celebrities sell, to look, sound, and "feel" like other Celebrities, and ultimately, to subject themselves to public scrutiny and approval/disapproval. It is a great deal of demand on people who, not that long before, were working as waitresses and car mechanics. Being a new Celebrity/*celebrity* commodity is strenuous work, but, as Kelly Clarkson remarks in S1E22, it is "so much fun," especially on a program like *American Idol*.

The culminating representation of how the *Idol* contestants have learned to represent the collective conceptualizations and public expectations of *celebrity* generally comes when the contestant pool has dwindled to the top three. In this episode (generally shown on the Wednesday results program), each of the contestants returns to his or her hometown to be adulated as the conquering hero. In these episodes, the contestants are expected to display the proper balance between wonderment at the amount of attention s/he is receiving at the same time as displaying detached grace in dealing with his/her *celebrity* status.

For instance, S4E38 chronicles the contestants' return home to Florida, Alabama, and Oklahoma. The segment begins with Seacrest's usual affirmation of the contestants' *celebrity* status — the contestants are receiving "star treatment," flying home in private jets to have fantastic *celebrity* experiences — then each of the contestants in turn are shown receiving their *celebrity* coronation. Vonzell Solomon's return to Florida consists of a stop at both local radio and local television stations, then a trip back to the post office in which she worked as a letter carrier prior to *American Idol.* Following the post office visit, Solomon is whisked by police-escorted limousine to an autograph session at a local Wal-Mart, taken for a ride on a luxury yacht, and finally delivered to a massive crowd in a park, where the mayor gives her the key to the city. Solomon is allowed a farewell dinner with her family before it is back into the limousine and onto a private jet for a return to Hollywood.

Bo Bice's return to Alabama is similar, although augmented by the fact that members of the legendary band Lynyrd Skynyrd await him at his hotel. Bice then takes a limousine to a radio station, and returns for a police escort to his own autograph session at Wal-Mart. Following this, he is driven to the Helena city hall, and the mayor presents a teary-eyed Bice with the key to the city. The crowd of 8,000 (as we are told) are finally treated to a performance of "Sweet Home Alabama" by Bice, who is joined on stage by Lynyrd Skynyrd.

Carrie Underwood's return to Oklahoma is even grander still. Not only does she receive the black stretch limousine, the police escort, and the appearance on the Tulsa Fox–affiliate morning show, but she also, upon arriving in her hometown of Checotah, is the guest of honor in a parade. While Checotah, Oklahoma, reports a population of 4,000, according to a sign shown in the segment, we are told over 10,000 people have turned out for the parade. Underwood exclaims, "My cheeks hurt from smiling!" as she is ushered to a podium where she sings the national anthem for the gathered crowd, and the governor of Oklahoma proclaims the day "Carrie Underwood Day." Underwood then also receives a key to the city, a

IV. When Someone's Down on the Floor, Kick Them

certificate of achievement from her university president, and is inducted into the Oklahoma Music Hall of Fame. From there, Underwood visits her former high school for a CD signing, then returns home to have dinner with her family and pets (the pets are an important part of Underwood's character development, as will be discussed later in this chapter), and finally, delivered to a private jet to return to Hollywood.

In all three cases, the work of being a Celebrity in public is showcased. Each contestant performs ritualized duties of the well-known — the autograph signings, parades, receiving the key to the city — as well as displaying access to certain *celebrity* privileges (private jets, limousines, police escorts, parades) that demonstrate his/her position along the celetoid/ Celebrity continuum. By this time in the season, just two episodes from declaring a winner, the *Idol* contestants demonstrate that they are prepared to meet the societal expectations of *celebrity* behavior, and can handle the rigors of public "well-knownness."

The second way in which *Idol* presents representations of collective conceptualizations of *celebrity* is through the constant messaging by the cast regulars — Simon Cowell, Paula Abdul, Randy Jackson, and particularly Ryan Seacrest. As the host of the show, Seacrest spends more time talking to the audience and to the contestants than the judges, and is tasked with keeping the show moving, leading into and out of commercials, and tying the program's various elements together through banter with the judges, contestants, and live studio audience members. Because of this relationship with the viewing audience and the increased screen time he receives, Seacrest is also often responsible for reinforcing what *celebrity* means in the eyes of the viewing audience. Whether it is a simple observation that the winner of *Idol* is going to end up "famous and rich!" (S1E19) or a more pointed reflection that Hollywood is a heartless place in which once you are out of sight, you are a "nobody," and "getting in good" with the final four while they are still accessible is a good idea (S1E20), Seacrest often emphasizes the stereotypical attributes and behaviors that are expected by the public of Celebrities: Celebrities are wealthy; Celebrities are "somebody." In S1E6, co-host Brian Dunkleman paints a picture of the type of life the *Idol* winner can expect: "fame, fortune, constant hounding by the press, endless speculation about their sexual preference, stalkers...." Celebrities are expected to subject themselves to the negative aspects of "well-knowness" (unwanted paparazzi, obsessive fans, prying into their personal lives) as well as enjoying the rewards of fame (i.e., financial gain).

Simon Cowell, in his (largely constructed) role as the dastardly British judge with little mercy for the contestants, also often reinforces what it means to be a Celebrity. In S6E4, eventual top 24 contestant Antonella Barba has just watched her best friend make it to the Hollywood round of auditions. When it is her turn, she meekly admits she believes her friend is a better singer than she is, because her friend has had more formal training. After Barba's audition, the judges roundly agree that Barba is a far better singer than her friend. Barba accepts the praise, but continues to adulate her best friend, to which Cowell responds:

> SC: Let me give you one lesson in show business: when someone's down on the floor, kick them.
> AB: Not my best friend. Sorry. I can't.
> SC: Always.

While Cowell is, in some ways, simply playing the role of the "bad guy" he has created for himself, he is also feeding into collective conceptualization stereotypes of Celebrities: that a Celebrity will do anything to achieve fame, even if it means selling her best friend short to get ahead.

Of course, Cowell often belies his role as villain with tempered yet seemingly genuine praise for contestants he believes in. The S1 finalists Kelly Clarkson and Justin Guarini were invited to present the Best New Artist award at the MTV Video Music Awards just prior to the finale of S1. Cowell attended the show, and on the next *Idol* program, remarked that Guarini was a genuinely nice person who, "after the horrors of some of the artists" Cowell met at the event, was a "credit to what pop stars are really all about" (S1E23). Cowell's use of the word "really" is interesting here, as it suggests that for all of the rhetoric about Celebrities kicking people when they are down or ignoring the "nobodies," what a pop star is "really" about is being a nice person — "nice" being an adjective that is not often at the top of the list when describing Celebrity behavior.

As Ryan Seacrest himself points out, however, Cowell may not have the most salient opinion on matters of what people are "really" about. In S5E36, Taylor Hicks performed Elvis Presley's "Jailhouse Rock" under the tutelage of music mogul Tommy Mottola and Presley's former wife,

IV. When Someone's Down on the Floor, Kick Them

Priscilla. After the performance, Cowell and Seacrest had an exchange in which Cowell notes that in the "real world," Hicks' performance would be seen as a horrible imitation of Presley. Seacrest responds by telling Cowell that he [Cowell] doesn't even live in the real world because of his staff, his chauffer, and his luxury Rolls-Royce.

Seacrest's comment has twofold implications. First, it speaks to the "one of us but not one of us" dichotomy discussed in Chapter III. Cowell is a member of society, but one who doesn't interact with other people in the same manner as "regular folks"; he has servants, a chauffer, luxury automobiles. The second implication is that because of his distance from the daily existence of "regular folks," he is in no position to judge how those "regular folks" will interpret the performance they have just seen. Ironic, since Cowell's entire function is to tell the audience how they should interpret the performance they have just seen.[3]

For all of the talk on *Idol* about what it "means" to be a Celebrity, perhaps the parents of Kelly Clarkson summed it up best. In S1E21, Clarkson's mother states, "To everyone else, she may be a Celebrity, but to us, she's always going to be Kelly." This comment reinforces the perception of the front stage/back stage separation; that the Kelly Clarkson everyone else sees on television is not the Kelly Clarkson her friends and family get to see, and that there is a sort of false veneer that *celebrity* brings which masks the true identity of the Celebrity. In essence, what it really means to be a Celebrity is to have alter ego; Kelly Clarkson the cultural commodity form is a distinct and different entity than Kelly Clarkson, daughter of Jeanne Clarkson.

And that commodity form brings with it a host of luxurious material goods, the third way *Idol* presents collective conceptualizations about *celebrity*. Celebrities have things — a lot of things — because Celebrities can afford them. Material acquisition and conspicuous consumption are major functions of *celebrity* commodities. Celebrities teach the public at large how to properly relate to goods for sale in a consumer culture, and *Idol* provides the contestants with the opportunity to behave in a manner expected of the new Celebrity. Because the program was so new and was debuting into an environment of a highly recognizable and culturally-ingrained reality show format where cast members on a reality show were expected to live together (e.g., *The Real World, Big Brother, Survivor*), during S1 of

Idol, the audience was continually shown footage of the contestants living together at a five-story mansion in the Hollywood hills. The mansion had 26 rooms across the five floors, with 13 bedrooms, 13 bathrooms, a swimming pool on the third floor, a spiral staircase in the center of the building, four-poster beds in the bedrooms, a foosball table made entirely of chrome — in short, the contestants were living in the kind of home one would expect a wealthy Celebrity to own. Throughout the season, contestants are shown shooting pool on the elegantly-appointed billiards table, relaxing by the meticulously-maintained pool, or grouped together on plush couches watching their big-screen television. The *Idol* contestants were in the process of becoming a part of the larger *celebrity* network through their acquisition of the material goods necessary to identify one's self as a Celebrity.

Seacrest also, through his voice-over work on various video packages shown throughout the shows, often highlights the material considerations of the contestants. For example, not only does he repeatedly, season to season, reference the wealth awaiting the winning contestant (e.g., "the whole fame and fortune thing" [S4E35]), but he makes clear distinctions between the former "ordinary" lives of the contestants and the new *celebrity* lives they are leading. In S4E38, the final four contestants are about to find out who is going to be eliminated and who is going to move on to the crucial "return home as the conquering hero" show. Seacrest tells the contestants that three of them will continue to have access to the material gains of *celebrity*, including access to a MarquisJet private jet and V.I.P. treatment, and one will, presumably, be returned to his/her "ordinary" life (however, this is not usually the case for the majority of top four contestants, who often go on to *celebrity* careers even without winning the show).

The final way *Idol* presents representations of the collective conceptualization of *celebrity* is through the status it affords certain Celebrities. These Celebrities are in possession of talent and "well-knownness" far beyond even other Celebrities. These select few are accorded legendary status; they are the Celebrities which other Celebrities worship. While some Celebrities are occasionally mentioned in this manner (SC: With Alicia Keys ... the problem is you become a bad impersonator because she's so current [S4E16]), on *American Idol*, there are three Celebrities which represent the ultimate avatars of *arête*, in hierarchical order: Mariah Carey,

IV. When Someone's Down on the Floor, Kick Them

Celine Dion, and the pinnacle of musical talent in the world of *American Idol*, Whitney Houston. To be compared to one of these three singers is the highest compliment that can be paid to a contestant, and to sing one of these artists' songs is to invite a host of unflattering comparisons and unpleasant remarks from the judges.

When the praise comes, it is normally in one of two varieties. First, there is the praise that comes to a contestant who has sung one of the "Big Three's" songs and done an admirable job. For example, Cowell's comments to Vonzell Solomon after she sang Houston's "I Have Nothing," were a sort of reluctant praise: "I would have thought, three weeks ago, you attempting Whitney would have been crazy ... you pulled it off" (S4E25). This form of praise is rare; not many contestants who have sung a Big Three song have fared well afterward with the judges.

The second form of praise is a comparative praise that is given to a contestant who has performed a song by someone other than the Big Three. By saying the contestant is *like* one or more members of the Big Three, the judges are according the contestant the highest praise possible on *American Idol*. This is very, very rare, and only a handful of contestants can boast they received this commendation from the judges. For example, in S1E19, Kelly Clarkson sings The Weather Girls' "It's Raining Men." Following a raucous standing ovation from the audience and effusive praise from Randy Jackson and Paula Abdul, Cowell tells Kelly Clarkson, "I think you've just put yourself up in the same league as Celine and Mariah Carey." Clarkson went on to win S1, and is one of the highest-selling artists *Idol* has ever produced. In recent days, Clarkson herself has become a name by which the judges can praise a contestant without referencing the Big Three; a minor avatar of sorts. For example, in S5E20, Cowell tells Katherine McPhee, "You know who you are beginning to remind me of? I remember the first time we saw Kelly Clarkson at this stage in the competition and there is something about you that has reminded me vocally of Kelly Clarkson." In S7E20, Cowell also remarks to Carly Smithson, "I have to say something. This reminds me: six years ago, exactly the same week, Kelly Clarkson." Clarkson's name has become the ultimate praise when speaking of talent within the context of *American Idol* in much the same way the Big Three are the ultimate praise of talent outside the context of *American Idol*.

More often, however, the Big Three are invoked as invective against a contender who has attempted one of their songs. Repeatedly since the first season, contestants have been warned against attempting the songs of the Big Three, lest they draw unwanted comparisons. Yet, season after season, contestants select songs by the Big Three and are publicly admonished for the choice. The criticism can be relatively mild and benign, such as the exchange between Randy Jackson, Paula Abdul, and S6 contestant Antonella Barba in which Barba is told that "less than one percent of the population can sing like Celine" (S6E15). Or, the criticism can (and does) get much harsher. When S5 contestant Heather Cox attempts Mariah Carey's "Hero," she receives a swift and harsh rebuke. In S5E14, Abdul says that singing Carey's songs invites unwanted comparison, and all it does is remind the audience how brilliant Carey is (and, by inference, how brilliant the contestant is not). Cowell then says Cox's performance is like one of those "ghastly pageants" where someone sings before the finalists are announced. As will be discussed later, one of the worst things one can be labeled on *American Idol* is "pageant."

However, even singers the judges are fond of, who are decidedly not "pageant," are subjected to damning comparison to the Big Three. Katharine McPhee, after singing Whitney Houston's "I Have Nothing," was told that by choosing it, she was effectively telling the world that she is as good as Whitney Houston. Cowell then quips, bluntly, "You're not" (S5E32). When singers attempt Big Three songs, there is a predisposition among the judges to reject the contestant, even when the contestant is someone who has previously garnered praise. The chances are far more likely that the judges will dislike the performance and judge it negatively than that they will enjoy the performance and give it a positive review. Even singers who are vocally capable of invoking a similar style to the Big Three are cautioned away from even attempting to sing the Big Three's songs.

Much like Kelly Clarkson is the former American Idol the judges cite when handing out high praise, S3 winner Fantasia Barrino is the former American Idol the judges caution contestants to stay away from. Barrino's unique style and highly recognizable voice are difficult to emulate, and the judges are far more likely to negatively review an attempt to sing her songs—no matter how much the judges may like the contestant. For

IV. When Someone's Down on the Floor, Kick Them

example, up until S6E32, S6 contestant Lakisha Jones enjoys consistently positive responses from the judges. However, after Jones performs Barrino's "I Believe" in S6E32, Paula Abdul remarks that Barrino is so "undeniably and wonderfully and magnificently unique" that she can't hear anyone else sing Barrino's songs but Barrino.

Of course, it's difficult for the singers to stay away from the Big Three when you enlist one of the Big Three to be the guest mentor for the week, as happens in S7E31, when *Idol* invites Mariah Carey to work with the contestants. Since each of the contestants are forced to sing a song written by Carey, it is impossible not to be compared to her. Even Seacrest notes the apparent uphill struggle the contestants face, saying to Randy Jackson that after years of name-dropping Carey and telling the contestants to stay away from singing her songs, how can he possibly judge a Carey theme night. Jackson responds that he is just going to try to be fair and hope the contestants don't try to sound like Carey (S7E31). Even on Mariah Carey night, you are not allowed to try to sing like Mariah Carey.

In the end, many contestants realize the place the Big Three occupy in public consciousness, and the legendary status accorded to them by the viewing audience and the judging panel. There is only so much a contestant can do — a contestant who is often not a professional entertainer, may be as young as 16 years old, and has never been on camera in front of millions of people on a program with one of the largest regular audiences in television history. Mikalah Gordon, on the verge of elimination, implores the audience:

> MG: Look, if I were a Mariah Carey or a Whitney, and I was perfect and didn't have to make mistakes, I wouldn't be on this show. I mean, we're all learning, we're all trying and that's what *American Idol* is. We're trying to get better and we're going to learn from our mistakes. Give me another week and it's going to be fabulous [S4E23].

Gordon did not get another week; she was voted off the next evening.

Collective conceptualizations of the meaning of *celebrity* abound within the *American Idol* text. In four very distinct ways, *Idol* consistently reinforces conventional societal notions about what it means to be a Celebrity. *Idol*'s contestants are given multiple opportunities to act out the ways in which America expects Celebrities to act, and placed in situations where they can have the types of experiences society assumes Celebrities have. *Idol*'s recurring cast, primarily Ryan Seacrest, remind the audience that the contestants are living the *celebrity* experience, without having to verbally express much more than "fame and fortune," relying on public "common knowledge" of the *celebrity* lifestyle to construct meaning in that arena. The *Idol* contestants are given the means to publicly consume other commodities, often shown shopping, driving new cars, living in lavish mansions and enjoying the other perks of *celebrity*, as the public expects them to do. Finally, the contestants are regularly reminded of the legendary figures within their field that the audience perceives as the pinnacle of talent and success. Contestants either place themselves on a similar path to greatness or fail miserably in the attempt, but in either case, it is the audience's perception of the greatness of the Big Three Celebrities which drives their interpretation of the contestant's performance. In all four cases, *Idol* is attempting to connect their contestants to the larger framework of collective conceptualizations of *celebrity* in a way that transcends the production of mere celetoids.

V

What's a Ballsy?

> *I can hear your voice from one note and know it's you, Brooke, so that's a great thing.*
> — Paula Abdul, S7E24

Categorical Types of Individuality That Are Expressed Through the Celebrity

On *American Idol*, the contestants each represent a specific form of identity and individuality that is promoted to appeal to multiple demographic segments of the audience in order to maintain viewership. However, because the *Idol* contestants, being only fledgling Celebrities, do not yet exist as intertextually as other, more established *celebrity* commodities, *Idol* must handle many of the functions of an intertextual existence in-house. To this end, the *Idol* performance program each week contains not only singing performances and judges' critiques, but a variety of feature and promotional packages designed to give the viewing audience a closer, more "spotlight" look at each contestant in turn. These packages may last up to two minutes each, and generally follow a prescribed format. For example, in the early stages of the competition, the content of the packages generally features an interview with each contestant in relation to the theme of the week: "Inspirational Songs," "The Year You Were Born," and so forth. In the later episodes of a season, when guest mentors are more frequently used, the packages tend to be footage of the contestant rehearsing with the guest Celebrity, then the guest Celebrity's (almost always kind) impressions of the contestant.

The result of a season's worth of these packages is that the audience is able to construct a categorical type of individuality for each of the contestants: this contestant is a "southern rocker"; that contestant is "the girl next door"; the contestant that just sang is the "former nerd turned smoldering crooner." Each contestant seems to have two different types of categories or labels that become attached to him/her: one that is musically centered, and one that is personality centered. For example, Carrie Underwood, from very early on in S4, was identified as the "farm girl" and as a country singer. The packages Underwood appeared in during the season affirmed these identity labels each week, showing Underwood carrying buckets of feed to cows on her home farm, as well as her repeated admissions that Martina McBride is her favorite artist and that she loves to sing country music. Since winning *American Idol*, Underwood has gone on to become one of the best-selling country artists in America, and her clear identity label as a country singer from an Oklahoma farm probably did not hurt her credibility with her target audience.

Because *American Idol* is as much reality television program as it is music showcase, these packages serve as a vehicle for character creation as well. In the process of presenting categorical identities and types of individuality for commodity purposes, *Idol* also generates characters for whom the viewing audience can root. While this process can last the course of the entire season, it is not always necessary to have a full run in order to establish a character. For example, in S2, there was a contestant named Frenchie Davis, a heavy-set woman who was disqualified from the competition, yet went on to great *celebrity* fortunes on Broadway. In S5, heavy-set Mandisa Hundley gives what is roundly regarded by the judges as an outstanding audition. However, as she is leaving the room, Cowell remarks to the other judges, "Do we have a bigger stage this year?" As Paula Abdul attempts to defend Hundley, saying, "She's got, like, a Frenchie...," Cowell cuts across her, stating, "Forget Frenchie. She's like France" (S5E2).

Hundley continues on throughout the auditions, finally making it to the final cut in Hollywood week where she appears before the judges. Before the judges can speak, Hundley sits down in the chair and calmly states that people have told her she should say something nasty back to Cowell, but all she wants to say is that he hurt her feelings, and she wept, and she's over it. She forgives Cowell, and she doesn't even need an apology.

V. What's a Ballsy?

She then invokes her Christian upbringing, stating that if Jesus could die for her sins, she can "certainly extend that same grace" to Cowell (S5E10). Cowell appears genuinely ashamed, and responds that he has been "humbled" and feels "one millimeter small." Cowell and Hundley hug, and instantly, her character has been established — the classy lady who can overcome anything — and the word "classy" is used repeatedly by the judges throughout her critiques for the rest of the competition.

Most contestants, however, take multiple episodes and multiple packages in order to firmly establish a character/identity. It helps if the contestant is amenable to playing whatever role surfaces for him/her. For example, one of the most successful character creations on *Idol* is that of Kellie Pickler. Pickler was, at the time, a 19-year-old waitress from Albemarle, North Carolina, who finishes in sixth place in S5. In Pickler's first appearance (S5E3), during the audition weeks, the foundation of her character is established: she lives with her grandfather because her mother abandoned her at two years old and her father has been repeatedly sent to prison for drug abuse. She then claims to have nothing to go back home for. This, of course, is continually refuted throughout Pickler's identity generation, however; her grandfather and little brother become important pieces of Pickler's storyline, and it is established regularly that she does, in fact, have a family to go back home to.

Pickler's next appearance, during Hollywood week, not only reinforces her lack of parents via Seacrest's voiceover, but begins to establish the key element of Pickler's identity on *Idol*: she is a country bumpkin, a fish out of water lacking the savvy to deal with the newfound wonders of big city life. Staring out of her hotel room, she is overwhelmed by the Los Angeles skyline and "can't really take it all in" (S5E8). Then, later, when meeting with the musical director, she states that she has never sung with a band, never had voice lessons, and does not even know if the piano player will follow her if she speeds up or slows down. She finishes this with what becomes a trademark of hers over the course of the season; she doesn't know what key she should sing in, and says, "You know, when I think of keys, I'm thinking of keys you crank the car with, you know?" (S5E8). Just a little down-home country humor.

Pickler's plucky personality combined with her thick southern drawl and wide-eyed amazement at every new experience makes her a quick favorite of both the audience and the judges. Repeatedly, the judges refer to how much they "love" her, and her crowd response is audibly greater than most of the other contestants. Pickler's love for her family (despite the fact that, recall, she had "nothing to go back home for"), and her family's love for her, become another endearing element of her character creation. Even her grandfather has become a celebrity back home. Seacrest asks her about this, and Pickler relates:

> KP: Yeah! Listen, listen, they, um, if you remember the, um, the Greensboro clip they showed me asking if he wanted something to eat and he said, "I'd like a sandwich," so now when he goes out in places, these women come and say, "Clyde, I'll make you a sandwich!" [S5E11].

Later in the season, *Idol* returns to Pickler's grandfather, airing a package in which Clyde the Grandfather and Pickler's little brother, Eric, are sitting on a bench swing. Clyde recounts how the town of Albemarle has gotten completely behind Pickler, and how all of the town's residents talk about how much they love her. Then he says that the first thing Eric asks every day is when Pickler is coming home.

It is a very sweet segment, but while the segment highlights Pickler's closeness with her grandfather and brother, it also briefly reveals another of Pickler's identity traits throughout her time on *Idol*: the evolution of her "country bumpkin" role from merely inexperienced to borderline-unintelligent naivety. In the segment, there is a shot of a sign out front of the Four Seasons Realty company that reads: "Good Luck Kellie Calamari and Spinach For U Here." This is a reference to the fact that, early on in the season, it is clear that Pickler just has not had many "worldly" encounters. In S5E14, she discloses that she feels like a "fish out of water," but has had fun and has gotten to try some new things, including a spinach salad ("tasted like picking a leaf off of a bush") and calamari ("I can live without ever eating that again") — which she pronounces slowly and phonetically "cal-ah-mar-ee." She is also amazed at the number of dogs in Los Angeles that wear clothes, like hats and jackets and booties. As the season continues, many more of Pickler's "firsts" are revealed, as she comes across more and more items and phrases she has never experienced. In S5E17, Cowell refers to her as "a naughty little minx," which he then has to explain means "kind of like a nice bad girl." Later, with Seacrest, she exclaims,

V. What's a Ballsy?

"I'm a mink!" Seacrest corrects her as Cowell nearly spits out his drink, laughing. Immediately, Seacrest asks Pickler about the lunch she had, because he heard she had a new fish that she'd never eaten before. She responds, "Yeah! I had a SAL-mon!" (S5E17).

Pickler's mispronunciation of words and misunderstanding of phrases becomes an important part of her "naïve charm." As her character continues to develop, misinterpretation becomes more and more central to her identity. In S5E22, Pickler returns to the minx/mink misunderstanding, saying she thought Cowell was calling her a jacket (which makes no sense). Later, during the same critique segment, Cowell tells Pickler that her performance was both ballsy and sexy. When Seacrest asks her how she feels or if she learned anything new this week, she responds that her eyelashes are better. Pickler is here referring to a question Seacrest asks her on a previous episode, wherein she explains that she is wearing false eyelashes that feel like there are tarantulas on her eyes (S5E20).

The next night, on the results show, Seacrest reminds Pickler (as he does with all contestants during the results show) of the previous night's judges' commentary, when Pickler interrupts with a question:

> RS: Simon called you — didn't he say ballsy and sexy?
> KP: What's a ballsy?
> RS: I don't have enough time this half hour... [S5E23]

Eventually, there began to gather increasing backlash in the media and, especially, on the Internet in blogs and forums about Pickler's character identity and whether the entire naivety aspect was genuine or pretense. *Idol* could have chosen to ignore it; however, instead, Seacrest confronts the issue head-on. He explains to Pickler that people are saying her whole bumpkin persona is an act. Pickler responds that she has heard the rumors, and that she really did believe that because there is an "l" in salmon, that she was supposed to pronounce it. She goes on to claim that her friends "didn't know what it was either" (referring to a salmon), and that what is being seen on *Idol* is the "real Kellie Pickler." While it might cause one to raise his eyebrows a bit at the thought that Pickler would rather seem authentically unintelligent than savvy about how she was being portrayed, Pickler's "country naivety" identity coupled with her country musical niche made her a quick star outside of *American Idol*. Her first album, *Small Town Girl,* was certified Gold, and produced three Top 15 singles on the Billboard country music charts ("Bio" n.d.).

Most of the contestants go through this character construction process, although the longer a contestant stays in, obviously, the more well-defined and well-established his/her character becomes. While there are those, such as Mandisa, that have a character type immediately thrust upon them at first viewing, most contestants take a longer episode arc to really begin to present a solidified commodity identity—and similar characters may not produce identical results. Carrie Underwood's commodity identity, for example, begins in exactly the same direction as Kellie Pickler's, but ends up quite differently. At first (S4E2), she is presented in much the same way as Pickler: as a small-town fish out of water in the big city. Her first introduction labels her as a "farm girl, " and as "the girl next door." She is shown in jeans and a t-shirt carrying a bucket on the farm, and in her voice-over, she says that she gets up early in the morning to help her father feed cows or put out hay. She has never had the chance to experience things that other people have—never gotten to fly in a plane or travel very far.

Like Pickler, Underwood is presented as having trouble understanding words and phrases, but unlike Pickler's, which is portrayed as a sort of unintelligent naivety, Underwood's difficulties are presented as more of a wide-eyed innocence. As Underwood and Seacrest walk the streets of Hollywood (S4E3), Underwood is taking photographs not of the sidewalk or the signs, but of the palm trees. When Seacrest asks her if she's seen any stars, Underwood replies, in a sort of distracted seriousness, "It's been pretty cloudy."

Underwood's "farm girl in the big city" image is strengthened throughout the Hollywood round episodes, from shots of her struggling through a hotel lobby with two immense suitcases to her lack of understanding of common slang. When one of her fellow contestants tells her, "Hey, little momma, you knocked it out the box," she has to ask Constantine Maroulis if it was a compliment. Underwood, from early on in the competition, understands and embraces the character being created for her with a reasoned approach:

> CU: During this competition, I've, you know, become known as [air quotes] farm girl and, you know, I'm fine with that. I'd much rather be, you know,

V. What's a Ballsy?

the sweet little innocent girl from Oklahoma than a lot of other things that I could be called. So I'm proud of it [S7E15].

Underwood's "farm girl" character goes hand in hand with her country music genre, and whenever she diverges from that pigeonhole, the judges are quick to rebuke her. Week after week, Underwood selects songs that challenge her. In S4E22, she chooses the song "Alone" by Heart. She explains that she wants to break out of her shell a little bit by signing a rock ballad. The judges, however, are intent on keeping Underwood locked into the country genre. In S4E15, Underwood sings "Take Another Little Piece of My Heart." The judges admonish her, saying that it's too hard for her to try to perform Janis Joplin, and wondering why she is "changing who she is" to do a rock song. Her performance quality when singing country music is reinforced at the same time, with Cowell in particular telling Underwood that her performance here was "reminiscent of what a local covers [sic] band would do." In juxtaposition, when Underwood sings country songs, she receives abundant praise from the judges. In S4E12, Jackson effuses that Underwood is a breath of fresh air and he cannot believe someone hasn't already "discovered" her; in S4E25, Abdul says that Underwood just feels "so natural" when singing country.

Underwood is not allowed to deviate from the commodity identity being constructed for her without reproach. She is from a farm, and farm girls sing country music. Farm girls do not sing Pat Benatar (S4E29), they do not sing show tunes (S4E27), and they do not sing Donna Summer (S4E31). The package in S4E32 further intensifies Underwood's farm girl persona; through her voice-over, she describes Checotah, Oklahoma, as a one-stoplight town, where there's not much "city folk" (she uses those exact words) would enjoy doing. She reveals that she is the youngest of her siblings, and that because there is a wide age gap between her and her sisters, she spent most of her time growing up with her mother and her animals.

The visual elements of this package contribute as much, if not more, to the development of Underwood's persona as the vocal commentary. The package opens on a sign bearing an image of a cowboy on a horse chasing down a steer, reading, "Welcome to Checotah — World Steer Wrestling Capital — Honey Springs Host City — Home of Grand Old

American Idolatry

Opry Star Mel McDaniel." A fading white water tower is shown, emblazoned with "CHECOTAH" in bold letters, while a train (complete with an American flag painted on the side) crosses the desolate scrubland. A shot from a moving automobile shows a wide-open plain streaming by the frame, then cuts to a pan shot of the town's one stop light — square brick buildings border the intersection, and everyone seems to be driving a pickup truck. When Underwood is finally shown, she is wearing a baseball cap and fishing on the banks of what appears to be a secluded pond. She casts a line, then moments later, pulls in a fish and exclaims, "Awesome!" After a moment, the image cuts to Underwood sitting on the porch of a brick farm house with a dog. Her father is shown driving a hay baler, then Underwood is shown carrying a bucket of feed to the cows. Her dog chases some cows, and then Carole Underwood is shown sitting on a porch swing, giving her interview. A moment later, the family is shown sitting and standing around a kitchen table with coffee mugs and plates of pie. The décor is stereotypically country — wood paneling, rustic table and chairs, checkerboard and flower patterns abounding. A still photograph of young Underwood in a flowered dress with her graduating older sister in cap and gown and a second, much older sister is shown, followed by a photograph of young Underwood in a baseball cap with her arms draped around her mother's neck. Underwood picks up striped cat and holds him; there is a sewing machine in the background and collages of family photos. Then, Underwood is shown tenderly picking up a baby rabbit and petting it on the head. Her mother fights back tears as she says, "She's a very good daughter."

The visual elements of the piece tie together to create an image of Underwood that the vocal commentary alone could not achieve. Instantly, we are told everything we need to know about Checotah, Oklahoma: it is a one-stoplight town, arid and reminiscent of an Old West village. Underwood's farm is a working farm, with cows and tractors, and maintaining the farm is a family affair. Underwood has an affinity with animals and is both kind and gentle — her interaction with the baby bunny buttresses her mother's comments that she may love animals more than people, but also gives Underwood an aura of sweet innocence. The Carrie Underwood of this *Idol* package is not only talented, but likeable and deserving — a story of transcending humble roots to pursue one's dreams

V. What's a Ballsy?

on the biggest stage in the country. She is the monomyth of the "American Dream" personified. The package attempts to make Underwood's commodity identity authentic, and authenticity is highly prized in the *Idol* environment, where so much of the proceedings are intricately constructed.

S7's Brooke White is rare among *Idol* contestants in that the authenticity of her identity/character begins to be established the first time she is presented. Whereas with both Pickler and Underwood, it takes several episodes to establish their "fish out of water" characters as "real" or "authentic," the veracity of White's identity is established almost immediately. In White's audition, she reveals that she is a professional nanny, and that, at 24 years of age, she has still never seen an R-rated movie. Cowell is flabbergasted by this, to which White responds, "So, basically, Simon has a challenge to bring me over to the dark side. I'm sorry to disappoint him, but that's just really not going to happen" (S7E12). White's fair complexion, long, wavy blonde hair, and sunny disposition immediately creates a "good girl" image — one that evolves throughout the season. Musically, White is able to tap into a singer-songwriter styling that gives her music a very organic feel. This, in turn, leads to the judges repeatedly granting her one of the most coveted of all *Idol* labels: "original." (Originality and authenticity are discussed at length later in this book.)

White's identity and character leads to an inevitable season-long struggle with Simon Cowell, whose own "prince of darkness" character stands in stark opposition to White's. While Cowell appreciates White's musical abilities, her personality is often a point of contention with the head judge, such as when White sings The Turtles' "Happy Together" in a yellow dress in front of a backdrop of a glowing sun. Abdul praises White's originality and the ease at which her voice can be identified. Cowell, on the other hand, feels it is "like I'm in like some commercial for washing up liquid in the 1960s" (S7E12). White's blonde hair, combined with all of the yellow and all of the happiness (both in the song and on her face) all lacked "relevance" for Cowell ("relevance" being another code word, which will be discussed more in depth later). Cowell's main concern, though, is simple:

SC: I presume you're just going to be ... nice ... throughout this competition, aren't you?
BW: Is that okay with you?

American Idolatry

SC: Not really, no.
BW: Well, I don't know what to tell you then [S7E12].

White's persona intensifies as the season progresses. Each week, she seems to be driven to introspection and, on occasion, tears by the magnitude of the audience and the opportunity she is being given. While there is often joy in her performances, White is particularly adept at infusing ballads with emotion and what Jackson repeatedly categorizes as "rawness." After her performance of The Beatles' "Let It Be" (S7E20), in which she not only sings, but plays the piano and performs most of the song without the accompaniment of the studio band, White is moved to tears before the judges can even deliver their critique. She is standing in front of the judges, barefoot (because she can't play with her shoes on), weeping and vulnerable, and the judges love her for it. Cowell calls it one of the best performances of the night and a brilliant song choice, pointing out that White's piece was both believable and showcased her talent. When Seacrest talks to her after the critique, she can barely get the words out, admitting that she has "hit the big time here." Singing The Beatles on national television behind a grand piano and a full string orchestra has reduced her to a sobbing, trembling wreck.

The humanizing moment of admitting that she cannot play piano while wearing shoes simply adds to White's organic identity; later in the season, White does the unthinkable on an *American Idol* performance show—she makes a mistake, forgets the words to the opening line of the song, and asks the band to start over. Normally, this would virtually guarantee a contestant would be voted out. However, what would seem unprofessional or unprepared for another contestant was endearing and somehow expected from White. The audience and the judges empathized with her nerves and her consistently overwhelmed state at the scale of her situation, and kept her in the competition.

In the end, Brooke White's "good girl" persona coupled with her "singer-songwriter" musical style makes for a powerfully "genuine" character—a fact that is repeatedly emphasized by the judges; Paula Abdul, in particular:

PA: What's great about you is that you're consistent. You are who you are—you put your heart and your soul into ... you have an emotional connection

V. What's a Ballsy?

with each song that you pick. I think that's what record companies and executives want. You are Brooke White. Excellent and wonderful [S7E26].

In another episode, Abdul commented, "Every ounce of you is totally authentic to who you are, and that's a beautiful thing. You're identifiable ..." (S7E31). The ability to be identifiable, to differentiate one's self from the other contestants — to stand out from the crowd — is often the difference between success and failure on *American Idol*. White's authenticity on a program that is highly constructed is an interesting dichotomy that one popular blogger described as follows:

> The nature of being truly gifted is to be awkward, especially in an environment designed to smack your gifts right the fuck out of you ... Brooke was in there fighting for authenticity in the most inauthentic environment yet conceived ... this was the perfect sing out for her, "I Am, I Said," because it's all about ending up in a scary place that is too hard and dark when you should have stayed safe... But I like the idea that this was a challenge for her, and that maybe she'll come away with a stronger sense of her own goodness, and how bad the place [is] she invested it. You don't bring a bird to a dogfight and expect the bird to fight. Birds are best at singing ["She Was, She Went," 2008].

VI

You've Got the X Factor

> *It kind of bothers me when people think about Asian singers, you think William Hung. And I'm not hating on William Hung, but I mean, come on. There are many talented Asian people out there. You just don't see them. I mean, they don't get an opportunity in the entertainment industry at all.*
> — Paul Kim, S6E8

The Cultural Industries' Construction of the Celebrity

Idol's relationship with authenticity is a tenuous one at best. While *Idol*'s regular cast members repeatedly profess to be looking for "original" contestants, they just as often refer to the specific "type" of person they would like to participate in *American Idol*. An American Idol must look commercial, must be (if the contestant is female) within particular weight parameters, must have authentic "star potential," and must be likeable. If a contestant cannot fulfill these appearance requirements, it is highly unlikely that contestant will even be placed in the top 24 to be voted on by America, let alone win the competition.

As Cowell often notes, "You've got to get this competition into perspective — we're looking for a superstar" (S1E11). This is not simply an existential quality; Cowell is often being quite literal when he references the look of a superstar. More than any other judge,[1] Cowell makes continual reference to the physical appearance of the contestants, often in a derogatory way, such as when he tells Carrie Underwood her outfit is too old-fashioned, saying, "It's like Barbie meets *The Stepford Wives*" (S4E31). Whether it is a snide aside in the middle of a critique (as when he tells Bo

VI. You've Got the X Factor

Bice, "You look like my chemistry teacher" [S4E42]) or the focal point of the critique itself (as when he reacts to Vonzell Solomon's choice to wear a cowboy hat and boots given to her by her father, and he comments: "I'm not quite sure what you're trying to be in this competition at the moment" [S4E18]), Cowell is much more likely than the other two judges to express concern over the way a contestant looks. In fact, Cowell nearly rejected eventual S5 winner Taylor Hicks in the audition round due to the fact that Hicks did not look commercial enough for the competition. Cowell insisted that Hicks could not be "commercial" because he looked like a back-up singer, not like a front man (S5E5).

Cowell definitely has an image of "an American Idol" in mind when selecting contestants, and he is not reluctant to share that image with the other judges, nor with the contestants. S5 contestant Kevin Covais was a small, wiry, bespectacled 17-year-old with whose inclusion Cowell just did not agree. The other judges by this time have come to know exactly what Cowell is looking for physically in a contestant. Cowell says that no one under 20 years old is going to relate to Covais, then pressures Paula Abdul into admitting that Covais does not look like "the next American Idol would look" (S5E7).

Because of Cowell's open honesty about physical appearance, and because most people living in a mediacentric society are fully aware of conventionally accepted standards of attractiveness and their relationship to those standards, many contestants come into the audition with an expectation of being eliminated because of how they look, and physical appearance is often the excuse contestants that fail use to justify their failure, as one contestant's mother demonstrates: "If [my son] had, like, famous clothes on and looked rich, he'd have made it. Simon goes by everyone's looks" (S5E3). The canonical *Idol* record seems to bear this statement out to some extent. From the very beginning of *Idol*, Cowell's preferences are in the open, particularly when it comes to women and their weight. On two separate occasions in the series pilot, Cowell takes issue with the weight of female contestants. First, he confronts 24-year-old Karma Johnson of Seattle, saying that when he thinks of an American Idol, there is an image he pictures, and it's not Johnson. Johnson responds that contestants should not be judged on "how tight their jeans are or how big their breasts are" (S1E1). Moments later, in the same episode, Cowell has a similar conversation with another young lady, 21-year-old Jacquette Williams. He asks her if she thought she would make it through the audition process, and Williams truthfully admits she did not because she is heavy.

Cowell relents and allows Williams into the Hollywood round of auditions. However, during the first round of Hollywood week, he returns to Williams' weight, telling her she does not look like an American Idol. He goes on to say that "the record-buying audience around the world" doesn't think Williams looks like an American Idol, and that music, as a business, is led by image. Randy Jackson[2] responds by reminding Cowell that Williams has just sung a song by Aretha Franklin, and asks if Franklin looks like an American Idol. Shockingly, Cowell responds, "I do not believe that if Aretha Franklin entered this competition she would win it now" (S1E12). Both Jackson and Abdul are outraged by this response, to which Cowell retorts that he does not make the rules.

Cowell's comments are interesting on multiple levels. First, Cowell states that the "record-buying audience around the world" has decided that music is an image-led business. However, as discussed in Chapter I, popular culture is, by far and away, industry-driven vastly more than audience-driven, and consumers are often stuck making choices between products to which there are no alternatives. If all consumers are given are stick-thin, blonde-haired, blue-eyed pop stars to choose among, then saying the audience has chosen to only purchase stick-thin, blonde-haired, blue-eyed pop stars is naïve at best and disingenuous at worst. Secondly, stating that Aretha Franklin, one of the biggest superstars in the history of the music industry as evidenced by her induction into the Rock & Roll Hall of Fame and multiple Grammies, could not win *American Idol* because of her looks categorically belies the repeated claims by the program that it is, first and foremost, a singing competition. *Idol* is an image competition in which singing plays a role, but it could be debated that the role singing plays is not even central but peripheral, especially in light of Cowell's comments. Finally, as an Artists & Repertoire (A&R) executive[3] for the Bertlesmann Music Group and the founder of S-Records and Syco Records, Cowell does, in point of fact, make the rules — or, at least, has a hand in the making of the rules.[4]

As one might expect, Williams was not selected for the next round.

VI. You've Got the X Factor

Sixteen-year-old Baylie Brown, conversely, is exactly the kind of contestant Cowell is interested in. Blonde, slender, and beautiful, Brown fits the picture of an American Idol as Cowell imagines it. She is told that she was born to be a music superstar. Her look, her personality, and her voice are all "commercial with a capital C," and she is "a record label's dream" (S6E7). "Commercial" is designated a compliment; this is never reconciled with the fact that *Idol* judges repeatedly state that they are looking for someone unique and authentic (nor is it reconciled with the fact that Brown fails to make the final cut and does not appear in the competition part of the show). Can authenticity and commerciality co-exist? "Commercial," as used by Cowell, implies a specific look and a specific type of personality, and also directly indicates that having a great voice is not a necessity. This would seem to run counter to most common definitions of authenticity. However, Brooke White, perhaps the most "authentic" contestant *Idol* has ever produced, is also slender, blonde, and beautiful; she looks great, her personality is fantastic. She is not all that different from Baylie Brown. Authenticity in the *Idol* world appears to be inextricably linked to commerciality.

Authenticity is a mercurial quality on *Idol*, however. If it were as simple as Cowell phrased it to Carrie Underwood—"You know who you are and what you're all about" (S4E12)—each contestant would have, at least, some small measure of claim to authenticity. Clearly, most contestants do not have equal access to the label of "authentic." Authenticity in the *Idol* context is a construct of a few key factors. First, the contestant must "know who s/he is"; s/he must inhabit a very specific genre and excel within that genre, and must venture out of that genre only briefly and begrudgingly, if at all. With Underwood, it is country music; with Brooke White, it is the singer/songwriter format (one person and an instrument with little or no additional accompaniment); with Bo Bice, it is Southern rock. Maintaining this allegiance to the chosen genre may lead to praise from the judges when the contestant has excelled within that genre (Cowell's comment to Underwood: "There are three people in this competition who actually know who they are musically and you are one of them" [S4E20]), and if the contestant can continue his/her genre allegiance, even when faced with a seemingly counterintuitive theme night, so much the better. For example, Chris Daughtry's metal-influenced alternative rock styling suit the open-selection weeks perfectly. However, faced with the prospects of Stevie Wonder as the guest mentor and Stevie Wonder songs as the musical theme, the judges are openly skeptical of his chances. Daughtry, however, discovers a Red Hot Chili Peppers' version of "Higher Ground," and performs that arrangement instead, earning him high praise from the judging panel. Jackson tells Daughtry that he always seems to find a way to "make it his own"; Cowell says Daughtry's performance was the only "real world" performance of the evening, and echoes that Daughtry "made it his own" (S5E20). It is ironic that Daughtry earns praise for "making the song his own" while performing a cover of a cover—Daughtry's arrangement comes from the Red Hot Chili Peppers' version of the song, not Stevie Wonder's.

Daughtry's praise is even further ironic, given that the second factor in being granted the label of authenticity is to sound unlike anybody else. Cowell's praise to Gedeon McKinney illustrates, as he tells McKinney that he sounds like "somebody Berry Gordy would have got hold of thirty/forty years ago" (S5E15). McKinney is placed in a category with Marvin Gaye and Sam Cooke, and that makes him special, unique, and authentic. Cowell actually used the word "authentic" twice in his effusive praise of McKinney.

Whether it's McKinney's throwback sound or Nadia Turner's reggae-infused pop rock style, contestants are often encouraged to sound unique (even as they are forced by the program's format to sing within themes that often have little or nothing to do with that performer's unique sound). So, when Nadia Turner spiked her hair into a Mohawk to deliver an up-tempo rendition of Cyndi Lauper's pop anthem "Time After Time," her response when discovering she was voted into the bottom three was expected; she says that she infused the song with rock and reggae because all she can do is stay true to her own sound. In essence, in order to maintain an original sound, the contestant must attempt to balance the requirements of their own style with the realities of the theme that has been chosen for them by the show's producers. A contestant may, on occasion, earn some measure of consolation in defeat by having stayed true to their own voice, as Selina Ray did following her ousting from the competition: "I felt great. I sang a song that I love. I sang music that I love. I went back to being me" (S4E16).

VI. You've Got the X Factor

Note that the judges do not necessarily have to enjoy the contestant or the performance in order to recognize the authenticity therein. It is not a question of merely "liking" particular performers; even contestants for whom the judges (particularly Cowell) clearly exhibit distaste are able to garner praise on the merits of authenticity, such as Anthony Federov in S4E33. Cowell's faces during Federov's performance would have been enough to ascertain exactly how he felt about the contestant. However, in his critique, Cowell says a very interesting thing. He calls Federov "a very brave man," and says that while he personally hated the performance, Federov has done what all great artists do: he has found the right kind of song to sing to the kind of people who are going to like him and vote for him. In that respect, Federov nailed a particular kind of *Idol* authenticity.

The third requirement for authenticity on *Idol* is a recognition that the *Idol* producers are ultimately looking for someone with whom they can make albums and produce concert tours and merchandise. *American Idol* is not a high school talent show; the winners of *American Idol* have produced 15 RIAA-certified albums (Gold, Platinum, and/or multi-Platinum) and another eight albums with sales over 100,000 ("Gold and Platinum" n.d.) — a total of more than 40 million records in all. If a contestant can give an immediate impression to the judges of the type of record s/he will make as the winner, it vastly improves their chances with the judges. Jackson, in particular, is often at the forefront of praise for artists who are adept at presenting their "true" nature, as illustrated in his comments to Bo Bice following a performance of The Ides of March's "Vehicle." Jackson says that the thing he loves about Bice is that when listening to him, Jackson can hear exactly the kind of record Bice should make. He calls it the only "authentically good" performance of the night (S4E31).

Jackson mentions this aspect — the type of record the performer will make — on multiple occasions across multiple seasons. For Jackson, it appears that this aspect of authenticity is the key distinction between those contestants that are ultimately successful with the context of the *Idol* competition and those that are not. If the contestants can show "songs that [they] could choose that would show us the kind of record that [they] would make" (S5E24), and the audience responds favorably, the contestant has just given the producers and the public insight as to the future commodity features of the product s/he will become.

American Idolatry

Finally, authenticity in the *Idol* context can be located in a contestant's personality, however that may manifest. Whether it is the confident swagger of experience exuded by Bo Bice (Cowell tells him that watching him is like watching someone who is already an established music star [S4E22]) or the unassuming modesty of Elliott Yamin, whom Abdul calls "a breath of fresh air," humble, understated, and true to himself (S5E26), a performer who can "be him/herself" in a way that is pleasing to the judges, presents an air of authenticity.

When one has authenticity, such as Chris Daughtry, Carrie Underwood, Blake Lewis, or the previously discussed exemplar of authenticity on *Idol*, Brooke White, longevity in the competition is much more feasible. A contestant without a measure of authenticity is most often doomed to a quick exit, as S7 contestant Robbie Carrico personally experiences. Cowell is all over Carrico from the beginning of the competition, and when Carrico is voted out in S7E16, Cowell rubs it in by telling Carrico he never "felt real."[5]

Of course, looking like a star is not simply a matter of having attractive physical features and an air of authenticity. Clothes certainly play no small part in presenting the image of a star. When the clothes are not packaging the artist in the way that Cowell thinks they should (i.e., the contestant does not look commercial enough), he is quick to criticize. For example, Cowell tells S7 contestant Carly Smithson to have a word with her stylist, because she needs to start dressing more like a star, and there has been no progression in her appearance (S7E26). Clothes can either detract from the contestant's commodity potential (SC: "You lost some star quality tonight" (S4E15)) or enhance it, blending with authenticity to create what Abdul calls, "The X Factor," as in the case of Nadia Turner. Jackson repeatedly refers to the way Turner looks, at one point telling her that she has "star potential," and "the X factor" that sets her apart from the other contestants (S4E18).

However, looking like a star is not only dependent upon clothing. For example, Katharine McPhee's performance of Queen's power ballad "Who Wants to Live Forever?" is enhanced not only by the beautiful outfit and elegant hair and makeup she is wearing (not to mention her own physical beauty), but by the way in which the artistic directors create the physical space in which she performs. Cowell immediately points out that the

VI. You've Got the X Factor

director and the lighting director deserve a great deal of credit for making McPhee look phenomenal (S5E28), and he is absolutely correct. Not only does McPhee look stunningly beautiful during this performance, but the smoke effect on the stage mixes with dramatic lighting, slow dolly and zoom shots, and blend editing to create an experience greater than merely the performance of McPhee.

Similarly, S7 contestant Kristy Lee Cook is able to prolong her tenure on *Idol* through a rousing rendition of Lee Greenwood's "Proud to Be an American," complete with a fluttering American flag on the screen behind her and red, white, and blue lights illuminating the stage. Cowell gives her a severely backhanded compliment in saying that Cook delivered the most clever performance in years, essentially saying that singing "Proud to Be an American" on *American Idol* in front of the American flag on national television is brilliant, and he is not wrong. To fail to vote for Cook on that night would be tantamount to saying one hates America. It is a stunt, to be certain, but a successful one — Cook stays in the competition that week, despite all signs previously pointing to her being the next to leave.

Clothing, lighting, authenticity, and physical appearance all factor into whether or not a contestant "looks like" a star, but in the end, a star is created through force of will — the personality and likeability of the contestant. If the contestant is particularly adept at interacting with the audience, like Ace Young is, it will certainly draw the attention of the judges. Jackson tells Young that all previous contestants who thought they were working the room and connecting particularly to female audience members were a pale comparison; Young is anointed the new king of working the audience (and, almost as an aside, "plus ... you can really sing!") (S5E12). Drawing the attention of the judges is not always a great thing, however. Personality can go a long way, but there is a fine line between impressing the judges and going too far, as Constantine Maroulis often finds. Cowell, at one point, tells Maroulis that his singing is only a 7, but his pouting is a 9½ (S4E27), calling it the best "pouting performance" in *Idol* history.

Likeability is a huge factor on *American Idol*, especially with the judges. Fairly early on in a given season, a contestant will often find him- or herself branded either "likeable" or "not likeable," and his/her fortunes in terms of "looking like a star" (i.e., commercial commodity viability) directly result from this labeling. For example, S4 contestant Jessica Sierra advances to the top 10. Following her first top 10 performance, Cowell notes that Sierra doesn't have the "likeability factor" the other contestants have, and needs to try harder to get the audience to like her (S4E25). On the next night's results show, Sierra is eliminated from the competition.

On the other hand, likeability can carry a contestant far into the competition. Kellie Pickler is branded as likeable after her first competitive appearance (as well as "unpretentious," not having "the diva attitude," "heartfelt," and "not a sort of stage-school monster"). She is told that she is a "very nice girl" who has "the likeability factor," and that people will fall in love with her personality (S5E11). Pickler remains in the competition until the top six, and until her elimination, never once is voted into the bottom three. Cowell especially often overlooks Pickler's vocal shortcomings in light of her personality and the fact that he likes her. For example, following her anecdote about her first encounter with calamari, Pickler sings Bonnie Raitt's "Something to Talk About." The judges respond that Pickler couldn't be any more adorable, and Cowell especially cannot help but like her. Pickler, for her part, responds that her heels are so high and her legs are shaking so much that she feels like she may fall down, adding to her unpretentious aura of cuteness (S5E14). It is only in passing that Cowell mentions that if he hadn't seen her pre-song package (involving her adventures with calamari), he would have thought her performance was rough and uneven — curious commentary for a program that is about "singing first."

Interestingly but perhaps unsurprisingly, likeability only seems to be a factor when the judges want it to be, just as the competition is not necessarily a singing competition all the time — often only when the judges want it to be. At other times, it is a performance competition, a popularity contest, and so on. Seacrest addressed this point directly at the beginning of S5, before the first elimination program (S5E13). Seacrest directly asks Jackson how much weight likeability carries with the home audience, to which Jackson responds that it matters quite a bit, and that it's about having something special. However, he adds, the further into the top 12 the competition goes, the more it's about signing and performing and less it's about likeability. Cowell is more pointed when he says that the person

VI. You've Got the X Factor

leaving that night is obvious because they were "terrible." When Seacrest asks, "But what if they were likeable?," Cowell responds that "*it doesn't matter how likeable you are*" (emphasis added), because America has been trained to be "good music critics."

If it "doesn't matter how likeable you are," why do the judges make repeated references to likeability, across multiple seasons with multiple contestants? If the American audience is being trained to be "good music critics," why is such an emphasis placed on "looking like a star?" If it is, as Jackson says, "all about the singing and the performing," how does this reconcile with Cowell's claim that Aretha Franklin could not win *American Idol*? So much of the viability of the *American Idol* Celebrity commodity is directly tied to the culture industries' stereotypical construction of what it means to look like a Celebrity. Once that viability has been established within the context of *Idol*, the process of legitimating those Celebrity commodities begins.

VII
Sugarfoot and Babyface

> *You know, the experience of this show, it's proven that people go on and achieve greatness, whether they win or not. Look what happened with Bo Bice; look what happened with Clay Aiken. Jennifer Hudson's starring alongside Beyoncé in Dreamgirls. This show allows you to change the blueprint of your life. Whatever happens — make the right record, go on, and keep your dreams alive. It's just the beginning.*
> — Paula Abdul, S5E23

The Relative Commodity Status of the Celebrity

The Celebrity commodity exists in relationship to all other Celebrity commodities, and competes for the same resources, attention, and capital in the audience market as every other Celebrity commodity. In order for the *Idol* commodities to have a reasonable chance at success in that attention economy market, it is vital that the commodity be legitimated — that is to say, the commodity must be shown to have worth and merit in relationship to other Celebrity commodities. *Idol* accomplishes this through six different mechanisms: having Celebrity mentors impart wisdom to the contestants to enhance their commodity value, having established stars perform with the contestants, having the judges proclaim "Idol moments," referencing the commercial success of former *Idol* contestants, bringing former *Idol* contestants back to the program to validate their successes, and constantly reminding the audience of the size and scope of the program.

Before *Idol* can fully introduce the Celebrity commodities they have created into the general attention marketplace, they must first legitimate those commodities. This legitimating process takes place in stages, begin-

VII. Sugarfoot and Babyface

ning with the Celebrity mentor construct. Each season, *Idol* recruits a number of established musical Celebrities to meet with and train the contestants for their immediate performances and for their futures in the music industry. The mentor episodes are all structured in basically the same way: the Celebrity mentor is introduced via a feature package highlighting the mentor's career achievements — in essence, reminding the audience of the mentor's own relative commodity status and his or her credentials for mentoring others on the art of becoming a musical Celebrity. Next, the *Idol* contestants are shown singing one of the mentor's songs (normally in a group crowded around a piano), paying homage to the master. The Celebrity mentor walks in during this homage, to the visible delight of the contestants. The mentor gives the contestants some general advice as a group, and then throughout the rest of the program, the mentor is shown meeting one-on-one with each contestant in turn, giving coaching, counseling, and advice. Finally, the Celebrity mentor gives one last assessment of each contestant before the contestant is sent out to sing. Frequently, the Celebrity mentor is brought back the next night, on the results show, to perform.

Idol's list of Celebrity mentors is long and varied, and includes some of the biggest names in the music industry: Mariah Carey, Carol Bayer Sager, Gwen Stefani, Neil Diamond, Dolly Parton, Lord Andrew Lloyd Webber, Stevie Wonder, Barry Manilow, Queen, Kenny Rogers, and Andrea Bocelli have all served in the Celebrity mentor role on *American Idol*, and this list is not exhaustive. The introductory packages for these superstar Celebrities often contain lists of achievements which even seasoned professional musicians cannot replicate. For example, Stevie Wonder's introductory package reminds the audience — especially the younger demographic, which may not be as familiar with his work — of a lifetime of achievements:

> RS: In 1960, child prodigy Steveland Morris was signed to Motown Records at the astonishing age of ten. He was nicknamed Stevie Wonder, as he quickly headed toward superstardom. He's sold over 100 million albums and has won more Grammies than any other solo artist — 24 in all, plus a Lifetime Achievement award. He even won an Oscar for Best Song. Stevie's music is just as influential today. His latest album, *A Time to Love*, can be added to his list of gold and platinum records. But it's his musical message of peace, love, and harmony that has made him a cultural icon and an inspira-

tion for generations of fans. This week he was happy to surprise 12 of those fans at a Hollywood sound studio.

SW: The great thing about this show is that you bring lots of people together in the spirit of song. Isn't that wonderful? [S5E20].

Wonder is ushered into the studio and sits at the piano. The contestants all maneuver such that Elliott Yamin is moved to the front, where he can sit on the piano bench next to Wonder. Yamin immediately begins to cry. It is later explained that Stevie Wonder is Yamin's greatest idol; Yamin is overwhelmed with emotion from merely being in Wonder's presence. This type of display reinforces Wonder's relative commodity value — even these newly-minted Celebrities are in awe of him. This, in turn, emphasizes the significance of Wonder's advice to and coaching of the *Idol* contestants. Their own relative commodity values are increased because of this brush with greatness; it is a modernized version of the old French ritual, "*Le Roi te touche, et Dieu te guérit*" — "The King touches you, and God heals you." Having sat at the side of the master, the student is imbued with a measure of the master's greatness.

Even when a Celebrity mentor is from outside of the world of popular music, the introductory packages are designed to quickly validate the Celebrity mentor's presence. For example, Lord Andrew Lloyd Webber's relative commodity status may not reach the level of Stevie Wonder in terms of the world of popular music, but his introduction quickly alerts the viewer as to his accomplishments: he composed some of the most important musicals of the modern theater, has received every major theater award available, and has opened a new show in Las Vegas. Lloyd Webber tells the contestants that he is there to help them find the story in their songs — as he says, "Words, words, words" (S7E33). In the case of Lloyd Webber, the contestants are expected to sing songs from musical theater — an interesting theme night, considering that, as will be discussed later, "musical theater" is a label often used by Cowell as a pejorative.

At the end of each season of *American Idol*, the final three contestants are introduced to Clive Davis. Davis, the chief executive officer of the United States branch of BMG, is responsible for signing the winning *Idol* contestant (and, increasingly, several of the losing contestants as well) to record contracts and releasing the contestant's first album. Davis's introductory package normally contains similar information every time it

VII. Sugarfoot and Babyface

appears: as the president of Columbia Records, he was responsible for discovering Janis Joplin, Chicago, Billy Joel, Earth Wind and Fire, Santana, Bruce Springsteen and Aerosmith. Davis founded Arista Records in 1975, and signed Barry Manilow, Patty Smythe, Aretha Franklin, Whitney Houston, and Babyface. As his company grew, he also signed Alicia Keys, Maroon 5, Annie Lennox, and Rod Stewart, made albums with Foo Fighters, Dave Matthews Band, and Christina Aguilera, and now oversees the music of Pink, Outkast, Justin Timberlake, and Usher. Clive Davis is arguably the most prominent music executive in the world.

Davis's standing is less that of the sage master and more that of the king-maker. Davis is, in many ways, one of the major gatekeepers in terms of access to superstar *celebrity* status. To work with Clive Davis is to immediately legitimate commodity status; Davis, as his package suggests, works with only the top-tier superstars in the music business. In choosing to work with the *Idol* winner, he immediately accords him/her similar status as an Alicia Keys or a Justin Timberlake — a status artists outside of *American Idol* normally spend years attempting to achieve. This instant boost to the relative commodity status of the *Idol* winner usually translates intertextually to increased record sales and music video rotation. In fact, the only *Idol* winner debut album to sell less than one million copies was that of Taylor Hicks, which still sold just over 700,000 copies. Every *Idol* winner, and many of the runners-up, is signed to some subsidiary label owned or operated by BMG: RCA (Clarkson, Clay Aiken, Daughtry, David Cook, Bo Bice), Arista (Underwood, Jennifer Hudson, formerly Taylor Hicks), J Records (Fantasia Barrino, formerly Ruben Studdard), Jive Records (Jordin Sparks, David Archuleta), Hickory Records (Yamin, Studdard), or BNA Records (Kellie Pickler). Each of those former contestants has had a debut album with sales of more than 600,000 units ("Gold and Platinum" n.d.). Working with Clive Davis is a proven path to success for *Idol* contestants.

Near the end of each *Idol* season, beginning with S4, the contestants are legitimated in a second way: by showing the audience that these *Idol* contestants can share the stage with an established Celebrity in a performance. By directly intermingling the new Celebrity commodities with recognized, reputable, existing Celebrity commodities, the program informs the audience that the contestants are now competitive in the attention marketplace. The first time *Idol* attempts this legitimating strategy, Ryan Seacrest notes that when the program let the music community know that the finalists wanted to perform with established stars, the stars came calling (not the other way around; *Idol* is so big that artists presumably are begging to perform on its stage) (S4E43). The first pairing, Carrie Underwood with multiple–Academy of Country Music and Country Music Association award-winning band Rascal Flatts, serves two purposes: first, it legitimates Underwood in terms of her being able to skillfully share the stage with a well-known and respected band; and secondly, it helps to establish Underwood in the eyes of her most likely target audience, country music fans.

During the S4 finale, contestants perform with Kenny G. (Anthony Federov and Anwar Robinson), George Benson (Scott Savol and Nikko Smith), Kenny Wayne Shepherd (Constantine Maroulis, Jessica Sierra, and Nadia Turner), Babyface (Lindsay Cardinale and Mikalah Gordon), Billy Preston (Vonzell Solomon), and Lynyrd Skynyrd (Bo Bice). The S5 finale more closely pairs the contestants with their likely target audiences, more in the Carrie Underwood/Rascal Flatts and Bo Bice/Lynyrd Skynyrd mold, with Chris Daughtry performing with the band Live (Daughtry covers Live's version of Johnny Cash's "I Walk the Line" early in S5), Elliott Yamin performing with Mary J. Blige (Yamin's R&B–influenced album went to #3 on the Billboard music charts), and Paris Bennett performing with Al Jarreau (Bennett's mother, Jamecia Venzett Bennett, is a member of the jazz ensemble Sounds of Blackness).

The finales of S6 and S7 continue in this vein, including such pairings as Blake Lewis (whose performances were almost always laced with his signature beat-boxing) and rap pioneer Doug E. Fresh (who is credited by many as inventing beat-boxing) (S6E41), and Brooke White (singer/songwriter style) with Graham Nash (of the 60s folk group Crosby, Stills, Nash, and Young). In every case, the *Idol* contestant is performing with an artist (renowned, familiar commodity) to which s/he can be favorably compared in the manner of, "Brooke White is like Graham Nash; I enjoy Graham Nash; therefore, I will probably enjoy Brooke White as well." This syllogistic association would seem, intuitively, to benefit the *Idol* contestant, helping to further define the Celebrity commodity within a particular genre. The fact that, for example, Chris Daughtry can sing

VII. Sugarfoot and Babyface

with the band Live and deliver a quality alternative rock performance without being completely outclassed marks Daughtry as "ready" to compete in the larger attention marketplace.

The third way *Idol* legitimates its contestants' commodity status is through recognition of "the Idol moment"; that is to say, occasionally, a contestant will give a performance that makes not only the judges, but (hopefully) the viewers at home forget for a moment they are watching a constructed competition. These "Idol moments" temporarily transcend the immediate proceedings; they are public displays of virtuosity that elevate the contestant to some measure of greatness (however loosely that term can be defined). While public acts of virtuosity are discussed in detail later in this chapter, it is important to recognize that the "Idol moment" has implications beyond simply entertaining the spectators; having an "Idol moment" reclassifies the contestant within the competition (occasionally moving a mid-range contestant into front-runner status, as happened with Kelly Clarkson in S1), and additionally, the judges' memory of that "Idol moment" becomes a standard by which other, future competitors are often judged (Clarkson's moment is, as pointed out earlier, still referred to, granting Clarkson a competition-internal version of The Big Three's aura of greatness).

It falls to the judges to declare an "Idol moment" has occurred — the moment is directly addressed and commended, as happens when Katherine McPhee performs "Somewhere Over the Rainbow," seated on stage under a single spotlight with minimal accompaniment (S5E38). Abdul calls McPhee "magic" and "natural"; Cowell tells her she has a "very, very special talent," and says it was "the single-best performance of the competition to date."(S5E38). So taken is Paula Abdul by the performance that on the next week's performance show, McPhee is asked by the judges to reprise the song, and the "Idol moment" is underlined. Abdul tells her that every little girl in America aspires to be McPhee (S5E40).

Simon Cowell pronounced Carrie Underwood's "Idol moment," halfway through S4 on "80s night," in terms one might expect from an A&R executive: he predicts she will be the top-selling *Idol* winner ever (S4E22). Cowell's prediction came true — Underwood is, indeed, the highest-selling artist of all *American Idol* winners.[1]

Fantasia Barrino's performance of "Summertime" (S3E27) from the musical *Porgy and Bess* stands out as perhaps the defining example of an "Idol moment." Barrino, by the end of the song, is in tears; the audience's standing ovation lasts nearly a full thirty seconds. The performance is reprised in the S3 finale; Cowell declares her the best contestant ever to compete on *Idol*—a list that includes over 70 American and international *Idol* champions from various global incarnations of the program (S3E42). The song is featured on her 2006 album, *Fantasia*, and was nominated for a Grammy award for a Best Traditional R&B Vocal Performance. On the strength of that performance of a musical theater standard, Barrino was cast in *The Color Purple* on Broadway, a role for which she won a Theater World award.

In terms of "Idol moments," Paula Abdul is correct when she tells the contestants, "It's about levels of greatness. You're judged on your level of greatness each moment you're up on that stage" (S1E16). However, *Idol* also goes to great lengths to create an environment in which those "Idol moments" can occur. In S7, *Idol* took this to the extreme, equating the final night of competition between David Cook and David Archuleta to a boxing match. The differences between *Idol* and a sport such as boxing are legion, but at the very least, the physical act of boxing has nothing to do with personality or with audience perception of the combatants' skills[2]; if one boxer is faster or punches harder than his opponent, he will likely win. There is no arbitrary or subjective evaluation process, unless the match goes to the judges, and even then, there are a strict set of rules and criteria for how a boxing match is scored. In *Idol*, the competition at hand is of a completely different sort. The two are only very loosely equitable. Yet, the S7 finale featured an introduction designed to replicate that of a boxing championship fight, complete with advice from long-time boxing analyst Jim Lampley and introductory announcement from iconic boxing ring announcer Michael Buffer—complete with weigh-in information (Cook: 180 pounds, Archuleta: 100 pounds, soaking wet). Both contestants appear in boxing robes and gloves, and with their own boxing monikers: David "Sugarfoot" Cook and David "Babyface" Archuleta (S7E41).

A moment later, after the first commercial break, the program begins with a segment in which Lampley reminds the audience that in any one-on-one conflict, there can only be one winner. Seacrest, via voiceover,

VII. Sugarfoot and Babyface

states that the two are fighting over a prize reserved "only for superstars," while black and white footage of Kelly Clarkson, Chris Daughtry, and Carrie Underwood is shown (S7E41). It is interesting that Chris Daughtry's footage is shown here, in that Daughtry did not hold this "heavyweight title reserved only for superstars." Daughtry did not win *American Idol*. In fact, Daughtry did not even make it to the final competition. The package continues with footage of the contestants interspersed with footage of boxers taping their hands, bobbing and weaving, and hitting a heavy bag. Seacrest announces them both as undefeated (neither contestant was ever voted into the Bottom 3), and ends with a two-shot of both of them raising their fists, squared off like a boxing match (S7E41).

This "Idol moment" environment is unique for two reasons: first, it is completely inorganic. Any subsequent "Idol moments" which occur following this type of introduction are, at least in some part, due to the way in which the night of competition has been framed. Secondly, the intercut boxing footage with the *Idol* contestants creates a false comparison; *Idol* is not a boxing match. *Idol* is very little like a boxing match. Visually equating the two sets up different parameters for viewing and interpreting than normally exist on *Idol*.

Despite this elaborate attempt to precondition the audience, neither Cook nor Archuleta managed to have a judge-declared "Idol moment" during the finale. David Cook fairly handily won the "heavyweight title" over David Archuleta, with 56 percent of the votes to Archuleta's 44 percent (S7E42).

Another way in which *Idol* legitimizes the commodity status of its contestants is by continuing to follow the careers of its former contestants, and bringing them back for guest performances on subsequent seasons. By showing that former *Idol* hopefuls have achieved longevity and continued success in the attention marketplace (and in the commercial marketplace as well), *Idol* validates its own selection processes and potential of current contestants to achieve similar results. This is especially true when a former *Idol* contestant wins a major award, such as the night S3's Jennifer Hudson won an Academy Award for her performance in the film *Dreamgirls*. Seacrest sends out congratulations to *Idol*'s first Oscar winner, and states that it really "validates the caliber of talent our judges discover and that you vote for" (S6E14). Seacrest's use of the term "validate" is important, because it is a recognition that such intertextual acclaim has a residual effect, not only for the former *Idol* contestant who receives the award, but for every other *Idol* contestant who receives a small boost in credibility. A competition that discovered a Jennifer Hudson (or a Kelly Clarkson, Carrie Underwood, Chris Daughtry, et cetera) must know what it is talking about.

Similarly, success in the commercial marketplace is another form of validation. When Jordin Sparks, S6 winner, returned to *Idol* to perform the single "No Air" with Chris Brown, the program staged an "ambush" of sorts to present her with plaques from the RIAA. One plaque commemorates the one millionth download of her single "No Air"; one commemorates a half-million sales of her CD, certifying it Gold. The last plaque commemorates one million downloads of her single "Tattoo." Seacrest ends the segment by declaring that *"American Idol* works," a point with which Sparks immediately agrees (S7E30).

American Idol is repeatedly shown to work in other venues as well, such as the package which follows former *Idol* contestants who have found their fortunes on Broadway (S7E34). Broadway is a popular route to success that many former *Idol* contestants take, despite the fact that Cowell often disparages those contestants whose voices sound like "musical theater." Numerous *Idol* contestants have been cast in major Broadway productions, as evidenced by the footage in this package; S3 runner-up Diana DeGarmo appeared in *Hair Spray*, Fantasia Barrino starred in *The Color Purple*, as did S6's Lakisha Jones. This particular package focuses on S1's fourth place Tamyra Gray and S2 runner-up Clay Aiken. Gray, at the time of broadcast, was appearing in *Rent* (her second Broadway show), while Aiken was starring in *Monty Python's Spamalot*.

Bringing former *Idol* contestants back to perform is one of the main ways *Idol* validates those contestants' Celebrity commodity status. Many former *Idol* contestants have been invited to participate in this exercise; it is a rite of passage for the previous season's winner, but other contestants are invited to perform as well (for some, multiple times): Clay Aiken, Kimberly Locke, Bo Bice, Katharine McPhee, Elliott Yamin, and Brooke White are all former contestants who appear and perform on programs in later seasons.

When performers are not directly brought back to perform, *Idol* still

VII. Sugarfoot and Babyface

legitimates their Celebrity commodity status through repeated references to their record and/or tour sales. At the beginning of S5E34, Seacrest reveals the theme of the night: *Billboard* Top 100 songs. However, the introduction is less about the *Billboard* charts than it is about the place *Idol* contestants have held on those charts. As of S5E34, *Idol* contestants had produced 90 Billboard #1 hits. Kelly Clarkson had also broken a 40-year Billboard record when her single "A Moment Like This" leaped 51 spots in one week — a record previously held by The Beatles.

This chain of success, with now more than 100 #1 hits and over 30 Gold and Platinum albums, reinforces the Celebrity commodity status of the former *Idol* contestants. As has been repeatedly pointed out throughout this book, *celebrity* is a commodity, and ultimately, commodities are evaluated on the financial rewards they reap. Worth in the commodity market of a capitalistic consumer society is calculated not existentially but fiscally. More album sales equates to more commodity status, and in that respect, recognizing the success of former *Idol* contestants commercially validates their Celebrity/*celebrity* commodity status. In S5E39, Clive Davis details exactly how much success the *Idol* contestants have achieved. Originally, Davis relates, no one thought a successful, long-term recording artist could be produced from a television talent show. However, Kelly Clarkson's first album sold over three million copies; her second sold over ten million copies — and she won two Grammy Awards. Ruben Studdard's album sold over two million albums and spawned a #1 hit on the R&B charts. Clay Aiken sold three million records and has a #1 hit. Fantasia Barrino sold two million records and garnered four Grammy nominations. Bo Bice's album went platinum. Carrie Underwood sold three million albums and spawned a #1 hit. The litany of hit records by *American Idol* alum as detailed by Clive Davis in S5E39 is impressive — and only covers the first four seasons. These comments are made at the end of S5, meaning that those commercial successes have been augmented in the ensuing three seasons. For example, at the time, Chris Daughtry's album had not yet been released; Jordin Sparks' not yet even competed (her album is also multi–Platinum), and David Cook's gold-certified album still two seasons away.

It is a never-ending feedback loop; *Idol*'s contestants generate commercial success which brings their fans back to *American Idol* to see who the next Idol will be, and so on. The commercial success legitimates the competition as a quality indicator of future commercially successful commodities. In order to keep this loop in motion, the show necessarily needs to continually remind viewers of the stars it has created.

Davis's comments also allude to the fact that the size and scope of the *American Idol* program is another way to legitimize the Celebrity commodities it produces. Whether it is a causal comment by Seacrest ("It's not the biggest stage in the music industry, but it's the most important" [S6E11]), or the fact that *Idol* was able to secure the rights to perform songs from both the Lennon/McCartney song book and the Michael Jackson collection for its contestants, *Idol* presents the message quite clearly that the program is a very big deal, indeed. Seacrest puts the magnitude of the S7 finale's voting public into perspective: 97 million votes were cast — more than the combined populations of Canada, Spain, Ireland, and Australia. The previous voting record was eclipsed by more than 23 million votes (S7E42).

The contestants, over the seasons, are taken to many places to illustrate the scope and ability of *Idol*: Elvis Presley's former home Graceland, the main stage at the MTV Video Music Awards, Sunset Sound studios, The Record Plant, the Rock and Roll Hall of Fame — all with insider access that non–Celebrities could not attain. The night *Idol* presented the songs of The Beatles, Seacrest began the show by stating, "The best songs in musical history and we've given them one of the best platforms in show biz. No pressure" (S7E20).

By persistently referring to the program as some variation of "the greatest stage in television history" and pointing out the number of votes cast each week (over one billion votes have been cast for *American Idol* to date), *Idol* legitimizes the Celebrity commodities it creates. These commodities are not, goes the sales pitch, created by some faceless corporate executive and foisted upon an unsuspecting public. These Celebrity commodities are created by you — 97 million of you.[3] Who knows better the quality of consumer commodities than the consumers themselves?

Even the judges disagree on the magnitude of the show, as illustrated by this exchange between Abdul and Cowell:

> PA: I got to be honest with you — at this stage of the game, I think every single one of them is going to be able to get a recording contract anyway. It

VII. Sugarfoot and Babyface

doesn't matter to me ... every single one of you are deserving of a record contract.
SC: I disagree with Paula. I think this is a competition you have to win [S4E26].

Clearly, Cowell has a vested interest in maintaining the illusion that *Idol* is a competition one has to win. However, history has proven that is not at all the case. In fact, in S3 and S5, a non-winner's debut album sold more copies than the winner's debut album; two of the top ten selling *American Idol* alumni debut albums ever are from non-winners (Chris Daughtry and Kellie Pickler).

In any case, *Idol* has a range of strategies for legitimizing the relative commodity status of its Celebrity contestants, and has shown great acumen in delivering to the attention and commercial marketplaces commodities that are able to compete with other, more traditionally generated Celebrity commodity products.

VIII

Wear the Least Amount of Clothes Possible

*I want my music to speak for me,
rather than the dress or lack of dresses I wore.*
— Christina Aguilera

Processual and Dynamic Changeability of the Individual Celebrity

One of the defining features of *celebrity* is the dynamism inherent in the Celebrity form; that is to say, a Celebrity may be reinvented and reinvented as many times and in as many different formats as necessary to continue to sell that Celebrity commodity. This is not necessarily only a metaphoric process; this can also manifest as a physical process as well. One of the main ways a Celebrity can instantly project a new image and generate new interest is through an image makeover — a literal attempt at reinvention. *Idol* is no exception; each contestant, in large and small ways, goes through a process of reinvention to present a new image of a commodity with which the public has already become familiar. It simply happens in a more protracted time frame. When we are introduced to the contestants at the beginning of each season, they are presented for several episodes as they "really" look; they have received no stylistic assistance from *Idol* and are filmed in their "natural" state. As the show progresses, the contestants receive more and more makeup, fashion, and hair design assistance from *Idol*'s "Glam Squad," until finally each contestant reaches his/her "packaged" state — a far cry from the "natural" state in which the

VIII. Wear the Least Amount of Clothes Possible

contestant first appeared. These changes in the reinvention process happen in the physical, attitudinal, and lifestyle loci of each contestant.

The amount of work necessary to transform the contestants from their "natural states" to "camera-ready" is normally, as described in Chapter III, an exercise in fetishized labor; that is, the amount of work that goes into the commodity product is normally masked by the product itself. *Idol* defetishizes this labor, to some extent, by reassigning the work of creating a Celebrity commodity from secret labor to spectator event in service to the concept of glamour.

The contestants' access to hair and makeup artists, personal stylists, and fashion consultants is framed as glamorous, as one of the benefits of *celebrity*. Dressing up, getting hair and makeup done, and "being beautiful," as put by Vonzell Solomon in S4E35, is seen here as a break from the norm, not as a specific part of a process designed to exact global changes in the contestant's appearance. However, some contestants appear to be perfectly aware of the metaeffects of these image makeovers; in S4E35, Scott Savol says that one of the best things about *Idol* is that a fashion coordinator works with him to pick outfits that make him look good on television and makes him "more appealing to people." Savol expresses the reality of the contestant makeover — the "natural state" of the contestant may not be "appealing to people" (i.e., commercially viable), but changes in clothing may help steer viewers in the direction of voting for or against a particular competitor.

As stated before, in addition to the fashion consultant, the contestants are also given access to professional hair and makeup artists as well, to enhance their marketability. In S1E17, the contestants are taken to meet with a beauty consultant at Sephora for an "image makeover." They meet with Celebrity makeup artist Charlie Green, which pleases Kelly Clarkson because she "never does makeup," so she is excited for someone to do it for her. Green says she wants to give Clarkson, "sexy, Bridget Bardot, smoky eyes." Green is attempting to further define Clarkson's Celebrity image by identifying her visually with another, visually recognizable Celebrity. This is a common practice in Celebrity reinvention — Madonna reimagining herself as Marilyn Monroe throughout much of the 1990s, for example. Clarkson's admitting that she "never does makeup" gives her access to the *celebrity* makeup artist that much more glamour — the labor involved is fetishized here, but in more of a vernacular usage of the term rather than a Marxist one. The makeup work is a commodity in and of itself to be coveted and desired; Clarkson's access to it increases her *celebrity* status. Simultaneously, the show reinforces her "regular girl" persona, further identifying her with the audience — any viewer at home could ostensibly be just as glamorous with the right makeup.

The stylists, however, are not infallible, and the contestants seem to be relatively free to help shape their own image, even against the wishes of the style team. For example, in S5, part of the stated charm of Taylor Hicks is the fact that he has gone prematurely gray-haired; Hicks is 29, but according to his story, his hair went gray at age 15. He is adamant that it's not a ploy to look different or to stand out; it is just his real hair. However, the gray hair is one of the defining physical characteristics of Hicks; it makes him stand out among the other contestants. The stylists, though, seemed to believe that he was standing out for the wrong reasons, and approached Hicks. In S5E20, Seacrest asks Hicks about his encounter with the hair stylist who wanted him to dye his hair — which is met with raucous boos from the audience. Of course, it didn't happen; Hicks' hair remained gray throughout the entire competition, and he went on to win the title of American Idol.

Contestants have to be careful of going too far with the physical changes, however, or they become fodder for the judges' critiques. For example, struggling S6 contestant Haley Scarnato performs in S6E28 wearing a revealing top, very short shorts, and very high heels. Cowell comments:

> SC: I think you have a very good tactic at the moment, Haley. Wear as least amount of clothes possible, because look, I'll be honest with you: you can't do well in this competition based on your voice, because there are much better singers. So all you can do is — it's true — all you can do is have fun [S6E28].

While Scarnato attempts to take Cowell's comments in stride, her face visibly shows consternation as Cowell uses her makeover against her. Quickly, however, she recovers, and by the time Seacrest announces her phone number, Scarnato has a smile back on her face. This is because one of the processual changes to the Celebrity commodity which takes place on *Idol* is attitudinal in nature. The *Idol* contestants find out, as the season

VIII. Wear the Least Amount of Clothes Possible

progresses, that this singing competition entails far more than just singing, as Jason Castro's comments illustrate. In S7E14, Castro admits that really what he likes to do is sing and make music, and *Idol* involves quite a bit more of "the not-music stuff" than he was expecting. He goes on to acknowledge that he is not very good at talking. Castro's utterly ineffective articulation skills eventually become one of the endearing qualities about him that the judges respond to, but clearly, Castro is overwhelmed by the amount of "not-music stuff" in which he is expected to participate. He must re-adjust his perception of his position within the competition. This is apparently a great deal of pressure; according to Seacrest, *Idol* employs "psychological coaching to [help] handle the pressures" (S1E5).

In addition to psychological coaching, the *Idol* contestants meet with press consultants to prepare them for life as a human commodity. In S1E19, the contestants are shown meeting with Alyssa Vitrano, Entertainment Director of *YM* magazine, and Abby Gardner, Beauty Director of *YM* magazine. The contestants are allowed to ask questions, since dealing with the media pressures of *celebrity* requires some basic training. Contestants asked questions ranging from how artists are selected for magazine features to how to control a photo shoot. Each contestant is forced to undergo a change in outlook and perception (although some probably more than others) as they transform from private citizen to Celebrity commodity. *Idol*'s coaches and psychologists work with the contestants to help them adjust.

The contestant must navigate through this attitudinal restructuring as best s/he can, sometimes more successfully than others, as illustrated by Carrie Underwood. Underwood, for weeks before this, has been called boring and robotic by the judges — Cowell, in particular. For this performance, Underwood appears in a black halter top, jeans and boots, singing Pat Benatar's "Love Is a Battlefield," much to the apparent surprise of the judges. Underwood explains that she is trying to shake the label of "boring"; Cowell retorts that her performance was like "watching a kitten who wants to be a tiger" (S4E29).

The judges can be fickle, but so can the consumer audience for which the Celebrity commodities are being manufactured, so learning to deliver what the judges are looking for is good practice for the future. In the end, the Celebrity commodity occupies a very different mental space than the original private citizen; Elliott Yamin, in S5E36, proclaims that his former self is "history"; he has effectively evolved into a different entity.

The transformation into Celebrity commodity also involves a change in lifestyle, from the contestants' former lives in various mundane occupations to the new *celebrity* life. Seacrest often points out the former occupations of the contestants (RS: "This girl, a year ago, driving a mail truck. Now she's going for the win on *Idol*" [S4E35]), in order to position them for comparison by the audience. Carrie Underwood, in S4E35, divulges that her transition from sitting in class, getting her degree, to singing in Hollywood has been a "complete fairy tale."

The "fairy tale" aspect of *Idol* is an important one in terms of displaying the processual and dynamic changeability of the Celebrity commodity. It is almost as though the contestants have been changed by magic — that a convergence of destiny and circumstance lifted Underwood out of her college classroom and placed her on stage in front of the largest television audience in contemporary American television. And in that convergence, Underwood's essential constitution has been altered as well — she is not the same person she was four months ago. Of course, this has larger ideological implications, which will be discussed in Chapter XII. However, as a marker of mutability, Underwood's transformation bodes well for her sustainability in the dynamic attention marketplace; she has shown the ability to adapt, to change, and to continue to thrive.

As the contestants evolve from private citizen to Celebrity commodity, the lifestyle changes serve to prepare them for their primary function as *celebrity* commodities: conspicuous consumption. *Idol* repeatedly places the contestants in situations, as noted earlier in this chapter, where this conspicuous consumption is possible, allowing them access to *celebrity* experiences they would not otherwise have. This serves the dual purpose of expressly demonstrating the contestants' readiness for conspicuous consumption and showing the contestants' adaptability to new situations and new experiences (a definite bonus when dealing with dynamic attention and commercial marketplaces). For example, in S7, the contestants are flown from Hollywood to Las Vegas to watch a performance of *Cirque Du Soliel*, but experience much more than that (S7E38). They are flown to Las Vegas on a private plane (complete with a bedroom), and visually recreate the image of The Beatles descending the airplane stairs on their

VIII. Wear the Least Amount of Clothes Possible

first trip to America. If the connection the program is trying to make has been lost on the audience, it is reinforced a moment later when footage of the contestants signing autographs in a crowd of screaming fans is intercut with The Beatles footage of the band signing autographs in a crowd of screaming fans. One woman reaches out of the audience and grabs Jason Castro, kissing him. Syesha Mercado is then shown dancing with the dolphins at the Mirage.

The range of new experiences for the contestants on this one trip — a luxury private plane, throngs of adoring fans, being accosted by a spectator, private admittance to the dolphin show — are not simply markers of wealth but markers of access. Living the *celebrity* lifestyle provides access to places and people to which private citizens are not privy. The contestants then receive a "V.I.P. red carpet makeover" (S7E38), and are ushered into the theater to watch the performance. After the show, the contestants are led backstage to meet the *Cirque du Soliel* performers, many of whom are just as thrilled to meet the *American Idol* cast as the contestants are to meet them. The contestants sign autographs for the cast (although it is *Cirque du Soliel*'s show; the contestants, however, are never shown receiving autographs, only giving them), and a large group photo is taken.

The complete change in lifestyle from private citizen to Celebrity commodity is summed up rather succinctly by Amanda Overmyer:

> AO: I'm from Mulberry, Indiana. It's a small, rural town outside of Lafayette. I work as a nurse in home oxygen and medical equipment sales... Now it's all brand new territory to me. It might be a photo shoot. It might be interviews. Who would have thought all these people would want to hear what I got to say? [S7E20].

The realization that now, people want to hear what one has to say is a major component of the change from contestant to Celebrity. It is not only a change in lifestyle, but a change in attitude regarding how one interacts with the surrounding world. Coupled with the physical changes each contestant goes through, the mutability of the *Idol celebrity* existence portends the dynamic changeability for which they must be prepared in their future careers as human commodities.

IX
Why Is She Special?

Normal is not something to aspire to.
It's something to get away from.
— Jodie Foster

Cultural Legitimation

Thus far in this book, discussion has focused on the successes of the *Idol* contestants, from what it means to be a Celebrity to what it means to look like an American Idol to how identities are constructed and commodities created and legitimated. However, there is a simultaneous process at work on *Idol*, a process that is in action every moment of every program, to one extent or another. That process continually legitimates certain cultural forms while symbolically annihilating others; in order for Celebrities to be constructed, anti–Celebrities must be destructed. *Idol* puts forth a single vision of what it means to be a pop music star; this vision legitimates a certain cultural view of *celebrity*, popularity, and what it means to be "cool," and takes great pains to obliterate all other forms of *celebrity*. This is a delicate balance to maintain, seeing as only one contestant will survive to become the American Idol, and other commodities need to be removed from the proceedings without sustaining fatal damage that would render them unfit for later sale and consumption.

Not all commodities on *Idol* are created equal; in the early episodes of each season, clearly there are people shown for the express purpose of distinguishing the actual contenders from the masses. However, even among the semifinalists, there are those whose inclusion appears to be specifically designed as what one might call "cannon fodder." These contestants are purposefully expendable; they are classic celetoids, in that most

IX. Why Is She Special?

of them will not receive recording contracts, and will fade into relative obscurity rather quickly. For example, S7 contestants Amy Davis and Colton Berry were early eliminations; they, along with six other S7 contestants, have had no major commercial endeavors since appearing on the show. They were offered no record contracts, and were never seen again on the program after their ousting. They were returned to their regular private lives, well-known for a very short period of time and then discarded — celetoids, by definition.

This process of symbolic degradation — of destroying the symbolic capital of some contestants in order to increase that of others — is constant; it could be said that as each contestant is being groomed for eventual commodity form, s/he is simultaneously undergoing subtle (and sometimes not-so-subtle) symbolic degradation in preparation for his/her removal from the competition. Each contestant who makes it to the top 24 only has approximately a four percent chance of winning *American Idol*. It is far, far more likely that a contestant will be voted out of the competition. Therefore, even contestants on which the judges are keen are subjected to negative criticism. However, the wording of the criticism is significantly different from contestant to contestant; those contestants who are included as cannon fodder receive no mercy, particularly from Cowell. A judge favorite may be criticized, but the amount of symbolic degradation that criticism represents is much less. Compare, for example, the criticism leveled at S7's Carly Smithson (a judge favorite) and that directed at S7's Kady Malloy (cannon fodder). Following her S7E12 performance, Cowell tells Smithson that because of all of the buzz and hype about her, his expectations are very high. He acknowledges that she is suffering from bronchitis, but was still expecting something incredible (here he invokes performances by Kelly Clarkson and Fantasia Barrino), and was disappointed. Contrast this with Malloy's S7E18 criticism, in which Cowell tells her that she has a "massive lack of personality," and calls her both a robot and a Stepford wife. He is bored with her "gloomy" performance, even though Malloy defends herself by reminding Cowell she was singing a sad song. Undeterred, Cowell counters, saying that there was no emotion in her song at all, sad or otherwise.

The subtext of each set of comments is clear: Smithson is expected to be a superstar; there is a "buzz about" her, and she has already generated "hype." While she did not give a great performance, it is attributed to the fact that she has bronchitis, and Cowell is disappointed because he expects her to perform at the same level as Kelly Clarkson or Fantasia Barrino. The underlying message is one of "excellent performer, bad performance."

Malloy, on the other hand, receives comments which frame her as "bad performer, bad performance." Cowell completely strips her of identifying features by declaring she has none; he robs her of the opportunity to show personality by announcing that she is boring. "Boring" is a charge that has been leveled at many contestants; even Carrie Underwood was considered a bit robotic in her performances. However, like with Smithson, those comments were tempered with praise, if not for the specific performance at hand; then at least for the body of work Underwood had produced up to that point and for the superstar qualities she otherwise possessed. With Malloy, there is no such temperance; she is boring, she has no personality, she is a Stepford wife, and, as such, she is not worth voting for. Perhaps unsurprisingly, Malloy is voted out the night after she receives those comments; Smithson is not even called into the bottom two on the night after she receives the above commentary. However, Smithson's symbolic capital has been slightly reduced by the negative commentary.

The difference is, while Malloy is in no way expected to last in the competition, and therefore can have her symbolic capital utterly degraded on an immediate basis, Smithson is presumed to be a long-term contestant, and her cache of symbolic capital needs to be allowed to remain viable. Smithson is notionally supposed to complete a transformation to Celebrity commodity; Malloy has no such future as far as *Idol* is concerned. She is a deliberate celetoid. In her dismissal, *Idol* reinforces its own vision of what it means to be a "star"; more specifically, it demonstrates precisely what types of attributes are *not* those of a star. As the judges tell Selina Ray in S4E16, there is a fine line between pop star and hotel singer (Cowell predicts Ray will end up as the latter), and Jackson can't help but think aloud, "Why is she special?"

Even those who are "special" in the eyes of the judges are, most likely, going to be voted out. When they inevitably are, it is important that the show allows them, in some way, to recover some measure of symbolic capital, even as that capital has been progressively downgraded. The process of symbolic recovery (or, at least, symbolic stabilization) begins when the

IX. Why Is She Special?

competition reaches the top ten; the top ten contestants are included in the *American Idol* tour, and therefore need to remain commercial attractions. If a contestant can survive long enough to make it to the top ten, his/her symbolic capital is slowly restored, whether by the judges through their commentary, or the Celebrity mentors through their endorsement, or by the contestant him/herself through the feature packages. For example, during Nadia Turner's ousting, she told the audience:

> NT: I want to be remembered that I kept it real the whole time. Like no matter what I said, no matter what the song choice was, that I don't leave here having any regrets and knowing that at the end of the day, Nadia was Nadia and that I stayed true to myself [S4E32].

In doing so, Turner reinforces for her fans that they have been receiving the "authentic" Nadia Turner. No matter what the judges have had to say about her, if fans have enjoyed her performances all the way into the top seven, they can be guaranteed that they will receive more of the same on the tour and in the studio. When one of the cannon fodder/celetoid contestants are voted out, his/her package is of a far different sort. It is made clear that merely being on the show is a fulfillment of a dream, because simultaneously, the message is being delivered that s/he will likely never be seen again.

The entire concept of dream fulfillment plays an enormous role in the construction of the show, particularly in the early stages when the episodes focus on the audition process. Seacrest normally directly emphasizes the dream fulfillment aspect from the beginning of each season, such as in the opener from S5. Seacrest, via voiceover, reminds the audience that for some people, winning *Idol* is about money; for others, it's about artistic merit, touching people's lives, or simply the experience. Then, Seacrest makes an incredible claim: he calls auditioning for *Idol* a "rite of passage," akin to going to prom, buying one's first car, or graduating from high school—just another part of growing up (S5E1). *Idol* is not only something people do to fulfill their dreams; it is ingrained in the very fabric of modern American society. It is as natural a part of the culture now as baseball and apple pie, according to Seacrest. People audition for *American Idol* because they are supposed to—to not want to audition for *Idol* is to refuse to be American. To make it onto the show is to fulfill a dream;

American Idolatry

American Idol is directly connected to the success myth as discussed in Chapter II. In fact, during the audition episodes, the word "dream" is used repeatedly, in every season, multiple times per episode — so much so that one might get the impression that dreams are what the program is really "about."

From the first season, when an unidentified contestant confesses that, "It's not supposed to happen this way or something. I don't know, but, like, dreams aren't supposed to come true. That's how we're raised and that's what we're taught" (S1E4), it is clear that even the cynical nature of modern youth can be broken down by the powerful pull of the success myth as presented on *Idol*. In every season, there are repeated references to dreams — by the contestants (Syesha Mercado: "It's like I'm living my dream right now. I am living my dream, so that's a beautiful thing" [S7E21]), the judges (Abdul: "Whatever happens, make the right record, go on, and keep your dreams alive" [S5E23]), and Ryan Seacrest ("Here in America people are going about their daily routine, fixing cars, waiting tables, selling real estate — but so many have one thing in common: a dream. A dream to make it on this stage and become one of the most famous people in the world. You can make that dream come true" [S5E1]).

The dream in question is relatively abstract, and varies from person to person. For some, the dream is specifically about music (R.J. Helton, for example, states, "It's my dream to sing and just to be known, I guess" [S1E18]); for others, it is more about the demands of *celebrity* (Justin Guarini: "We've all dreamt of doing photo shoots, doing appearances, doing these interviews and it's just mind-blowing that now we're finally here" [S1E13]). But whatever the specifics of the dream, the fact is that *Idol* spends a great deal of time focusing on the success myth aspect of the program — winning *American Idol* is not simply a matter of becoming a Celebrity commodity or getting to be on television or getting to go on tour. It is about the fulfillment of a dream, in public, for all to see.

This makes Randy Jackson's comments to Michael Johns in S7E28 naïve at best and outright disingenuous at worst. Johns, an Australian-born singer now living in the United States, sings Aerosmith's "Dream On"; it is his first opportunity to sing with the full orchestra, and his performance is exuberant. Jackson does not like the performance at all. Johns responds that with the 20-piece orchestra and the huge stage, he just had

IX. Why Is She Special?

to perform "Dream On." Jackson counters by reminding Johns that he could have chosen any song that he wanted to. Johns responds by saying that he is now living in America and making his dreams come true, to which Jackson pointedly responds: "Let me just add that this show is about being the best singer — undiscovered talent — we can find. Not about dreams. Being the best singer" (S7E28).

This statement is simply factually incorrect, to the point of being ludicrous, based upon the history of the program and the manner in which *Idol* has been constructed. Clearly, the show *is* about dreams, and it could be argued that the show is also patently *not* about finding the best singer. Dream fulfillment and the success myth are integral, essential elements of the program's construction. Otherwise, why the need (from the very beginning of the series) for an announcer state: "The kids gave it their all ... two dreams are about to end right now" (S1E10), if not to remind the viewing audience exactly what is at stake?

For some contestants, those dreams go far beyond fame, television time, or even a music career. Because of its positioning as one of the biggest ratings successes in American history and its track record for producing great commercial success, *American Idol* provides the opportunity for lottery-like hope; it can change one's life circumstances. For example, S7 hopeful Angela Martin auditions after telling the story of her infant daughter, who suddenly developed severe physical handicaps. As Martin accepts her ticket to continue on in the audition process to Hollywood, she explains that, for her, it is not about fame; her child can neither walk nor talk (S7E1). Her participation in *American Idol* could generate the kind of financial resources and access to medical care for her child that she cannot afford on her own. This is a common refrain among contestants (e.g., Suzanne Toon (S7E6), who believes *American Idol* can ease her struggling and allow her to provide more easily for her daughter); many young parents without financial stability seem to view *American Idol* as a possible road to salvation.

Sixteen-year-old Temptress Brown auditions because she believes it will make her mother happy (S7E1). Her mother is morbidly obese, confined to a wheelchair and using an oxygen tank. Brown is a heavy-set girl, with dark ebony skin and bright orange hair, draped in a brown, striped shawl, and she appears to be painfully shy. Seacrest interviews her just prior to her audition, and Brown reveals that she is auditioning for her sick mother, whom Brown takes care of every day. Brown's mother is then shown, separate from her daughter, and discloses that she feels guilty because Brown should be concentrating on other things besides her sick mother. In a heartbreaking moment, Brown's mother tells her that she loves her, and thanks her for trying. Brown, nearly in tears, enters the audition room and is visually overwhelmed. She can barely speak to the judges, and her rendition of "I Am Telling You I'm Not Going" from the musical *Dreamgirls* is poor. However, not even Cowell can bring himself to disparage Brown; he appears to recognize this is not the average bad audition.[1] Cowell calls her a sweetheart, and a nice girl, and the judges take it in turn to bolster her confidence and praise her courage and spirit. Brown begs for a second chance to try harder; instead, she receives a hug from Paula Abdul that sends her into tears. Brown tells the judges she cannot face her family, and all three judges walk Brown out to her parents. Abdul tells the Browns that they have "raised a beautiful daughter"; Brown's father is concerned that Cowell may have been "rough on" Temptress. Cowell, of course, was categorically, comparatively kind to Brown, as he is to most contestants for whom appearing on *American Idol* is a chance at hope — perhaps circumstances, financial and otherwise, could change if only one can make it to the "big stage."

For others, the pragmatic benefits of *Idol* are beyond financial. For example, Yuliya Matyus explains, as she prepares to enter her audition, that she only has a six-month visa, and if she cannot secure a performer's visa, she has to return home (S5E1). Matyus is not selected to continue in the process, and presumably is forced to return to Ukraine.

The display of pursuit of the success myth and the symbolic degradation of both celetoids and future Celebrity commodities are not mutually exclusive. In fact, the two are often intertwined on *Idol*. When a celetoid is symbolically degraded, it is often framed in the "dream coming to an end" theme; the dream has ended because the contestant is expected never to be seen again. When a contestant with a greater supply of symbolic capital is symbolically degraded, it is normally framed in a "dream fulfilled" theme, since that person is expected to continue to be a successful consumer commodity. The grand archetype for the struggle over symbolic degradation on *American Idol* is the story of Sanjaya Malakar,

IX. Why Is She Special?

because Malakar is representative of what happens when someone slated for celetoid status manages to stay in the competition far longer than expected. Malakar was voted out in seventh place, earning a spot on the lucrative *Idol* tour, much to the mounting disquiet of the judging panel. In fact, the episode of Malakar's ousting was the highest-rated episode of S6; the week after he was voted off, ratings fell nine percent ("NBC's Worst Week?" 2007). Cowell would eventually disavow the entirety of S6, stating, "It just wasn't one of our better seasons, and you get that on all these types of competition shows ... you get great years and not-so-great years" (Washburn, 2008). However, Malakar plainly found some connection with the audience, as despite the judges' increasing efforts to engage in symbolic degradation, Malakar remained in the competition, week after week.

When Malakar is first presented, he (age 17) and his sister Shyamali (age 19) are auditioning in Seattle. Shyamali auditions first and receives a ticket to Hollywood. Sanjaya enters second and exchanges with the judges, admitting that he believes Shyamali is a better singer than he is (S6E2). Malakar then sings "Signed, Sealed, Delivered" by Stevie Wonder. After he is finished, of particular importance are Cowell's comments, as Cowell will, in the main, be the person responsible for Malakar's symbolic degradation. First, Cowell says that Malakar is a lot better than Shyamali; he follows this by saying, *"You're like a shy little thing who's got a good voice"* (S6E2, Emphasis added).

Remember for later that Cowell, on first hearing of Malakar, declares that the contestant has a good voice. Malakar subsequently makes it through round after round of eliminations during Hollywood week; he is one of the early selections for the top 24. If, as Jackson repeatedly offers, the show is about finding the best undiscovered singing talent in the country, and about nothing else but singing, then Malakar's inclusion in the top 24 must, logically, have been based purely on the qualitative merits of his singing ability. In short, Malakar must have been among the 24 best undiscovered singers in the country who auditioned for *American Idol* in 2007. If he were not, it would be an open admission on behalf of *American Idol* that the competition is about more than simply singing. The fact that Malakar was obliged to successfully endure multiple eliminations during the audition process is an unambiguous indication that the judges and producers had ample opportunity to hear Malakar sing and determine his suitability for the competition. Malakar did not make the top 24 as the result of a fluke; his inclusion was deliberate and premeditated.

From Malakar's first performance critique, his symbolic degradation begins.[2] Cowell remarks that Malakar's singing was "dreary," "dull," and a "waste of time" (S6E11). The minute and a half song felt like an hour to Cowell. Cowell's comments escalate in intensity in the ensuing weeks. In week two of the competition, he tells Malakar that he sounds like a party where the parents have forced the children to dress up and sing, calling it "weak" and "weird" (S6E14). Remember, Cowell's initial impression was that Malakar possesses a good voice — good enough to make it into the top 24 out of over 100,000 potential contestants.

After two weeks of Malakar continuing on in the competition, despite brutal reviews from Cowell and Jackson, Cowell decides to take a different tack in criticizing Malakar — a decision that would come to define Malakar's symbolic degradation. He tells Malakar that he thinks his "Paula hairstyle" is weird, and that in this singing competition, maybe Malakar's hair is what is making him so popular (S6E17). Cowell's recognition that Malakar is popular, despite the ongoing criticism of his voice, renders that line of symbolic degradation impotent. If *Idol* is a pure singing competition, and Malakar's vocals are as bad as Cowell has said they are, then Malakar should already have been voted out. This means Cowell must begin to degrade the perceived source of Malakar's symbolic capital — his physical appearance.[3]

From S6E18 through Malakar's eventual departure in S6E31, his hair becomes the focal point of his character — as the judges increase the amount of references to his hair, Malakar adopts wilder and wilder hair styles (from slicked-back crooner style to his infamous and inventive Mohawk made of small ponytails). In S6E20, Jackson comments that Malakar's singing as "almost unlistenable," but that every week, he looks forward to what hair style Malakar is going to wear. He tells Malakar that in *Hair Idol*, he wins. In referring to Malakar as "Hair Idol," Jackson has made it clear that it is on these terms and these terms alone that Malakar is to be evaluated for the remainder of the season. His vocals will just be assumed as sub-par; the only thing of interest or value about him will be his weekly hair style.

However, the judges seriously underestimate Malakar's drawing power. S6E22 can be termed as one of the defining moments of *American*

IX. Why Is She Special?

Idol; it certainly stands as Malakar's "Idol moment." Malakar takes the stage to perform The Kinks' "You Really Got Me." As his song begins, the cameras cut to the audience, where 13-year-old Ashley Ferl is so overcome by her excitement at seeing Malakar that she bursts into hysterical tears. She weeps through Malakar's entire performance, and, at the performance's conclusion, Malakar descends from the stage to hug Ferl, completing the "Idol moment" between fan and Celebrity. After this occurs, the judges cannot possibly say anything negative about Malakar's performance; he has literally reduced a fan to tears on live national television simply by performing in her presence. This type of event had never happened previously on *American Idol*, and has never been replicated since.

Jackson comments that Malakar has come out of his shell, and calls it his best performance to date; Cowell simply states a noncommittal, "I think the little girl's face says it all" (S6E22). For one moment of *Idol* history, Sanjaya Malakar is the greatest rock star the program has ever produced; he is in league with acts such as Michael Jackson and The Beatles in the fact that he can reduce a fan to hysterical weeping in pure, overwhelmed excitement — something no other *Idol* contestant before or since has done on the live television broadcast.

After that incident, Cowell all but gives up when it comes to Malakar. While Jackson continues to engage Malakar on the subject of his hair, and even Seacrest joins in the follicle debate (speculating at the beginning of each show on how Malakar will wear his hair), Cowell forfeits the battle of symbolic degradation. As quickly as the judges can destroy Malakar's supply of symbolic capital, he seems to be able to rebuild it; Cowell eventually concedes, "Sanjaya, I don't think it matters any more what we say, actually. I genuinely don't. I think you are in your own universe, and if people like you, good luck" (S6E24). The next week, Jackson too surrenders, stating that he can't even comment on the vocals any more, but as an entertainer, Malakar has become a break-out star (S6E26).

Malakar's victory over the attempts at symbolic degradation are, of course, short-lived. Eventually, like 96 percent of *Idol* contestants, he is voted out. As he goes, Malakar recovers one last bit of symbolic capital; his final song is Bonnie Raitt's "Something to Talk About," the words of which Malakar changes to, "Let's give 'em something to talk about/other than hair" (S6E31).

X
Are You Drunk?

> *I think most of the people involved in any art always*
> *secretly wonder whether they are really there*
> *because they're good, or because they're lucky.*
> — Katharine Hepburn

Perceived Virtuosity and Performative Excellence

Although contestants such as Malakar do achieve remarkable results in the semifinals of *Idol* on their own terms, such contestants are more of an anomaly than the norm. *Idol* is a machine which produces packaged, commodified Celebrity products; contestants are concurrently exhorted to be unique and original, yet chastised to stay within recognized boundaries. (Cowell, in S8E20, states unequivocally, "It's fine being artistic, just not on this show.") Not only are the contestants expected to be unique and original, but relevant and "current," and display personality in their performances. The performative aspect of the competition is where, ostensibly, the focus of the program lies; perform well, and one might find him/herself described as having the "It factor;" perform poorly, and one might be compared to a wedding singer or a drunken patron of a karaoke bar. A contestant's Celebrity commodity status is directly dependent upon his or her ability to navigate the pitfalls of performing in order to display enough virtuosity that s/he develops an aura of *arête* — *arête* which can be exchanged for symbolic capital with which to secure one's commodity future.

At its very core, the markers of performative excellence (i.e., virtuosity) on *American Idol* are a collection of a few key principles, the first of which is the concept of originality. Jackson and Cowell's criticism of

X. Are You Drunk?

Angelica Puente's audition (S7E5), in which she sings Celine Dion's "Power of Love," illustrates the definition of "originality" that *Idol* attempts to present. Cowell asks her plainly how many times she has listened to the song. When Puente admits it has been quite a few times, Jackson calls it a "mimic," and suggests that she stop listening to Dion before she ends up a sound-alike. Cowell agrees, and tells Puente to decide who she is, because "this is not a sound-alike competition."

Idol's stated definition of "originality" is "not sounding like anybody else." However, when Cowell states, "It's about being an original. It's not about copying. It's about being an original, and that's what's going to get you to win this competition" (S4E19), he is really using the term "original" in a very specific connotation; "original" here means, "still recognizably marketable and easily categorized." For example, Chris Daughtry and David Cook both were labeled "original" in their respective seasons. However, Daughtry's most highly acclaimed performances were either covers of other artists' covers of songs (Live's version of Cash's "I Walk the Line"; Red Hot Chili Peppers' cover of Stevie Wonder's "Higher Ground") or very similar versions of original work (his version of Fuel's "Hemorrhage" sounded so much like the original that the band approached him about replacing the lead singer). David Cook, too, performed covers of covers (Chris Cornell's version of Michael Jackson's "Billie Jean" was an "Idol moment" for Cook; Cook covers Doxology's version of The Beatles "Eleanor Rigby"), but gained much of his symbolic capital by putting his own arrangements on well-known songs such as Lionel Richie's "Hello" and Dolly Parton's "Little Sparrow"—arrangements that all fell within specific parameters of alternative-rock styling in the mode of Soundgarden, Audioslave, and Foo Fighters.

This specific version of originality occasionally leads some contestants who actually are original—in that they do not fall into neat genre categories and/or have voices that are unlike any other mainstream artist— to question their futures within the competition, as Chris Sligh does just before his audition (S6E5). Sligh notes that there has never been anyone who sounds like him on the show, then insightfully points out that usually when people say that, it's really because they aren't very good.

Sligh is good enough to make it to the top 24, but eventually (as he, in a way, predicted), the fact that his voice did not fit into a predetermined musical category eventually leads to Cowell's criticism. However, Sligh defends his unique style, retorting, "Obviously the audience is digging it. This kind of music is very popular right now. And what I have to say is just because I don't sing Il Divo or *Teletubbies*, doesn't mean that I can't sing" (S6E11). The comment is especially barbed for Cowell; in his early career, Cowell produced an album for the children's television program *Teletubbies* and created the operatic pop group, Il Divo ("Simon Cowell Biography" n.d.). In essence, Sligh directly challenges the notion that his actual originality is inferior to the constructed version of originality in use on the program, and questions Cowell's positioning to judge such claims as well.

Amanda Overmyer is another contestant whose originality earns her a place in the top 12, yet proves to be too original/different for the competition. First, in group performances, it appears that Overmyer's microphone is either not turned on or has a significantly lower volume — her voice is distinct and powerful, yet she cannot be discerned from the chorus of other voices, despite the fact that her tone is considerably lower in pitch than the other female singers. Secondly, Overmyer refuses to sing ballads and selects only up-tempo numbers. As will be discussed in detail a bit later in this section, a contestant must sing both ballads and up-tempo numbers to have success on *Idol*; refusing to do one or the other is self-defeating. However, Overmyer steadfastly eschews slower songs, insisting that ballads are boring and that she would rather use her ninety seconds to show the audience what they would get if they attended her concert (S7E22). Cowell retorts that Overmyer's tickets aren't on sale just yet, but Overmyer counters that even if she's only singing in a local bar, she would still perform the same way.

Overmyer does not tidily conform to a preconceived notion of what a classic rock singer "should" be; her voice doesn't harmoniously blend with the other singers. She will not follow the prescribed *Idol* format of singing ballads with "big notes" at the end. She cannot win *American Idol*; her symbolic capital will necessarily be degraded long before she is a contender for the top honor.

Idol, essentially, subscribes to a vision of "originality" which favors the most marketable version of a particular archetype. This allows the program to maintain the illusion of free and democratic choice without actu-

X. Are You Drunk?

ally providing free and democratic choice. *Idol* will almost always favor the more marketable incarnation of classic rock singer (Bo Bice) over the less marketable version (Amanda Overmyer); Bice "plays by the rules," while Overmyer does not. Chris Sligh's alternative rock is too far out of the mainstream; David Cook's more sanitized version has more potential appeal and receives a bigger judge "push."

One rejected contestant during an audition episode summed it up succinctly after the judges declined to invite her to Hollywood:

> You're telling me that you want me to be unique. So I want you to bring out a product that is unique, so we can ... you know, have something to measure with. America does not get to select the top 32. America does not [S5E1].

The winners of *American Idol*, with one distinct exception, win precisely because they are not unique; they fit into easily identifiable categories which have proven appeal to the consumer audience. Kelly Clarkson sang radio pop songs; Ruben Studdard and Fantasia Barrino sang mainstream urban R&B. Carrie Underwood's pop country and Jordin Sparks' "Radio Disney" styles and David Cook's alternapop all fit into recognized, salable categories. The only exception among the winners has been Taylor Hicks, and it is no real surprise that he is the lowest-selling artist of all *Idol* winners to date; artists that fit into prescribed category boxes are easier to package and market. If the promoters can say, "Our new American Idol sounds a lot like this artist, so if you like this artist, you'll like our new American Idol, too," the audience can quickly identify and categorize the consumer commodity. If the promoters have to take the time to explain the commodity to the audience without a point of reference, there is more of a chance of the commodity's failure. When the contestant above states that "America does not get to select the top 32," and that the judges say they want uniqueness but the commodities they produce do not reflect this desire, she has a legitimate argument.

In addition to being "original," contestants are also exhorted to be "young" and "relevant." Unlike "original," however, both "young" and "relevant" are ill-defined in terms of meaning given by the judges. For example, Cowell chastises Colton Berry in S7E11, telling him that although he sang well, his career path is likely musical theater because he has "no relevance" to today's charts. Berry is told that he is not a recording artist, and that his performance was a waste of time — he is neither special nor "current." His performance was basically good karaoke.

According to this commentary, "relevant" means, "like a recording artist," and not like "musical theater." However, in the same commentary, Cowell says Berry sang "quite well," but also "very karaoke." Cowell never defines what he means by "sound like a recording artist." Similarly, he uses the term "current" repeatedly, although he never provides a clear definition of what the term means. In S5E4, Cowell tells Katharine McPhee, "You're very current. You're very, very current. You're on the money. It's not stage school. It's not wanna-be-ish. It's just very, very what is happening today." "Current," in this context, is an indistinct term. By "not stage school," it intuitively appears he means delivered in a way that is neither stilted nor overly styled. By "wanna-be-ish," one might assume the performance does not come over as desperate or overwrought. However, these are speculative definitions at best.

As with Chris Sligh's questioning of Cowell's standing to criticize originality, a shadow of doubt could be equally cast on his (and the other judges', as well) position to identify that which is young and current, despite his standing as an A&R executive. For example, S6 runner-up Blake Lewis performs "All Mixed Up" by 311 in S6E17. The judges are full of praise, but also inadvertently reveal their own limitations. Jackson calls Lewis "current," but also admits he did not recognize the song (but he loved it). Abdul didn't know the song either, but was interested. Cowell not only failed to place the song, but didn't understand any of the lyrics — still, he found Lewis "current."

Lewis is labeled "individual" (i.e., unique) and "current." The judging panel, though, could not recognize a song by 311 — a song which was released some 11 years before Lewis performed it on *American Idol*, from an album that went triple–Platinum (over three million copies sold). Three long-time professionals from the music industry could not identify a song that produced one of the highest-rotation music videos of 1996 ("Capitol Gains" n.d.). Lewis's version is nearly identical to 311's 1996 version; his performance is qualitatively neither unique nor current. This reveals that when the judges state they are looking for relevant and current artists, they have a particular conception of those terms in mind that may not reflect actual relevance or currency in terms of the larger collection of artists in

X. Are You Drunk?

the music industry. For example, Jackson tells Chris Daughtry that he is very current, comparing him to Jon Bon Jovi and Matchbox Twenty (S7E12). However, this statement is delivered on February 22, 2006, and Matchbox Twenty had not released an album for nearly four years; Jon Bon Jovi, at the time, was 44 years old. The artists Jackson uses to describe Daughtry were, in one case, not young; in the other, not current.

"Young" (and, by extension, "not old-fashioned") may be the easiest of the terms from which to extract a precise definition (at least, as the judges define the term). For example, Cowell assesses Garrett Haley (S7E11), calling him boring, whiny, terrified, and haunted. Cowell goes on to say that Haley looks like he's been locked in a room for a month. In S5E34, he tells Katharine McPhee that her performance was younger because it showed more personality (S5E34), and in S4E27, he remarks to Carrie Underwood that she is too old-fashioned and reminds him of a soap commercial from the 1960s (S4E27). Being "young," then, appears to be connected both to physical appearance and to personality. "Young" is the opposite of "boring," Cowell seems to mean, "energetic" or "animated."

However, showing too much personality can be a detriment. Like every other construct on *American Idol*, the showing of personality is only a positive factor when the judges want it to be. Otherwise, the program is "only about singing." For example, Jackson chides Alaina Alexander, when she says she picked her song because it best displayed her personality, that it is not *"Personality Idol,"* but a singing show (S6E12). Much like the show that clearly ritualizes dream fulfillment is "not about dreams," the show that regularly centralizes and privileges personality is "not *Personality Idol.*" From Cowell's claim that Kady Malloy is a "Stepford wife" to his comments to Jason Castro in S7E22, it is clear that personality (as conceptualized by the program) is a central characteristic intrinsically tied to performative excellence/virtuosity on *American Idol*. Castro is told that he is lucky *Idol* is a television program and not a radio show, because his goofy charm carries him through weaker vocals. Cowell tells him if he wasn't looking at Castro, and was just listening on the radio, he would have turned it off.

Castro's performance is elevated because of his personality, despite the fact that Cowell believes his singing was not up to standard. The measure of his excellence/virtuosity in this case is, therefore, directly linked not to his musical ability but to his charisma. This is why, in the same season, Kristy Lee Cook is told she ultimately cannot win *American Idol*. In S7E18, Cowell calls her "forgettable" and says that on the larger stage with the more powerful voices and the brighter personalities, the best she can hope for is to come in tenth. Cook is told she does not have the voice to compete musically with the other contestants, but she is also, importantly, told that she is also unable to compete with the other contestants in terms of personality, because personality clearly factors into the audience's perception of virtuosity.

In fact, Cowell has plainly stated he believes personality is a central factor in audience voting. In S5E14, he tells Katharine McPhee point blank that the show is about more than singing—it's about picking the right song, it's about personality, and it's about connecting with the audience. Personality is certainly intertwined with performative excellence on *American Idol*; this makes it curious that Jackson is repeatedly surprised that personality is such a factor—and that contestants consider personality and stage presence when performing for America. For example, in S4E33, Jackson comments to Constantine Maroulis that while he acknowledges Maroulis is "a good-looking kid," his number was local-bar-level quality, with lots of showmanship and not a lot of vocal ability—a five out of ten. Abdul agrees that Maroulis's showmanship was "amazing," but defends his bum notes on the basis of performance.

The judges agree that Maroulis's vocals are sub-par; however, Abdul defends his performance on the grounds of personality, while Jackson uses "high on performing" almost as an insult. This echoes Jackson's incredulousness just episodes earlier, when he comments on the bottom two; he is upset that two of the best singers are in the bottom, and claims that people should be voting only on singing—not on looks, personality, or performance (S4E26). As the series progresses, Jackson never quite loses his selective naivety, despite repeated examples of how *Idol* is not, and never really has been, strictly a singing competition.

If *Idol* presents a clear picture of what it means to exhibit performative excellence and virtuosity, it also is very clear about juxtaposing that picture against what does not constitute excellence. Cowell, in particular, employs a vast array of insults and derogatory comments to place boundaries

X. Are You Drunk?

around what is considered to be quality performance and what is considered to be not right for the competition. Cowell refers to performances as "student in a bedroom at midnight" (S7E20), "someone busking outside of the subway station" (S7E24), "what a local covers band would do" (S4E15), and "like an office party when someone tries to get up and entertain and fails" (S4E20), but there are five categories of performance for which Cowell has repeatedly expressed disdain — his favorite insults, if you will: "wedding singer," "karaoke," "pageant," "theme park/hotel singer," and "musical theater."

Cowell's disdain for musical theater has been documented in this chapter; his typical comment in this vein might inform the contestant that s/he appeared desperate, or manic, or "shrieky" (S5E36).

As with his comments earlier in this chapter to Selina Ray, there is a fine line in Cowell's estimation between pop singer and hotel lounge singer. This is a very common insult from Cowell; he uses it often to remind contestants that there are singers in hotel lounges every night who could perform as well as the contestant (apparently, Cowell has been in a lot of hotels where there are singers in the lounge; I have yet to personally experience this outside of Las Vegas). He is also fond of telling contestants he could have seen their performance in Disneyland, where theme park performers sing cute songs passably but never in any commercially viable way.

"Pageant singing" is *Idol* vernacular for a stilted, stiff performance marked by seemingly false emotion, normally in the context of a ballad. This is a criticism usually directed at a contestant who has attempted to sing one of the Big Three's songs, and is always directed at women. The talent portion of a beauty pageant is some sort of nightmarish torture in Cowell's mind.

"Karaoke" is another common criticism. It appears to be used as a catch-all for any performance which "exhibits zero originality" and is "a completely and utterly forgettable performance" (S5E15). As Cowell tells Scott Savol, an ordinary guy (like Savol) can stand up at any karaoke bar and entertain an audience, but that kind of performance doesn't necessarily sell records (S4E31).

"Wedding singer" is a clearly defined insult. Cowell explains to Angela Martin, after her audition, that she has bad habits from her days performing with a wedding band: corny ad-libs, too many "heys" and "woos," and she seems to be desperate to encourage people to like her. She is exhorted to "de-wedding-ize" (S7E1).

Cowell's insults range from relatively benign ("Musical wallpaper — you notice the wallpaper but you don't remember it" [S4E29]) to the outright mean:

> SC: Taylor, are you drunk?
> Taylor Hicks: No. Not at all.
> SC: I thought it was ridiculous [S5E28].

However, the insults serve two purposes. The first, of course, is to constitute Cowell's "evil British judge" character; he insults the contestants because he's supposed to insult the contestants — he's the "mean" judge. The second purpose, though, is to clearly delineate what is an unacceptable performance, and, in turn, reinforce what is considered performative excellence and virtuosity on the *Idol* stage. Cowell's insults are (normally) not idle; like his use of the terms "young," "current," "relevant," and "original," they are doing specific work in constructing the Celebrity commodity.

XI

I Want to Break Free

> *I lose all respect for celebrities when they back a candidate. It's saying that the American public isn't smart enough to make their own decisions. I would never want anybody to vote for anything or anybody just because I told them to.*
> — Carrie Underwood

Advocacy/Endorsement of Other Commodities

As discussed in Chapter III, one of the essential functions of *celebrity* is to not only engage in conspicuous consumption, but to serve as de facto advocates for particular products and services through personal use of those commodities. Via these endorsements, Celebrities connect their respective fan groups to other commodities which those fans are encouraged to buy out of symbiotic attachment to their chosen Celebrity. In the larger *celebrity* commodity marketplace, Celebrities carefully select those commodities to which they attach; an endorsement of a particular product is not simply a consumer choice but a direct statement about the Celebrity's tastes, beliefs, and values. The *Idol* Celebrities, on the other hand, do not have this luxury. The commodities they endorse are chosen for them, as the creators of those commodities are often sponsors of the show. AT&T (formerly Cingular Wireless), Coca-Cola and the Ford Motor Company are the three main sponsors which engage in extensive product placement on *American Idol* (at $26 million each [Lindstrom 2008]), but the contestants are often called upon to endorse other products as well — on occasion, even other *celebrity* commodities. The contestants also receive Celebrity endorsements, confirming their status as viable *celebrity* commodities.

American Idolatry

AT&T's product placement is the most streamlined of all of the three major sponsors. Each week, viewers are given an option to text message their vote, but only if they are AT&T subscribers. The AT&T logo appears next to each contestant's phone number, and Seacrest is often shown walking through the audience with an AT&T phone, encouraging people to text the word "vote" from their AT&T wireless phone. While AT&T does not provide the same amount of physical merchandise to the show that the other sponsors do, the company's logo appears dozens of times in a given episode, and the company's name is repeatedly mentioned by Seacrest throughout each episode.

Coca-Cola's sponsorship of the program provides ample opportunity for product placement. Since the very beginning of the series, Coca-Cola's signature red and white motif and logos have featured prominently in the visual construction of the show. The ubiquitous Coca-Cola cups which are omnipresent on the judges' table — always with the logo facing the camera — are the most subtle of the product placements. Coca-Cola sponsors the contestants' holding room, in which the contestants wait until it is their turn to perform. This room contains not only bright red carpet and walls, but a full Coke machine, tables cut into the Coke signature "swoosh," pictures in the shape of Coke bottles on the wall, and the Coke "swoosh" patterned into both the shape of the wall treatments and the shape of the red couches and chairs (FIG. 9). Dubbed "The Red Room" by Seacrest, the product placement therein is normally passive (and clever. For example, in S5, a coffee table appears in the center of the room — a coffee table made from a Ford Motor Company tire). However, on rare occasions, the product placement in The Red Room is active — in S1E13, Tamyra Gray is given a birthday party in The Red Room and contestants are shown holding Cokes; in S4E26, Carrie Underwood is holding a Coke bottle and Nikko Smith is physically drinking a Coke. Throughout S1, Coca-Cola also sponsors "the Coca-Cola moment," a regular segment that includes Gray's birthday party, the contestants' trip to the Nickelodeon Teen Choice Awards, and the contestants' visit to Sunset Sound Studios.

Ford Motor Company is another major product placer, although the product placement is generally of a more active sort than Coca-Cola. For example, in the first season, it is repeatedly alluded to that the contestants

XI. I Want to Break Free

have been loaned an undisclosed number of Ford Focus automobiles for their own use; in introducing one package, Seacrest "reminds" the contestants that they all received cars to use for the summer (S1E10); in another, Tamyra Gray announces to the other contestants that there are new cars outside (S1E16), and then the contestants are seen driving away in a Ford Focus. Whether these automobiles were truly at the contestants' disposal or simply arranged for the various package shoots is debatable. However, the implication is clearly that the contestants are driving Ford Focuses for the summer, which is a direct endorsement of the Ford Focus line of automobiles. Throughout S1, there is a regular segment called "Focus on the Contestants," wherein the contestants are asked questions and give their responses while seated in a Ford Focus. In this case, there is no actual use of the automobile; it is stationary. In S1E13, the Ford Focus is featured in the photo shoot in which the contestants are participating for *US Weekly* magazine.

In all seven seasons, the top 12 contestants participate weekly in the production of a commercial advertisement for Ford. This commercial is shown during the results episode, generally after the first commercial break. The theme of the commercial varies from week to week, and always features the contestants singing a song as a group. The song relates to the theme of the commercial[1]; for example, the commercial featuring Queen's "I Want to Break Free" casts the contestants as office workers, dressed in 1950s clothing, moving slowly and robotically from cubicle to cubicle. When the Ford automobile is parked outside, color and vibrancy flows through the office, and the contestants "break free" from their menial tasks and run outside to enter the automobile (S7E31). Initially, all of the automobiles featured were Ford Focuses; eventually, the commercials would feature Mustangs, Fusion hybrids, and other models in the Ford line.

Because *American Idol* is a Fox Broadcasting Company product, one of the regular benefits the contestants receive is an opportunity to screen upcoming Fox films — with cameras present to record the proceedings. By S7, the number of film premieres in which the contestants have participated becomes something of a joke. When Jim Carrey appears in the *Idol* audience the week of the premiere of his animated movie *Horton Hears a Who!*, Seacrest plainly asks him, "This wouldn't be a Fox film, would it?" to which Carrey responds (perhaps too honestly), "It's a bit of cross promotion. You know, when you a do a movie with Fox, you're contractually obligated to do a certain amount of that" (S7E21). Of course, the contestants are later invited to appear on the red carpet at the film premiere, which, as discussed earlier in this chapter, provides an opportunity to practice living up to public expectations of Celebrities, as well as serving as a product endorsement.

S1's contestants were invited to the premiere of the film *Swimfan*; S6's contestants attended the sneak premiere of *The Simpsons Movie*. S5's contestants not only attended the premiere of *Ice Age 2: The Meltdown*, but the stars of *X-Men: Last Stand* hand-delivered preview copies of the film pre-release to the contestants. Rebecca Romijn and Hugh Jackman are shown backstage, sitting with the contestants. Both Romijn and Jackman confess that they are fans of the show, and then offer the contestants sneak peek DVDs of the unreleased *X-Men* movie (S5E39).

In one way, Romijn and Jackman are promoting their new film by appearing on *Idol* and giving the contestants exclusive sneak previews of the film. In another way, Romijn and Jackman are lending their enormous *celebrity* endorsing power to the contestants.[2] By appearing just before the release of the #4 highest-grossing film of 2006 ("2006 Yearly Box Office" n.d.). and stating that they are entertained by the contestants and find the contestants to be amazing, Romijn and Jackman provide credibility and support for the contestants' *celebrity* commodity status — even other Celebrities are entertained by these *Idol* Celebrities.

This is not an uncommon occurrence on *Idol*. Celebrities regularly appear in the audience.[3] When Jennifer Lopez guest mentors in S6E28, she reveals that she watches *Idol* at home, and is rooting for the contestants, and even has her favorites (whom she refuses to reveal) (S6E28). That Lopez is as invested in the program as the average viewer is another comparative endorsement — if multi–Platinum recording artist Jennifer Lopez is entertained by the contestants, and I am a fan of Jennifer Lopez, I may be inclined to take the contestants more seriously. If the beautiful actress Jennifer Love Hewitt says that she might have to tackle Justin Guarini on the red carpet at the Teen Choice Awards because he is "pretty hot" (S1E17), he must be. The Celebrity endorsement contributes to the commodity credibility of the *Idol* contestants, which, in turn, increases their own endorsement power for the products placed by the sponsors. It also allows

XI. I Want to Break Free

the contestants to endorse other Celebrities and have those endorsements matter to the audience; if this contestant whom I really enjoy is influenced by this particular artist, maybe I will enjoy that artist as well. In S6E31, the contestants run down the artists they are currently listening to: Kirk Franklin and Fred Hammond for Melinda Doolittle, Incubus for Blake Lewis, Fergie for Jordin Sparks, Maroon 5 and Jason Mraz for Chris Richardson. By extension, *Idol* makes a connection between the contestants and those particular artists: Like Jason Mraz? You're going to love Chris Richardson!

Commercial endorsements, conspicuous consumption, and product placement all have prominent places on *American Idol*. The contestants' *celebrity* status both influences and is influenced by their relationship to other *celebrity* commodities, and a wide array of products benefit from their endorsement.

XII
Look at This! I'm Unique!

> *"I didn't get a lot of exposure that I thought in the beginning I should have had. You know people early in the competition, they gain favorites and people they see and you know, I haven't gotten shown and I just felt that it was kind of against me."*
> — Melinda Lira [S4E13]

Idol Thoughts

In S6E4, a curious thing happens. Auditions seem to be going as they normally do — some great singers have been given golden tickets to move on to Hollywood; some not-so-great singers have been given their two minutes of television time and been shown the door. Then 20-year-old Sarah Goldberg of New York, New York, enters the audition space. Dressed in a red cowboy hat and cowboy boots, her hair draped in braided pigtails at the side of her head, Goldberg begins to sing Selina's "Dreaming of You" for Randy Jackson, Paula Abdul, and guest judge Carol Bayer-Sager.

A few lines into the audition, Bayer-Sager stops Goldberg and asks if she really feels, in her heart of hearts, that she can sing. When Goldberg admits that she does not, Jackson asks why she is auditioning. Goldberg's response is a lengthy conversation that, in many ways, is the inevitable end result of the *American Idol* processes detailed in this book.

Goldberg responds that she is not a singer, then chides Abdul for shaking her head and laughing at her while she auditioned. Jackson sug-

XII. Look at This! I'm Unique!

gests that the only reason Goldberg is auditioning is because she wants to be on television.

At this point, Goldberg begins to tear up, and her voice becomes more and more strained as she gets louder and louder. She confides that she is tone deaf, and that her friends make fun of her, but even if she doesn't sing, she can still be the next American Idol. How?

> SG: Because I've never sung before, and so you can teach me how to sing.
> RJ: Huh?
> SG: Yes! I think I practice. I practice with, like, music. I practice — I can't believe I'm crying this much — I think you don't have to sing to be an American Idol. I really don't. I think Paris Hilton can't really sing. I think that there's...
> RJ: She's not an American Idol.

At this point, there is a moment of uncomfortable silence. Then, the judges begin to try to usher Goldberg out. Paula Abdul actually bangs her head a few times on the table in front of her. Suddenly, Goldberg screams, "LOOK AT THIS! I'M UNIQUE! WOOO!" In saying this, she throws her arms up into the air and begins to dance around wildly.

Jackson tells Goldberg that since she doesn't sing and entered a singing competition, she has to go. He says that Goldberg got what she wanted — a little fame. Goldberg vehemently spits that fame is not what she wanted. She wanted to be the next American Idol.

Goldberg leaves the audition space, the judges commiserate about having to sit through her audition, and Seacrest does his normal duty of framing Goldberg as just another "crazy" auditioner. However, Sarah Goldberg is not just another "crazy" auditioner. She represents the direct by-product of a machine that is designed to turn people into things to be bought and sold, where actual authenticity is eventually punished while the appearance of authenticity earns high praise and judges demand currency and relevancy while simultaneously exhibiting a remarkable lack of knowledge of contemporary recording artists. Goldberg is labeled as "crazy" for recognizing she is an active participant in what Baudrillard calls "the Simulacra"— and for openly stating that it hardly matters if she can sing; the American Idol could be anyone, anywhere, because s/he is going to be made into the program's version of *celebrity* eventually anyway.

To Recap

This book began by asking the question, "What is popular culture?" The answer was shown to be complex; popular culture is a means for reproducing constitutive social relations, a vehicle for constructing hegemonic structures, and a site for social stratification. Popular culture is also inextricably consumer culture, and popular cultural objects possess both economic and symbolic aspects which can be either complementary or in conflict. These cultural products reflect particular ideologies, not only for the producers of cultural objects, but for the consumers as well. Ultimately, though, popular cultural objects are commodities, and commodities must sell in order to remain viable.

Some scholars (primarily Theodor Adorno and some members of the Frankfurt School) believe that popular culture has been almost completely co-opted by what has been termed "the culture industries"; that is to say that corporate interests have taken over cultural production en masse and reduced the amount of intellectual engagement necessary to consume those products to the lowest possible level in order to coerce people into submissiveness. This false sense of happiness in turn leads to the creation of false needs — needs which can only be satisfied by consuming more culture industry commodities. While containing quite a large measure of validity, this position has also been criticized for its elitist pessimism and for generalizing in areas where it can be clearly shown intellectual challenge and engagement still exist, even within a culture industry model of cultural production.

Within popular culture, reality television has come to occupy over 50 percent of the television market share in the United States. Reality television has been a popular target for critics, who hail the format as a triumph of banality and have gone so far as to label reality programming "stupid" and "moronic." However, this myopic stance fails to consider that "reality television" is a widely-encompassing, generic term that includes many programs which are both intellectually stimulating and aesthetically challenging.

Reality television has a long history, dating back to the early 1950s. The format of the modern reality program began to take shape in the 1970s, and boomed in the 1990s with the debut of MTV's *The Real World*.

XII. Look at This! I'm Unique!

Reality television has generated major changes to the production of television programming, including increased exporting of programming frameworks instead of specific content, increased importing of European formats for American broadcast, and increased exploration of multimedia companionship of television programming. These changes helped facilitate the creation of *American Idol*, which has dominated not only the Nielson television ratings, but the music charts as well.

Parallel to the development of modern popular culture has been the evolution of the modern Celebrity. Originating from a sort of heroic fame, *celebrity* in time diverged in definition from fame with the rise of media. In fact, *celebrity* has been likened to the underbelly of fame, a debased version of fame in which no heroic act need be performed or quality of virtue exhibited in order to attain it. However, the history of Western civilization is ultimately the history of *celebrity*; Western society's history is a catalogue of individual achievements that exhibit varying levels of heroism and virtue — and some exhibiting neither at all.

In contemporary American society, this manifests as "the success myth"; any one of us could be a Celebrity if we only work hard enough, persevere, and catch a lucky break. This is one of the main functions of *celebrity*— to sustain the ideology of the success myth, which keeps people producing in a capitalistic society. Additionally, the Celebrity is called upon to transmit the ideology or consumerism and to serve as a model for appropriate cultural behavior. However, the primary role of the Celebrity is to exist as a commodity, and to remain economically viable in the marketplace. Those in the media who cannot generate or sustain market viability may only briefly experience *celebrity*hood; they are celetoids, minor constellations in the universe of stars.

It is at this nexus between popular culture/reality television and *celebrity*/commodity that my research begins, questioning the nature of the contestants on *American Idol*, their place on the celetoid/Celebrity spectrum, and the process by which the program constructs their commodity future.

My research followed a Foucaultian discourse analysis and a set of considerations developed by P. David Marshall, which I refer to as "Marshall's toolbox." The entire seven-season canon of *American Idol* was examined. This in-depth analysis revealed information about the nature of

American Idolatry

American Idol which can be grouped into the eight categories of *celebrity* text presented by Marshall's toolbox.

First, the program adheres closely to contemporary collective/audience conceptualizations of *celebrity*. The contestants are, over the course of each season, trained to "act like" Celebrities, including opportunities to interact with fans outside of the competition, and repeated "behind-the-scenes" glimpses into their daily lives. During this naturalization process, the contestants are kept together, living, working, and playing in the same space, so that the show can monitor their progress and control access to the contestants. Once the handful of contestants lucky and skilled enough to reach the top three have had the entire season to practice being a Celebrity, they are returned to their hometowns to display their *celebrity* behavior and status. In addition, the judges and the host repeatedly verbally enforce what it "means" to be a Celebrity — wealth, access, and special treatment are showcased regularly as benefits of being an *American Idol* contestant. The program provides a vast array of material goods to the contestants, exhibiting the contestants as conforming to audience conceptualizations of consumerism and conspicuous consumption by the contestants, as Celebrities are expected to engage in. Finally, the program awards certain Celebrities elite status, using them to designate the highest end of the celetoid/Celebrity spectrum and position contestants along that continuum by comparison. To be compared to Whitney Houston or Celine Dion in terms of talent and ability is to be placed higher on the spectrum. Even other *American Idol* contestants are eventually awarded this elite status, reinforcing their cultural capital beyond their stay in the *Idol* competition — Kelly Clarkson and Fantasia Barrino are two contestants who enjoy this status.

Celebrities also express specific types of individuality which help establish their cultural significance intertextually. Because *Idol* is a fairly insular program (in that the contestants do not yet exist intertextually), much of the establishing of the contestants' individuality happens through the construction of the program itself. Contestants are quickly given easy-to-remember labels based on personality characteristics and singing genre types. For example, a contestant may be labeled as a "farm girl turned country star" or a "quirky folk singer." The construction of individual identity can be clearly charted by following the progress of S4's Carrie

XII. Look at This! I'm Unique!

Underwood and S5's Kellie Pickler — two contestants that have achieved lasting commodity success outside of the *Idol* competition — and S7's Brooke White, who continually defied attempts to "package" her and eventually earned the label of "authentic."

The culture industries also have their own methods of constructing *celebrity*, and *American Idol* attempts to adhere to those constructions in the transformation of their contestants. In order to be successful on *American Idol*, a contestant must fit certain physical characteristics — the more "commercial" the contestant looks, the more likely it is that s/he will be selected to compete. If the contestant has a great look and also meets certain personality requirements — an outgoing nature, a bright smile, the ability to connect with the audience — s/he will be labeled as having "star potential." However, *Idol* makes a clear distinction between that "star potential" and authenticity. *Idol*'s version of authenticity is superficial; contestants who display the ability to appear unique while still remaining commercial and appealing to a broad demographic fare better than contestants who are truly unique and resist the sanitizing of their aesthetic. Ultimately, a contestant must prove to be "likeable"; in many ways, likeability can maintain a contestant's stay in the competition even farther than his/her singing talent seems to warrant.

A *celebrity* text must clearly delineate the Celebrity's commodity status relative to all other *celebrity* commodities in the attention marketplace. *Idol* attempts to provide this delineation by reinforcing for the viewing audience the successes of past contestants. For example, on multiple occasions, former *Idol* contestants are brought back to the program to perform and to receive accolades and awards for their commercial successes. The program often references the sales totals of former contestants to remind the audience that an *American Idol* contestant can look forward to continued marketplace achievement outside of the competition. In addition, *Idol* makes constant reference to the scope of the program — how many people are watching, how many votes have been tabulated, and so forth. Not only does the program keep track of the successes of past contestants in order to delineate relative commodity status, it enhances the commodity status of the current contestants by exposing them to a stream of well-known Celebrity mentors, who impart wisdom and performance techniques to the contestants. This, in turn, creates an aura of endorsement which elevates the contestant — if Stevie Wonder says a contestant is a good singer, that contestant must be, because who would know better than legendary performer Stevie Wonder? Finally, relative commodity status can be enhanced by the proclamation of an "Idol moment": a performance so masterful that the contestant appears to be a polished, established artist rather than a contestant on a reality show.

A Celebrity must also exhibit a dynamic and processual changeability; that is, the Celebrity must be adaptable and able to be reinvented as needed to stay fresh and current and viable. Contestants on *Idol* undergo this reinvention process before the public eye, transforming not only physically, but attitudinally and in terms of lifestyle. *Idol* employs a "Glam Squad"— a team of stylists, hairdressers, makeup artists, and coaches — whose function it is to take the contestant from "natural" state to "camera-ready." The contestants also receive psychological coaching and consultation with media professionals to prepare them for life in the public eye. Finally, the contestants are gradually accustomed to the benefits of *celebrity* life — access to red carpets, private jets, and an increase in the importance of the things they say. These changes prove to the audience that the contestant can adapt and transform.

Celebrity is designed to represent and legitimate certain forms of cultural expression, but the opposite side to that is the symbolic degradation of other forms of cultural expression. As *Idol* puts forth one specific notion of what it means to be culturally relevant, it, by extension, obliterates all other notions of relevance. This is quite apparent through the audition episodes, where great pains are taken to poke fun at those who do not live up to *Idol*'s standards. However, even among the top 24, some contestants appear to be included specifically to symbolically degrade them — they are cultural cannon fodder. Throughout this process, constant references are made to the dreams of the contestant, and the ability of *Idol* to fulfill those dreams. For some contestants, this dream fulfillment goes beyond simple fortune and fame. The process of symbolic degradation can be charted by following the rise and fall of S6 contestant Sanjaya Malakar.

Contrary to Boorstin's proposition that a Celebrity can be well-known for being well-known, most Celebrities must exhibit some form of performative virtuosity and excellence in order to receive recognition. An *Idol*

XII. Look at This! I'm Unique!

contestant must appear to be original (but not too original), young and relevant. Simon Cowell arbitrates these characteristics through a series of insults and praises which frame the manner in which performative excellence is evaluated on *American Idol*.

Finally, a Celebrity's main purpose is to endorse, both symbolically and materially, other commodities and to transmit the ideologies of consumerism and conspicuous consumption to the audience. In this respect, not only does *American Idol* allow direct product placement from corporations like Coca-Cola, Ford Motors, and AT&T, but the contestants regularly participate in movie premieres for Fox. In addition, other Celebrities endorse the *Idol* contestants, strengthening the contestants' status as commodities.

Idol Reflections

Two research questions were posed at the outset of this research: What is the final product that *American Idol* creates, and what does the triangulation provided by Marshall's "toolbox" tell us about the contestants on *American Idol*? The first question is more easily answered by beginning with the second question.

What does Marshall's "toolbox" tell us about the contestants on *American Idol*? According to Marshall, there are six traits exhibited by a *celebrity* text, and the degree to which that text exhibits each of the traits is the degree to which the text represents *celebrity*. If the text exhibits only one or two traits, one is probably not dealing with a Celebrity. To Marshall's "toolbox," I added two more traits based on all of the literature on *celebrity* available to me, in order to even further narrow a definition of *celebrity*. For purposes of this book, in order to be a *celebrity* text, *American Idol* would not only have to exhibit all six of Marshall's traits, but would also have to display some aspect of performative excellence/virtuosity (i.e., the Celebrity would have to actually be actively "doing something" in order to generate "well-knownness") and would have to be directly engaged in the act of promoting consumerism and the advocacy of commodities other than itself. In the back of my mind, I also had a loose, ninth criterion: all eight of the other traits should have to be exhibited by every contestant that makes it into the top 10 each season (the *Idol* summer tour group); otherwise, the interpretations could only be localized to specific contestants rather than globalized to the entire program.

The top 10 contestants each season universally display all eight traits of Marshall's "toolbox"—some more than others, obviously, depending on length of stay in the competition and relative front-runner status as pronounced by the judges. Some of the time, those displays are collective; all of the contestants are advocating the same product/commodity simultaneously, such as when they are all waiting together in the Red Room. Mostly, though, each facet of Marshall's "toolbox" are displayed by each individual repeatedly over the course of the season — a contestant's video package is shown, wherein she talks about growing up on the farm (expressing individuality and creating identity), walks onto the stage in stylist-chosen clothing with professional hair and makeup (displaying dynamic changeability and looking like a Celebrity is "supposed" to look, reinforcing the culture industry standard of *celebrity*), and gives a wonderful performance (displays performative virtuosity). She is declared a superstar by the judges, compared to Whitney Houston (reinforcing audience conceptualizations of *celebrity* by comparison), and her performance is labeled an "Idol moment" (enhancing her relative commodity status), then Ryan Seacrest asks her how she feels right now, and she says she is living her dream (culturally legitimating the success myth). Seacrest gives out her voting phone number, which is displayed with the AT&T logo (de facto endorsement of another company's product/service). The contestant is, at that moment, a Celebrity—whether or not she can sustain that *celebrity* status past the end of the competition and avoid becoming a glorified celetoid is another matter.

According to the leading theories on the relationship between *celebrity* and society, the very term *celebrity* implies undeservedness—*celebrity* exists as a sort of false praise, the meaningless thronging of people to an individual for reasons that have little to do with word or deed. Fame is reserved for those whose deeds are heroic and *celebrity* is for those whose deeds are manufactured. Even when an individual's deeds are considered heroic enough to generate fame, any act of self-promotion of those deeds immediately drifts the individual toward *celebrity*. *Celebrity*, then, requires effort on the part of the Celebrity. However, media have a great deal to do with

XII. Look at This! I'm Unique!

the relative *celebrity* status of that individual as well. In essence, a Celebrity is a Celebrity because media say s/he is. We, the consumer public, have very little say in the matter — the only way we can vote is with our wallets. We can either buy the *celebrity* commodity or not. But in terms of media attention, we are quite literally stuck with whatever "media darling" is currently popular among content producers; Britney Spears yesterday, Paris Hilton today, Miley Cyrus tomorrow — whether we like it or not.

American Idol, though, attempts to circumvent that process by presenting the illusion that the contestants are Celebrities because *we* say they are. It suggests that it is removing the sphere of influence over who gets to become a Celebrity from the media and moving it to the audience. Once the competition begins in earnest, the audience is never again reminded that the judges pre-selected all 24 contestants upon which they get to vote. *American Idol* is, at heart, basically a Morton's Fork, or what I call a stick-or-brick proposition: if I were to tell someone that I wanted to hit him, and he could choose whether to be hit by a stick or by a brick, does he really have a choice? Avoiding the hit altogether is not an option; in removing that option, I have limited the number of choices available to the person in question. So, too, on *American Idol*, the choice is given between 24 contestants, each with a particular look, style, and musical ability. However, each of them has been selected by someone else; in many ways, each represents the most sanitized version of whatever genre s/he has been chosen to represent. David Cook is "alternative," but in a safe way, not in a Trent Reznor way. Chris Daughtry sings metal-tinged rock, but sings it like Fuel, not like Suicidal Tendencies. Carrie Underwood is far more Shania Twain than Patsy Cline. The default position for *American Idol* is, as Cowell has said on numerous occasions, what is "commercial."

For all of its fencing in of the audience's choices, though, the fact remains that from the top 24 onward, the audience *does* make the decisions. Many times, the judges have been upset or even shocked at which contestant has been voted out (the night Chris Daughtry leaves the competition, the audience sounds downright fit to riot). In the end, the audience, through pseudo-democratic process, selects the new American Idol, and historically, that winner goes on to enjoy legitimate *celebrity* status.[1]

American Idolatry

It is this relocation of the power base from media to audience which, I believe, places *American Idol* in its own category of *celebrity* text. We (the consumer public) do not get to decide whether Peyton Manning plays football on Sunday, appears on *Saturday Night Live,* or endorses the United Way. We have no control over the number of times in a given week Oprah Winfrey will be on television (other than to simply turn off the television, but she is still there, whether we watch or not). Much to my personal dismay, we cannot control the number of times in a week Soulja Boy's new single will be played on the local radio station. These people are awarded *celebrity* status by someone else, the culture industry (if one is inclined to subscribe to that theory), or, at the least, mass media outlets. On *American Idol,* however, the consuming public is told it is in direct control over the production of the next commodity it is going to consume. When David Cook defeats David Archuleta in the finals of S7 by a margin of three to two, the public is categorically saying, "We prefer the David Cook commodity!" This is not to say that they will not also consume the Archuleta commodity as well; by making it all the way into the finals, Archuleta has built up considerable symbolic capital in his own right.

This is part of the reason why *American Idol* is so dominant in the music industry as well as the television industry. In saturating the top 24 contestants with singers with easily recognizable genre categories (and often multiple contestants in any one category), the show virtually guarantees that there will be at least one singer that an audience member can, at the least, enjoy, and at best, identify with. Once this connection is made, although the viewer's favorite contestant statistically will most likely not win the competition, the attachment is encouraged to continue later, outside of the competition. The viewer is simply urged to temporarily transfer his or her allegiance to a different contestant for the remainder of the competition. In this way, *Idol* can attach a single viewer to multiple contestants, making multiple commodities viable simultaneously. At the end of the season, when David Cook's album is released, a viewer may be likely to purchase not only that album, but possibly David Archuleta's album and download Brooke White's single and perhaps buy a ticket to the *Idol* concert tour to see Chikeze Eze, since he has no album release scheduled and the viewer really liked him way back at the beginning of the top 10.

XII. Look at This! I'm Unique!

Looked at on a macro level, across seven seasons, *American Idol* reveals distinct thematic and ideological patterns which help to somewhat explain its monumental success — and its cultural/symbolic significance. *American Idol* is one of the most successful television programs in recent history, in terms of commercial profit, ratings domination and intertextual renown. This is hardly surprising, given its ability to encompass so many facets of American culture and its machine-like generation of *celebrity*/Celebrity commodities.

It is remarkable how *Idol* is able to encapsulate three of the most dominant ideologies in American society into three hours per week. In providing a venue for participatory democracy, *Idol* reinforces a perception of societal control — that we, the people, are behind the metaphorical driver's wheel in America. By erasing the distinction between citizen and consumer through the (s)election of commodity forms, *Idol* couples democratic process with purchasing power — the commodity that most of the viewing audience wants is the commodity they are going to get, ready-made for their own personal tastes. And, in putting the process of converting that commodity from the raw materials of "ordinary people" out in the open, *Idol* strengthens and legitimates the success myth — a myth that is fundamental to the very structure of American society.

It is important to remember, though, that the version of participatory democracy presented by *Idol* is only illusory. The same could be said for larger democratic processes in America as well, up to and including presidential elections, for the same reasons. First, as earlier noted, when one enters into the democratic process, one has a direct impact on the amount and quality of democracy s/he gets to practice. On *Idol*, this manifests as judge/producer control over the top 24. By the time the viewing public is allowed to vote, the candidates have already been pre-selected without the option for a metaphorical "write-in" candidacy. One can only vote among the choices given. Similarly, in American politics, one is told, "You may vote for Candidate A or Candidate B. You could, theoretically, vote for Candidate C or D, but to be honest, Candidates C and D have absolutely no hope of winning. We are not even going to allow Candidates C and D to directly debate Candidates A and B. So vote for C or D if you like, but you are throwing your vote away." In severely narrowing the practical options for casting a vote, what might be considered "true" democracy is overtaken by an illusion of democracy wherein the voter still gets to vote, but only for the candidates presented as "realistic" or "viable." As earlier noted, this is a "stick or brick" proposition. However, in mirroring larger democratic processes, *American Idol* helps legitimate the illusion — *Idol*'s version of democratic participation and that of American politics writ large are simultaneously legitimized.

The confluence of democracy and consumerism *Idol* is attempting to legitimate should be of serious concern to anyone with even a passing interest or investment in American politics. There are much larger, more serious societal implications that reach far beyond selecting the nation's favorite singer. First, *American Idol* has no age requirement to cast votes. In a very real sense, programs like *American Idol* will be many, many Americans' first foray into the democratic process. Participatory competition programs like *Idol* are inculcating a spirit of democratic ideals in American youth. The message currently being translated is, "If the candidate's face is on the television more, if that candidate has the right look and the right amount of confidence and says (sings) the right thing at the right time, it automatically infers the candidate is superior to others, regardless of the candidate's actual skill or talent." *Style over substance* may not be the ideology American society wants as the foundation of its future voting public.

Secondly, the ease with which *Idol* equates election and selection (as well as product and person or voting and purchasing) should be of monumental alarm to anyone interested in U.S. politics. *American Idol* is the most watched television program on the air, and the most successful reality television program in history. Well over a billion votes have been cast during the show's seven seasons — votes which were cast for packaged commodities. The conflation of democracy and consumerism, where one can buy and own his/her favorite candidate, has large-scale societal ramifications — particularly among the younger viewers who are approaching, but have not yet reached, voting age, one would think.

As television is one of the leading vehicles for the dissemination of dominant ideology — particularly that of consumerism — and since one of the major symbolic functions of a Celebrity is to be a commodity him- or herself, *Idol* is ideally situated to blur the lines between participatory citizenship and commodity consumer. *Idol* encourages its audience to vote

XII. Look at This! I'm Unique!

with a promise of future reward in the form of their favorite contestants' faces on T-shirts, tour date appearances, CDs in stores and singles for purchase on iTunes. In short, the audience is *electing a product*. This has profound implications for society as a whole. When the lines are blurred (or erased) between candidate and commodity, style and substance become the same thing. That is to say that on *Idol*, the choice really does not reduce to, "Vote for the best singer." It reduces to, "Vote for the singer whose future merchandise you will want to buy" and, "Vote for the person you like the most." Discussion of performance content is tangential. It is about likeability, about "looking like a star," about connecting with the audience — much like presidential politics has, in many ways, been reduced to "looking presidential," appearing to identify with the struggle of the "common man," and whether or not one wears an American flag pin on his lapel in public. The similarities should be chilling to anyone with interest in American politics as a whole.

The *Idol* contestants, in addition to representing commercial commodities, also serve the function as ersatz Adamic heroes. That is, before our very eyes, they become the living embodiments of the success myth — hard work, perseverance, talent, and a little luck are all that stand between the ordinary person and superstardom. The American Idol is drawn from the people, elevated by the people, and performing for the people. However, the contestants are artificial Adamic heroes because, unlike the original conception, the contestants are directly involved in self-publicity. The public acclaim which the *Idol* contestants receive lies at the intersection of attributed and achieved *celebrity*. They are not entirely the product of their own deeds, nor are they entirely the product of media construction. They are a hybrid form. These hybrid forms patently do not discount individual talent or skill. However, what the hybrid form does do for the person in question is distinguish him or her from contemporaries within the same field. The attribution is a layer — a veneer — on top of achieved *celebrity* status. In all public fields, from Bill Gates in the business world to Barack Obama in the political world to Peyton Manning in the sports world and Stephen King in the world of publishing, there are those for whom simply being the best at what they do is not the sole rationale for public acclaim. True, Bill Gates would still be a computer genius and perhaps even a commercial mogul without media attention, and would possess some form of achieved *celebrity*. However, the additional media consideration elevates his standing on the celetoid/*celebrity* continuum. Likewise, it is possible that Barack Obama may have been elected president on the basis of oratory skill and policy position. However, it would be a dubious argument to suggest that his media savvy and likeability played no part in his rise from first-term senator to President of the United States. Likewise, playing in local bars and clubs may have eventually led to David Cook's discovery by a major record label and a successful, multi-platinum album and a lucrative concert tour. Certainly, other artists have found success in exactly that manner. However, *American Idol* and the media attention it can generate changed things considerably for Cook and his musical future.

Idol's relative success in masking its own construction also probably contributes greatly to its success. For example, the show was able to present Carrie Underwood as the "farm girl making it big" with the expectation that the manner in which her narrative was constructed would go largely unexamined. Underwood is shown assisting her father in the operation of the family farm, feeding cows by hand with a bucket and tending to bales of hay. Was this exhibition staged for the cameras? Is Underwood always a willing participant in the daily operation of the family farm, or must she — as many, many children must when presented with family chores — be coerced or forced into labor? Is that really how she dresses to feed the cows? In full hair and make-up? And, by the way, was she not actually studying at Northeastern State University at the time she was cast for *American Idol?* How much work could she possibly be doing on the farm? These questions go unanswered; they lie outside of the character construction of the show, with the expectation that no one will seriously ask them.

In order to set up constructions such as Underwood's, it is vital that *Idol* also set up constructions like Temptress Brown. The heart-wrenching manner in which Brown reluctantly steps before a metaphorical firing squad in order to make her extremely ill mother happy — a proposition that can end nowhere but with failure and hurt feelings — is exactly the sort of selfless Adamic act which lends verisimilitude to the rest of the proceedings. We, in the audience, can feel the pain of young Ms. Brown; we understand how hard auditioning is for her, and how much she really just wants to help her mother (even without the requisite skills and talent

XII. Look at This! I'm Unique!

to successfully complete her "mission"). When Brown bursts into tears at the end of her audition, it is not a construct — she appears to be genuinely heartbroken. The "reality" of the moment lends credibility to the rest of the *Idol* program, in much the same way the "reality" of Sarah Goldberg or William Hung or Angela Martin is intended to lessen our collective cynicism about the construction of *Idol*. These are real people displaying real emotions. In presenting them in their raw emotional state, *Idol* is attempting to assure viewers that what is being presented is "real" at all times. It is thematic sleight-of-hand.

It could also be (again, cynically) suggested that sequences such as Brown's are designed to give *Idol* a soul. That is, in treating Brown with tender kindness, the judges are humanized and the show itself is presented as caring for the well-being of its participants. Not *every* contestant is berated, made fun of, or dismissed as talentless. Some contestants transcend such treatment. This is a common occurrence in competitive reality television; from Paul Potts on *Britain's Got Talent* (a bumbling, overweight cell phone salesman who is revealed to be a brilliant opera tenor) to Heather Kuzmich on *America's Next Top Model* (who makes it to the show's top five contestants despite struggling with Asperger's Syndrome) to actress Marlee Matlin on *Dancing with the Stars* (who makes it to the show's top seven contestants despite being completely deaf), the inspirational contestant civilizes the competition and, in turn, lionizes America's core values: determination, overcoming obstacles, and, in the case of someone like Brown, selfless action.

As transmitter of ideological constructs, *American Idol* occupies a central place in the televisual matrix. Coupled with the vertical integration *Idol* has achieved (i.e., ownership over not only the contestant, but the television program, the merchandise distribution company, the record label, the tour management firm, and so forth), the final product that *American Idol* appears to produce is not "just" a Celebrity; it is a commodity form that has "skipped to the front of the line." That is to say, the *Idol* commodity doesn't have to endure the years of singing in bars and coffee houses, followed by opening for more well-established bands until someone discovers him/her and gives him/her a developmental recording contract that results in a first album very few people have heard until a single from the album breaks out with wide radio play and so on and so on until superstardom is attained. By virtue of winning *American Idol* (or placing highly in the competition), the contestant is more favorably positioned to enter the marketplace with a higher degree of desirability and a greater chance at success. The *celebrity* commodity created by *American Idol* appears to be more durable and recognizable than the celetoids created by other, similar programs, and has distinct advantages over existing *celebrity* commodities due to the vertical integration of the show's production and the illusion of the democratic process present in the commodity's generation. Comparing *American Idol* to other television programs may not even be the most accurate or pragmatic relationship. The closer association may be professional sports leagues, such as the National Football League or the National Basketball Association, that are in the business of selling not only the players, but the game itself as a separate and distinct but wholly symbiotic commodity and a wide range of related ancillary merchandise.

In essence, *American Idol* is very good at what it does. However, whether or not "what it does" is good for society is complicated. Some of *Idol*'s more insidious practices are glossed over or unexamined by the program itself, and naturalized as a part of the star-making process. But for all of the illusion of democracy and promulgation of the success myth that *Idol* attempts to convey, the truth remains that *Idol* is extremely particular about who does and does not receive opportunity. Randy Jackson's constant refrain that it does not matter how old a contestant is, as long as that contestant can sing, is at best a half-truth: it matters very much how old a contestant is. From 16 years of age to 29 years of age, Jackson's statement could be seen as accurate (if not willfully naïve). If it in no way matters how old a contestant is, as long as the contestant can sing, why the need for the arbitrary cut-off age of 29? What *Idol* explicitly is offering are parameters around the success myth: in order to be a successful pop music star, one has to be within these age limits. In *Idol* parlance, an American Idol must be *young* and *relevant*.

The same could be said for "looking like a star." A female contestant must fit certain body type requirements; if she doesn't, she is subject to a stream of degrading references to her size. Eventually, she may be "accepted," as Mandisa Hundley is in due course, but this does not preclude the initial assumption that her weight is a major obstacle to her

XII. Look at This! I'm Unique!

success. Male contestants, on the other hand, undergo no such scrutiny. Remember that for several overweight male contestants, including S2 winner Ruben Studdard and S4 top five finalist Scott Savol, size was a part of the contestant's charm. In this respect, *Idol* is incredibly sexist.

Race is also a site for unequal treatment on *Idol*. It could be argued that if a contestant is visually identifiable as Caucasian, s/he is fine. If a contestant is visually identifiable as African-American, s/he is probably fine. If, however, a contestant is "brown" (i.e., Latino/a, Asian-American, Middle-Eastern-American, or any one of a number of biracial or multiracial combinations with darker complexions), the contestant is in trouble from the outset. Chances are, the contestant is never going to be placed in a position to be voted on by the public in the first place. If the contestant does manage to slip into the top 24, the contestant's chances of making the top 10 are exponentially slimmer, and the chances of making it to the top 5 are nearly statistically non-existent. Only 13 of the 84 top 12 contestants across the first seven seasons of *American Idol* were neither visually identifiable as Caucasian nor African-American[2]; of those, only S3's Jasmine Trias and S7's David Archuleta and Jason Castro were voted into the top 5.

"Brown" people are also often the contestants for whom some of the most pointed symbolic degradation is reserved. S2's Vanessa Olivarez was dismissed amid controversy over a comment she made to Cowell that appears to have been scripted, but may have cost her with voters and she was voted out at number 12. S3's Camile Velasco went from being "probably the best out of the group" in the words of Cowell to enduring weekly berating about her nerves and lack of self-confidence until she was voted out at number nine. S4's Jessica Sierra was branded "unlikable" by Cowell and was voted out at number ten; S6's Sanjaya Malakar is the foremost example of symbolic degradation in the *Idol* canon. Race and gender image issues permeate *Idol*, reinforcing the dominant cultural hegemony that in order to be successful, one must be thin, attractive, and belong to a racially "safe" category. This belies the success myth in an insidious and significant way — when the success myth says that we all could be rich, famous, and thriving, the "all" in question quite often is qualified by race, gender, age, sexual orientation, and so on.

While class is not expressly talked about in relation to the contestants in any significant way on *Idol,* it does appear to play a part, particularly in the audition episodes. The poor are often conspicuous by their absence, and those who are featured are normally there to be made fun of. Obviously, it seems intuitively more difficult for one of lower social class to participate fully in the *Idol* experience — taking days away from work or school to audition, possessing the clothing and make-up to "look like a star," and so forth.

Race, age, and gender may be an area for future research. These are my preliminary thoughts, but certainly there is room for a more in-depth study of these themes throughout the show's seasons. Additionally, although I have focused mainly on race, age, and gender here, certainly there are other issues at play on *Idol:* class, sexual orientation, ability/disability, and more. The fact that *Idol* makes it seem as though "anyone can make it" without a full consideration of the systemic obstacles inherent in American society glosses over the darker side of the success myth — the side rooted in reality.

The S8 addition of songwriter and A&R executive Kara DioGuardi as a fourth judge has greatly changed *American Idol,* particularly as relates to the intrinsic commercial nature of the program. DioGuardi is, by and large, much more open and circumspect about her motives in judging. She refers to "package artists," often referencing the type of record a contestant would make or the manner in which *Idol* could market him/her. DioGuardi is quick to enforce the genre boundaries for contestants, even more so than Jackson or Cowell have been in seasons past. While it remains to be seen if DioGuardi is a permanent fixture on *Idol* or a temporary addition, it is clear that she has made the focus of *Idol* much more plainly stated in the short time she has inhabited the judge's chair. DioGuardi is interested in the commercial prospects of each contestant; all other matters in regards to *Idol* appear to be secondary concerns. Whether this honesty of purpose is refreshing or depressing is, I believe, a matter of individual opinion.

For all of its positive and negative qualities, the fact remains that *American Idol,* both as *celebrity* text and as entertainment media, is iconic of the current state of popular culture. It is currently the Greatest Show on Earth. For 20 weeks, from January to May each year for close to a decade, *American Idol* is the biggest thing happening in America. More

XII. Look at This! I'm Unique!

than the Super Bowl, more than any other televisual text, *American Idol* is consumed and enjoyed by Americans. It occupies the national consciousness, and in doing so, it tells us who we are, what we value, and what it means to be an American. *American Idol* universalizes, gives people something ostensibly innocuous to discuss — but in those discussions are imbedded narratives of race, class, gender, sexual orientation, patriotism, individuality and individualism, consumerism and democracy. It is the most salient, most constant of contemporary American narratives: the drive to be adored, to be adulated, to be attractive, to achieve. *American Idol* keeps alive the success myth, gives us our Adamic heroes to invest with our own hopes and dreams in the aspiration that one day, our dreams might too be fulfilled. Emerson's representative man is alive and well on *Idol*; these performers whom we cheer because they, in some way, are just like us — a "better" version of us. The narrative of fighting for one's hopes and dreams resonates with Americans who have been deeply entrenched in the success myth. Add in something that, despite individual tastes, is almost universally adored — music — and *Idol* has a clear path to the soul of America.

The purpose of this research was to take one specific, successful property and discuss the nature of the *celebrity* product it creates and the mechanisms by which it achieves success. In doing so, this research expands Marshall's theoretical "toolbox" for *celebrity* text analysis, codifies Rojek's theories of *celebrity* through concrete application, and rejects Boorstin's proposition that a Celebrity need do nothing in order to attain *celebrity* status. Additionally, it introduces the idea of democratic process to the generation of commercial commodity entities — a concept with implications beyond the television and music industries. Finally, it attempts to historically and rhetorically situate the entire concept of *celebrity* by drawing upon disparate facets of the discussion of fame and *celebrity* and condensing them into a more streamlined set of principles by which to engage *celebrity* texts.

Looking Ahead

This study of *American Idol* reveals *celebrity* to be a complexly faceted construct. There are many avenues of research in this area which are still viable and may prove interesting for future scholarship. For example, the supposition is made on multiple occasions in this work that the contestants on *American Idol* tend to be more recognizable to the average non-viewer than those of other reality television properties. Illustrating this through direct study, either quantitatively or qualitatively, would strengthen the conclusions drawn about the durability of the *Idol* commodities.

Additionally, this book is ultimately a work of interpretation. While I have engaged in embedded research, attempting to marry theoretical and methodological knowledge with first-hand, in-depth situations within the culture of the product's intended audience, I concede that, like all cultural products, *Idol* is open to a vast array of interpretations. Replicating this research with multiple observers, both embedded and not, and using their interpretations to triangulate an analysis of *Idol*'s *celebrity* commodity production could be a valuable contribution to understanding the nature of this unique program.

Finally, there is a parallel, away from which this book has attempted to stay, between the democratic processes on *American Idol* and other, larger democratic processes within society. If one were to juxtapose the visual presentation of the finale of *American Idol* and the visual presentation of the last night of the Democratic or Republican National Convention, some very obvious parallels could probably be drawn. There are probably other similarities as well, from the nature of coalition-building in terms of candidacies/contestants to the role of image and back story in the construction of the candidate/contestant to the value of punditry/judging in the formation of viewer/voter opinion. The comparison between *American Idol*'s creation of a *celebrity* commodity and the manner in which a presidential candidate secures office is fertile ground for inquiry.

Conclusion

The history of the Western world is the history of the individual, and stories that define Western culture are the stories of Celebrities. *Celebrity* is the prism through which nearly all cultural and societal achievement in the modern West is framed,[3] from the triumphs of Barack Obama to the

XII. Look at This! I'm Unique!

advancements in technology of Bill Gates and Steve Jobs to the struggles of Nelson Mandela and the tragedy of Princess Diana of Wales. It is not capitalism or democracy that is given credit for ending the Cold War between the United States and the Soviet Union; it is Ronald Reagan. Scientific inquiry and a team of laboratory assistants did not cure polio; Jonas Salk cured polio. The study of the nature of *celebrity* is far from trivial; it is the study of the very nature and constitution of the history of Western society.

In turn, the study of *American Idol* cannot merely be essentialized to the study of a successful television program. *American Idol* represents the commercialization and reification of identity in modern America; the (loosely) democratic election of the American Idol is the end result of a month-long process of turning a human being into a product to be bought and sold on the open market. Understanding the ways in which *American Idol* undertakes this process and achieves commercial success is invaluable in the understanding of the way cultural relevance is attained. In a society in which media occupy a central role in the dissemination and ingratiation of ideology, and in which Celebrities are key instruments in cultural and ideological instruction for "the masses," any deeper understanding of the manner in which those Celebrities are developed and introduced to the public can only further our understanding of the fundamental structure of American society.

Chapter Notes

Introduction

1. The term "celebrity" is, as will be pointed out throughout this book, an elusive and multifaceted thing. The reader will note the word "celebrity" used in three forms in this book: "celebrity" (with a lower case "c"), "Celebrity" (with an upper case "c"), and *celebrity* (italicized). "Celebrity" refers to the actual human being represented by the term, "celebrity" refers to the theoretical concepts and definitions given to the social phenomenon, and "*celebrity*" refers to the mediated construction and tradable commodity that a Celebrity generates.

2. To be fair, even Paris Hilton's Celebrity status is based upon the ascribed *celebrity* of wealth and inheritance. More on ascribed *celebrity* follows.

3. In some respects, the difference between a Celebrity and a celetoid may also be understood as the difference between a "public figure" and a "limited public figure." The Supreme Court, in *Gertz vs. Robert Welch, Inc. 418 U.S. 323 (1974)*, established that "some [people] occupy positions of such pervasive power and influence that they are deemed public figures for all purposes." These "all-purpose" public figures could be thought of as Celebrities (Of course, not all public figures are Celebrities; some are politicians, law enforcement or judicial appointments, etc.). This same case defined a "limited public figure," stating, "[limited] public figures have thrust themselves to the forefront of particular public controversies in order to influence the resolution of the issues involved." *22 MLR 2147 (DC E Wis. 1994)* further established that an actress or a model may be classified as a limited public figure. The celetoid may not have the "pervasive power" of a Celebrity, but within the narrow scope of his/her duties as a reality show contestant, the celetoid is a limited public figure. This distinction may help in later understanding the particular construction of *celebrity* with which this book is concerned — and is covered more in depth in Chapter II.

4. To be fair, Turner does not make this distinction — this is an inference based on the reverse of his argument.

5. The Recording Industry Association of America designates a platinum album as having sold one million copies.

6. In actuality, in the first audition cut, potential contestants sing for a variety of *Idol* employees, from production assistants to assistant producers, and many are released from the competition before they ever see the on-air judges.

7. While Season 8 of *American Idol* will be discussed very little in this book, as it is currently in broadcast at the time of this writing, it should be noted that the program returned to the Season 1–3 top 36 format in Season 8.

8. Note that media attribution does not only happen within the confines of the program; *Idol* also generates coverage in other media outlets. However, while these other media outlets may be discussed, the examination will be limited only to the program itself.

Chapter Notes

Chapter I

1. The problem with this is that, as Crane (1992) points out, those core media products are largely produced by small, elite groups of media producers who are normally vastly out of touch with the rest of society. Because the enclave of media producers is so numerically limited, they cannot possibly see the rest of society as anything other than a mass of poll numbers, ratings/shares, and demographic categories. This, according to Crane, means that media producers are often wildly unsynchronized with the rest of society in terms of taste and interests. This is why a large number of television series are cancelled in the first season (and many after broadcasting only one or two episodes). Media producers often have no idea what people will like, and are just throwing things against the wall to see if they stick.

2. "Uses and Gratifications" research has a long and storied tradition, beginning with early studies on radio listeners and their connection soap operas (Herzog, 1944). This line of research presumes that people receive much more than just information from the programs they consume; the programs fulfill some other psychological need, such as emotional release, advice, security, structure, or the like. Seminal texts in this line of study include Lazarsfeld & Stanton (1949), McQuail, Blumler & Brown (1972) and Katz, Blumler & Gurevitch (1974).

3. Often, but not always. There are numerous programs on television which exhibit both artistic merit and commercial success. Unfortunately, they are most often the exception rather than the rule. More on this in a moment.

4. *Dancing with the Stars* is a similar program, but certainly not the same. The level of technique and intricacy of choreography present on *So You Think You Can Dance* is vastly superior to that of *DWTS*. In fact, many former *SYTYCD* contestants have gone on to perform as the professional partner for the celebrities on *DWTS*. Additionally, the program itself is a much less serious affair, and is presented more as "all in good fun," while *SYTYCD* is a professional competition for professional dancers. This is not to say *Dancing with the Stars* is not an entertaining or quality program — it is simply different.

Chapter II

1. As Epstein (2005) reminds, "True celebrities need nothing said of them in apposition, fore or aft. The greatest celebrities are those who don't even require their full names mentioned: Marilyn, Winston, Johnny, Liz, Liza, Oprah, Michael (could be Jordan or Jackson — context usually clears this up fairly quickly), Kobe, Martha (Stewart, not Washington), Britney, Shaq, JLo, Frank (Sinatra, not Perdue), O.J., and, with the quickest recognition and shortest name of all — trumpets here, please — W" (p. 18). Anyone from Denver can quickly corroborate: Elway needs no other identifier.

2. The word "is" is used consciously here. It seems that in mainstream American language, people have forgotten that the word "media" is a plural. However, in vernacular discussions of "The Media," distinctions between various forms and formats are often rendered irrelevant, as though "The Media" were a single, monolithic (and malevolent) entity.

3. These are not necessarily outright lies, but more a creative restructuring of the environment that man makes for himself to make his environment more enjoyable.

4. Admittedly, some may pejoratively refer to this as "the lowest common denominator."

5. It is interesting that a succession of individuals is the manner in which history has always been written, as it seems to stand direct contrast to the manner in which capitalism has been established as the dominant form of social organization in the Western world. Dyer (1986) argues:

> Capitalism justifies itself on the basis of the freedom (separateness) of anyone to make money, sell their labour how they will, to be able to express opinions and get them heard (regardless of wealth or social position). The openness of society is assumed by the way

that we are addressed as individuals—as consumers (each freely choosing to buy, or watch, what we want), as legal subjects (free and responsible before the law), as political subjects (able to make up our mind who is to run society). Thus even while the notion of the individual is assailed on all sides, it is a necessary fiction for the reproduction of the kind of society we live in [p. 9].

For a more complete discussion of societal lies that everyone recognizes as lies but do not really want to know the truth about, see Harry Frankfurt's *On Bullshit* (Princeton: Princeton University Press, 2005).

6. For example, Homer repeatedly used the term "*kleos afthiton*," which translates to "imperishable fame," long before Alexander the Great was born (Giles, p. 3).

7. Although, as Giles reminds, "the historical evidence demonstrates quite clearly that fame has, to some extent, always been regarded as essentially amoral and frequently undeserved. As early as Virgil's *Aeneid*, fame was portrayed as a 'filthy goddess' that circulates rumour and establishes certain individuals in the public eye for no 'good' reason" (Giles, p. 4). As will be illustrated later, this notion of underserved recognition continues to this day, with many scholars adopting an attitude that, "celebrities ... needn't have done—needn't do—anything special. Their function isn't to act—just to be" (Gamson, p. 10). It is this (often erroneous) concept of Celebrities as human *beings* rather than humans *doing* that pervades much of the scholarship about *celebrity*.

8. See if you can spot the parallels to the manner in which *American Idol* contestants are contracted.

9. In fact, in 1944, one writer for *American Mercury* argued that *celebrity* was becoming a "lush, weedy thing," choking "many a rare plant of genuine accomplishment." In the years following, this would become a common refrain from cultural critics of *celebrity* (Gamson, 38).

10. Which explains how even the most exploitative of reality televisions shows are still able to find cast members; as discussed earlier in this chapter, it does not seem to even matter what one is well-known for any more, as long as one has had his/her five minutes of opportunity to be on national television. If that means eating a bowl full of bugs on *Fear Factor* or letting a deranged sociopath push one down the stairs in a shopping cart on *Jackass*, people appear to be ever-willing to subject themselves, as long as they can be on television. As Andy Denhart, blogger and reality TV junkie, writes, "With the number of reality shows out there, it's inexcusable to not be famous if you want to be!" (Flora, p. 38).

11. Much of modern Celebrity *ethos* is drawn from *arête*: sports stars become stars largely because they excel at their sport, for example.

Chapter III

1. In this regard, Celebrities operate as a sort of "symbolic product of television that provides totems of personality types for the audience. In this way, the personality system is configured around its ideological work to draw the viewer into an acceptance of a capitalist culture and political structure" [Marshall, 1997, p. 122]. Celebrities tell the rest of us how to conduct our daily lives in accordance with the hegemonic structure of society.

2. A former professor and now colleague of mine continues to admonish me for my continued "allegiance to the Marxist catechism" in this respect. I concede that the commodity itself (in this case, Alyssa Milano) is not the *cause* of abstract desire, but rather is the product of a capitalist system that is exploited by the consumerist nature of our culture. However, this does not eliminate the fact that abstract desire is a necessary piece of capitalism in general and consumerism specifically—perhaps not in the original Marx/Engels texts, but certainly in capitalism's contemporary form. There are other likely, proximate, and historically traceable causes of abstract desire, but that is a larger discussion space would not permit here.

3. Admittedly, this is an educated observation, but it is still an assumption, and one of the limitations of this particular study. A longitudinal study of the contestants

on several different competitive reality programs and their post-competition *celebrity* success levels may be an interesting research opportunity for another intrepid scholar.

Chapter IV

1. An embarrassed Clarkson repudiated this statement two episodes later, saying, "I want to defend myself. They edited that. I'm not that snobby. The whole, 'I'm an American Idol!' I'm not like that" (S1E8).
2. The term "choose" is used loosely here. The number of songs from which contestants are allowed to sing is limited, and some contestants can be left with slim pickings if they are among the last to select.
3. There is also irony in Seacrest making this comment to Cowell, as though he has no staff, luxury automobile, and existence outside of "regular folks" of his own.

Chapter VI

1. Season 8 of *American Idol* was not directly included in the research sample due to the fact that it has not completed its run as of this writing. However, in Chapter VI, new S8 *Idol* judge Kara DioGuardi is discussed, and her addition has brought a more pointed, blatant emphasis on commerciality, particularly in terms of physical appearance, than even Simon Cowell has had over the first seven seasons. DioGuardi is extremely concerned about the commercial prospects of each contestant, and makes constant references to physical appearance in almost every critique she gives.
2. It should be noted that Randy Jackson is not exactly svelte himself; in 2003, Jackson underwent gastric bypass surgery after being diagnosed with Type II diabetes.
3. The A&R division of a record company is in charge of finding new talent and signing them to the company — the A&R executive is the chief talent scout for the record label.
4. Perhaps (but unfortunately) unsurprisingly, weight is only an issue for women. Ruben Studdard, winner of Season 2, at the time of the finale weighed over 400 pounds. Not only is weight never directly addressed with Studdard, the judges make repeated references to the fact that his weight is part of his charm, such as when Cowell tells him that the way he looks is reminiscent of Luther Vandross and is "great" (S2E4), or when Paula Abdul, after Studdard's performance of Billy Joel's "Just the Way You Are," states that every woman wants to hear words like Studdard has just sung, and that the song is reflective of how America feels about Ruben — that they love him just the way he is (S2E25). Studdard's size is always framed as a positive, beneficial trait. No woman on *American Idol* has ever enjoyed the same luxury.
5. Interestingly enough, Paula Abdul immediately counters Simon Cowell by stating, "I bet it could drive you crazy having someone say, 'It's not authentic. It's not who you are.' How does anyone know who you are but you?" (S7E16). This larger existential question is never really addressed by *American Idol*, but ranks among the most self-aware, truthful and revealing statements ever uttered on the program.

Chapter VII

1. Over an equal number of releases, that is. Clarkson is still the top seller overall, but has released two more albums than Underwood. Clarkson's first two records, however, sold a total of 8,760,000 copies; Underwood's first two albums sold 9,420,000 copies. No other *Idol* winner comes close. ("Gold and Platinum" n.d.)
2. It could be argued that the hype surrounding boxing matches, in which promoters and the fighters themselves attempt to draw a crowd to the match, is very similar to *Idol*. It could also be legitimately argued that boxers are commodities as well as athletes. However, once the bell rings, one fighter is going to get punched in the face more than the other, and this has nothing to do with personality or commodity status whatsoever.
3. *Idol* rarely points out that a single viewer may vote multiple times. Anecdotally, as a sort of completely unscientific experiment, I once attempted to discern how many times I could vote in the two-hour

time window given for voting, using two cell phones programmed with redial features. I was able to vote 127 times. To reach 97 million votes, 763,780 people would have to also vote at that rate (I concede that a younger voter with more nimble fingers may be able to vote even more than I did.). Intuitively, one suspects the average *Idol* voter is not using two cell phones non-stop over the course of a two-hour period. While 97 million people are probably not voting for *American Idol*, the number of actual voters is probably still quite considerable.

Chapter IX

1. Whether Cowell has been coached on Brown's situation prior to her audition is not revealed; I am inclined to believe the producers told him to lay off Brown.

2. Paula Abdul's commentary throughout Malakar's presence on the show has been intentionally omitted. Abdul's function on the judging panel is to provide almost exclusively positive commentary; her role in symbolic degradation, not just of Malakar but of all contestants, is minimal at best.

3. This, of course, requires the assumption that voters agree Malakar's singing is terrible. *Idol*, however, has no mechanism for determining on what basis viewers are casting their votes; Cowell simply takes for granted that viewers agree with him. It should also be noted here that there were other mitigating factors for Malakar's continued presence in the competition. The website "Vote For the Worst" championed Malakar and provided thousands of votes; Howard Stern also undertook a radio campaign on his own program to keep Malakar in the competition. There could also be some backlash effect happening here, as by Season 6, one would assume many viewers are savvy to the way in which Cowell operates, and may have simply been voting for Malakar to spite Cowell. This is speculative, of course.

Chapter XI

1. One commercial is particularly clever in promoting multiple commodities simultaneously. The song is "I Want You to Want Me" by Cheap Trick. The *Idol* contestants are digitally inserted onto t-shirts, CDs, posters, and jackets while singing the lyrics. Not only does this commercial promote the Ford automobile, but it also promotes the *Idol* contestants as *celebrity* commodities and concurrently promotes an entire line of *American Idol* Celebrity-imprinted merchandise.

2. Rebecca Romijn's films have averaged $85,054,454 in gross returns ("Rebecca Romijn" n.d.); Hugh Jackman's films have averaged $90,113,862 in gross returns ("Hugh Jackman" n.d.). *X-Men: Last Stand* earned $234,362,462 at the box office. These are two Celebrities with significant fan bases and endorsement power.

3. A list which includes Todd Bridges, Gavin DeGraw, Mandy Moore, Christina Applegate, Taye Diggs, Ben Stiller, Heather Locklear, Emily Deschanel, David Boreanaz, David Hasselhoff, Quincy Jones, Jeff Foxworthy, Brad Garrett, Eva Longoria, Vanna White, Sarah Michelle Gellar, Brandy Norwood, Rachel Bilson, Whoopi Goldberg, Mickey Dolenz, Camryn Manheim, Marilu Henner, Mimi Rogers, Sela Ward, Tori Spelling, Carmen Electra, Jerry O'Connell, Rebecca Romijn, Hugh Jackman, Melissa Rivers, and Zac Efron, among others.

Chapter XII

1. "Legitimate" here meaning "commercially successful" and often "critically acclaimed." *Idol* winners are usually not Celebrities in name only; they are musicians who sell albums — lots of albums — and have traditionally reaped the rewards of such sales in the form of Grammy/CMA awards, RIAA designations, and concert tour success.

2. Admittedly, attempting to visually identify ethnicity is always a dicey proposition at best. Loosely, however, the list as referred to here includes R.J. Helton, A.J. Gil, Jim Verraros, Ejay Day, Vanessa Olivarez, Jasmine Trias, Camile Velasco, Jessica Sierra, Sanjaya Malakar, David Archuleta, Jason Castro, Ramiele Malubay, and David

Hernandez. Arguments could be made about the visual identities of a few other contestants, but the point is that the number still remains a significantly minute segment of the overall *Idol* contestant population.

3. To be certain, there do exist types of accomplishment that are not filtered through the prism of *celebrity*. For example, one may set a personal goal and accomplish that personal goal in private. However, I would argue that personal accomplishment is not societally valued, particularly in the United States. In order for an accomplishment to "matter," it must be recognized as accomplishment by others. This is primarily due to the pervasive influence of *celebrity*, which demands public adulation for even the most minor of achievements. Is a goal accomplished in private still an achievement? Undoubtedly. Is it an achievement society as a whole "cares about?" This is another matter altogether.

Bibliography

Adorno, T., and J. M. Bernstein (2001). "On the fetish character in music and the regression of listening." In T. Adorno (author), *The culture industry: Selected essays on mass culture*. New York: Routledge.
Agrawal, J., and W. A. Kamakura (1995). "The economic worth of celebrity endorsers: An event study analysis." *Journal of Marketing, 59*(3), 56–62.
Alberoni, F. (2006). "The powerless 'elite.'" In P. D. Marshall (ed.). *The celebrity culture reader*. London: Routledge.
Alperstein, N. M. (1991). "Imaginary Social relationships with celebrities appearing in television commercials." *Journal of Broadcasting & Electronic Media, 35*(1), 43–58.
"American Idol highest price regular season ad buy." (2007, January 16). Retrieved September 9, 2008 from http://www.mediabuyerplanner.com/2007/01/16/american-idol-highest-price-regular-season-ad-buy/.
Andrejevic, M. (2004). *Reality TV: The work of being watched*. Lanham, MD: Rowman & Littlefield.
_____. (2002). "The kinder, gentler gaze of big brother: Reality tv in the era of digital capitalism." *New Media & Society, 4*(2), 251–270.
Ashe, D. D., and L. E. McCutcheon (2001). "Shyness, loneliness, and attitude toward celebrities." *Current Research in Social Psychology, 6*(9). Retrieved May 2, 2008, from http://www.uiowa.edu/~grpproc/crisp/crisp.6.9.htm.
Barron, L. (2006). "'Elizabeth Hurley is more than a model': Stars and career diversification in contemporary media." *The Journal of Popular Culture, 39,* 523–545.
Barthes, R. (1981). "Textual analysis of Poe's 'Valdemar.'" In R. Young (ed.), *Untying the text: A post-structuralist reader* (pp. 133–161). Boston: Routledge.
Batra, R., and P. M. Homer (2004). "The situational impact of brand image beliefs." *Journal of Consumer Psychology, 14*(3), 318–330.
BBC News. (2008, April 30). *Abdul makes gaffe on US idol show*. Retrieved May 5, 2008, from http://news.bbc.co.uk/1/hi/entertainment/7375002.stm.
Bennett, J. (2008). "The television personality system: Televisual stardom revisited after film theory." *Screen, 49*(1), 32–50.
Berman, M. (2007, January 16). *The programming insider*. Retrieved September 9, 2008 from http://pifeedback.com/eve/forums/a/tpc/f/63310451/m/73710482/p/1.
Billig, M. (1987). "Protagoras and the Origins of Rhetoric." In M. Billig (author). *Arguing and thinking: A rhetorical approach to social psychology* (pp. 31–50). Cambridge: Cambridge University Press.
"Bio." (n.d.) Retrieved February 24, 2009, from http://www.kelliepickler.com/?content=bio.
Biressi, A., and H. Nunn (2005). *Reality TV: Realism and revelation*. London: Wallflower Press.
Boorstin, D. J. (1962). *The image: Or, what happened to the American dream?* New York: Atheneum.

Bibliography

Bourdieu, P. (1984). *Distinction: A social critique of the judgement of taste* (R. Nice, Trans.). Cambridge: Harvard University Press.

_____. (1977). *Outline of a theory of practice*. Cambridge: Cambridge University Press.

Brando, M., and R. Lindsey (1994). *Brando: Songs my mother taught me*. London: Century.

Braudy, L. (1997). *The frenzy of renown: Fame and its history*. New York: Vintage.

Brenton, S., and R. Cohen (2003). *Shooting people: Adventures in reality TV*. New York: Verso.

Brockington, D. (2008). "Celebrity conservation: Interpreting the Irwins." *Media International Australia*, (127), 96–108.

Brookes, H. J. (1995). "Suit, tie and a touch of Juju: The ideological construction of Africa: A critical discourse analysis of news on Africa in the British press." *Discourse & Society*, 6(4), 461–494.

Burke, K. (1950). *A rhetoric of motives*. Berkeley: University of California Press.

_____. (1969). *A rhetoric of motives*. Berkeley: University of California Press.

Calabrese, A., and C. Sparks (2004). *Toward a political economy of culture*. Oxford: Rowman & Littlefield.

"Capitol Gains." (n.d.) Retrieved March 9, 2009 from http://www.ew.com/ew/article/0,295000,00.html.

Carbine, J. (2001). "Unmarried motherhood 1830–1990: A genealogical analysis." In M. Wetherell, S. Taylor, and S. J. Yates (eds.). *Discourse as data: A guide for analysis* (pp. 267–310). London: Open University and Sage.

Carter, B. (2007, February 20). "Rivals say 'Idol' remains a 'schoolyard bully.'" *AOL Entertainment News*. Retrieved March 5, 2007, from http://news.aol.com/entertainment/tv/articles/_a/rivals-say-idol-remains-a-schoolyard/20070220070509990001?cid=918.

_____. (2008, January 14). "Reality TV is no lightweight in battle to outlast strikers." *The New York Times*. Retrieved 3 February 2009 from http://www.nytimes.com/2008/01/14/business/media/14ratings.html?_r=1.

Cavender, G., and L. Bond-Maupin (1993). "Fear and loathing on reality television: An analysis of 'America's most wanted' and 'Unsolved mysteries.'" *Sociological Inquiry*, 63(3), 305–317.

Chaudbry, L. (2008). "Mirror, mirror on the web." In T. J. Fitzgerald (ed.). *Celebrity culture in the United States* (pp. 157–163). New York: H.W. Wilson.

Choi, S. M., and N. M. Rifon (2007). "Who is the celebrity in advertising? Understanding dimensions of celebrity images." *The Journal of Popular Culture*, 40, 304.

Cohen, J. (2003). "Parasocial breakups: Measuring individual differences in responses to the dissolution of parasocial relationships." *Mass Communication and Society*, 6(2), 191–202.

Collins, R. (1990). *Culture, communication, and national identity*. Toronto: University of Toronto Press.

Collins, S. (2008). "Making the most out of 15 minutes." *Television & New Media*, 9(2), 87–110.

_____. (2008, May 22). "'American Idol' finale ratings surprisingly high." *Los Angeles Times*. Retrieved September 9, 2008 from http://latimesblogs.latimes.com/showtracker/2008/05/american-ido-20.html.

Cooper, B. L. (2005). "Tribute discs, career development, and death: Perfecting the celebrity product from Elvis Presley to Stevie Ray Vaughan." *Popular Music and Society*, 28(2), 229–248.

Couldry, N. (2002). "Playing for celebrity: Big brother as ritual event." *Television & New Media*, 3(3), 283–293.

Cowell, S. (2003). "All together now! Publics and participation in 'American Idol.'" *Invisible Culture*, (6). (2003). Retrieved November 11, 2008, from http://www.rochester.edu/in_visible_culture/Issue_6/issue6title.html.

208

Bibliography

Cowen, T. (2000). *In praise of commercial culture*. Cambridge: Harvard University Press.
Crane, D. (1992). *The production of culture media and the urban arts: Feminist perspective on communication*. Minneapolis: Sage.
Creeber, G. (2006). "The joy of text?: Television and textual analysis." *Critical Studies in Television*, *1*(1), 81–88. Manchester: Manchester University Press.
"Daughtry once again locks down #1 spot on Billboard top 200." (2007, March 7). Retrieved September 10, 2007 from http://www.daughtryofficial.com/news/daughtry-once-again-locks-down-1-spot-billboard-top-200.
Dellinger, B. (1995). "Critical discourse analysis." Retrieved September 3, 2008, from http://users.utu.fi/bredelli/cda.html.
Derakhshani, T. (2008). "Our celebrity madness: A reflection of consumerism." In T. J. Fitzgerald (Ed.), *Celebrity culture in the United States* (pp. 29–32). New York: H.W. Wilson.
DeRose, J., Fursich, E., and E. Haskins (2003). "Pop (up) goes the blind date: Supertextual constraints on 'reality' television." *Journal of Communication Inquiry*, *27*(2), 171–189.
Dickey, J. L. (2008, April 30). "Paula Abdul's gaffe confounds everyone on 'idol.'" *Orange County Register*. Retrieved May 5, 2008, from http://www.ocregister.com/articles/abdul-cowell-song-2030556-thought-first.
Dyer, R. (1986). *Heavenly bodies*. London: Routledge.
_____. (2006). "Stars as images." In P. D. Marshall (ed.). *The celebrity culture reader*. London: Routledge.
_____, and P. McDonald (1998). *Stars* (2nd ed.). London: British Film Institute.
Elias, J. (1996, December 1). "An actor whose face offers real-life lessons." *The New York Times*. Retrieved December 12, 2008 from http://www.nytimes.com/1996/12/01/arts/an-actor-whose-face-offers-real-life-lessons.html?sec=&spon=&pagewanted=all.
Emerson, R. W. (2004 [1876]). *Representative men: Seven lectures*. New York: Modern Library.
Engle, Y., and T. Kasser (2005). "Why do adolescent girls idolize male celebrities?" *Journal of Adolescent Research*, *20*, 263–283.
Epstein, J. (2005, October 27). "The culture of celebrity: Let us now praise famous airheads." *The Weekly Standard*. Retrieved November 11, 2008, from http://www.weeklystandard.com/Content/Public/Articles/000%5C000%5C006%5Cl87rmfyj.asp.
_____. (2008). "Celebrity culture." In T. J. Fitzgerald (ed.). *Celebrity culture in the United States*. New York: H.W. Wilson.
Fairchild, C. (2006). "Australian idol and the attention economy." In P. D. Marshall (ed.). *The celebrity culture reader*. London: Routledge.
_____. (2007). "Building the authentic celebrity: The 'idol' phenomenon in the attention economy." *Popular Music & Society*, *30*(3), 355–375.
Fairclough, N. (2003). *Analysing discourse: Textual analysis for social research*. New York: Routledge.
"Fashion's red carpet ride." (2006, February 16). Retrieved from http://www.cottoninc.com/lsmarticles/?articleID=472.
Featherstone, M. (2007). *Consumer culture and postmodernism*. London: Sage.
Ferris, K. O. (2001). "Through a glass, darkly: The dynamics of fan-celebrity encounters." *Symbolic Interaction*, *24*(1), 25–47.
_____. (2004). "Seeing and being seen: The moral order of celebrity sightings." *Journal of Contemporary Ethnography*, *33*(3), 236–264.
Fishwick, M. W. (2002). *Popular culture in a new age*. Binghamton: Haworth Press.
Fitzgerald, T. J. (ed.). (2008). *Celebrity culture in the United States*. New York: H.W. Wilson.
Flora, C. (2008). "Seeing by starlight." In T. J. Fitzgerald (ed.). *Celebrity culture in the United States* (pp. 33–39). New York: H.W. Wilson.

Bibliography

Fornäs, J. (1990). "Moving rock: Youth and pop in late modernity." *Popular Music, 9*(3), 291–306.

Franzosi, R. (1998). "Narrative analysis: Or why (and how) sociologists should be interested in narrative." *Annual Review of Sociology, 24,* 517–554. Retrieved October 21, 2007, from http://arjournals.annualreviews.org/doi/full/10.1146/annurev.soc.24.1.517?cookieSet=1.

Friedman, J. (2002). *Reality squared: Televisual discourse on the real.* New Brunswick: Rutgers University Press.

Gabler, N. (1998). *Life, the movie: How entertainment conquered reality.* New York: Knopf.

Gamson, J. (1994). *Claims to fame: Celebrity in contemporary America.* Berkeley: University of California Press.

"George Clooney." (n.d.) Retrieved December 20, 2008 from http://coolspotters.com/actors/george-clooney.

Giles, D. (2000). *Illusions of immortality: A psychology of fame and celebrity.* London: Macmillan.

———. (2000). *Illusions of immortality: A psychology of fame and celebrity.* New York: St. Martin's Press.

Goffman, E. (1959). *The presentation of self in everyday life.* New York: Peter Smith Publisher.

"Gold and Platinum." (n.d.) Retrieved February 23, 2009 from http://www.riaa.com/goldandplatinum.php.

Goldsmith, R. E., B. Lafferty, and S. J. Newell (2000). "The impact of corporate credibility and celebrity credibility on consumer reaction to advertisements and brands." *Journal of Advertising, 29*(3), 43–54.

Gramsci, A. (1978). *Selections from the political writings* (Q. Hoare, Trans.). London: Lawrence and Wishart.

Grossberg, L. (1997). *Bringing it all back home: Essays on cultural studies.* Durham, NC: Duke University Press.

Gubrium, J. F., and J. A. Holstein (2000). "Analyzing interpretive practice." In N. K. Denzin & Y. S. Lincoln (eds.). *Handbook of qualitative research* (pp. 487–508). Thousand Oaks: Sage.

Gunster, S. (2004). *Capitalizing on culture critical theory for cultural studies: Cultural spaces.* New York: University of Toronto Press.

Halbert, D., and A. F. Wood (2003). "Who owns your personality: Reality television and publicity rights." In M. J. Smith (ed.). *Survivor lessons: Essays on communication and reality television.* Jefferson, NC: McFarland.

Hall, S. (1998). "Notes on deconstructing the popular." In J. Storey (ed.). *Cultural theory and popular culture: A reader.* Athens: University of Georgia Press.

Hau, L. (2007, November 13). "Celebrity holiday megaspenders." *Forbes.com.* Retrieved September 30, 2008 from http://www.forbes.com/2007/11/08/celebrity-holiday-spending-biz-media-cx_lh_1108celebspending.html.

Hearn, A. (2004). "Image slaves." *Bad Subjects, 69.* Retrieved April 2, 2008, from http://bad.eserver.org/issues/2004/69/hearn.html.

Henderson, A. (2008). "From Barnum to bling: The changing face of celebrity culture." In *Celebrity culture in the United States.* New York: H.W. Wilson.

Herzog, H. (1944). "What do we really know about daytime serial listeners?" In P. F. Lazarsfeld (ed.). *Radio research 1942–3* (pp. 2–23). London: Sage.

Hibbard, J. (2008, April 30). "Paula Abdul hits a sour note." *The Hollywood Reporter.* Retrieved May 5, 2008, from http://www.hollywoodreporter.com/hr/content_display/news/e3i8ccff8ef2246288d518e4021f91c470b.

Hill, A. (2002). "Big brother: The real audience." *Television & New Media, 3*(3), 323–340.

———. (2005). *Reality TV: audience and popular factual television.* New York: Routledge.

Bibliography

Holmes, S. (2004). "Reality goes pop!" *Television & New Media*, 5(2), 147–172.

———, and S. Redmond (2006). *Framing celebrity: New directions in celebrity culture*. New York: Routledge.

Horkheimer, M., and W. A. T. (2002). *Dialectic of enlightenment: Cultural memory in the present*. New York: Stanford University Press.

Horton, D., and A. Strauss (1957). "Interaction in audience-participation shows." *The American Journal of Sociology*, 62(6), 579–587.

———, and R. R. Wohl (1956). "Mass communication and para-social interaction." *Psychiatry*, 19, 215–229.

Houlberg, R. (1984). "Local television news audience and the para-social interaction." *Journal of Broadcasting*, 28(4), 423–429.

Huff, R. M. (2006). *Reality television*. Westport: Praeger.

"Hugh Jackman." (n.d.) Retrieved March 9, 2009 from http://www.boxofficemojo.com/people/chart/?id=hughjackman.htm.

"Jacob" (2008, April 30). "She was, she went." In *Television Without Pity*. Retrieved January 13, 2009, from http://www.televisionwithoutpity.com/show/american_idol/season_7_top_5_results.php?page=5.

Jacobs, K. (2004). "Waterfront redevelopment: A critical discourse analysis of the policy-making process within the Chatham maritime project." *Urban Studies*, 41(4), 817–832.

Jacoby, M. B., and D. L. Zimmerman (2002). "Foreclosing on fame: Exploring the uncharted boundaries of the right of publicity." *New York University Law Review*, 77(1322).

Jay, M. (1996). *Dialectical imagination: A history of the Frankfurt School and the Institute of Social Research, 1923–1950*. Berkeley: University of California Press.

Jhally, S. (2006). *The spectacle of accumulation: Essays in culture, media, and politics*. New York: Peter Lang.

John., B. (1972). *Ways of seeing based on the BBC television series*. New York: Penguin (Non-Classics).

Jordan, C. (2006). "Marketing 'reality' to the world: Survivor, post–Fordism, and reality television." In D. Escoffery (ed.). *How real is reality TV?* Jefferson, NC: McFarland.

Joshi, H. (2000, December 3). "Discourse Analysis of Media." In *Suite101.com: Online Magazine and Writers' Network*. Retrieved September 10, 2008, from http://www.suite101.com/article.cfm/mass_communication/42498/4.

Kahle, L. R., and P. M. Homer (1985). "Physical attractiveness of the celebrity endorser: A social adaptation perspective." *Journal of Consumer Research*, 11(4), 954–961.

Katz, E., Blumler, J. G., and M. Gurevitch (1974). "Utilization of mass communication by the individual." In J. G. Blumler and E. Katz (eds.). *The uses of mass communications: Current perspectives on gratifications research* (pp. 19–32). Beverly Hills: Sage.

Keats, J. (2008). "Open-source celebrity: The wisdom of the audience." In T. J. Fitzgerald (ed.). *Celebrity culture in the United States* (pp. 155–156). New York: H.W. Wilson.

King, N., Touyz, S., and M. Charles (2000). "The effect of body dissatisfaction on women's perceptions of female celebrities." *International Journal of Eating Disorders*, 27(3), 341–347.

Koch, G. (1999). "From kingdom to stardom." *Constellations*, 6(2), 206–215.

Kripalani, C. (2007). "Trendsetting and product placement in Bollywood film: Consumerism through consumption." *Journal of Contemporary Film*, 4(3), 197–215.

Lahusen, C. (1996). *The rhetoric of moral protest: Public campaigns, celebrity endorsement, and political mobilization*. Berlin: Walter de Grutyer.

Lazarsfeld, P. F., and F. Stanton (1949). *Communication research 1948–9*. New York: Harper & Row.

Lee, J. (2006). *American idol: Evidence of same-race preferences?* (Working paper No. 1974). Austin, Texas: SSRN — http://ssrn.com/abstract=884482.

Bibliography

Leets, L., DeBecker, G., and H. Giles (1995). "Exploring expressed motivations for contacting celebrities." *Journal of Language and Social Psychology*, 14(1), 102–123.
Lemke, J. L. (1995). *Textual politics discourse and social dynamics*. London: Taylor & Francis.
L'etang, J. (2006). "Public relations and sport in promotional culture." *Public Relations Review*, 32(4), 386–394.
Levy, M. R. (1979). "Watching tv news as para-social interaction." *Journal of Broadcasting*, 23, 69–80.
Lindlof, T. R., and B. C. Taylor (2002). *Qualitative communication research methods*. Thousand Oaks: Sage.
Lovell, T. (1998). "Cultural production." In J. Storey (ed.). *Cultural theory and popular culture: A reader*. Athens: University of Georgia Press.
Lunt, P., and S. Livingstone (1996). "Rethinking the focus group in media and communications research." *Journal of Communication*, 46(2), 79–98.
Magder, T. (2004). "The end of TV 101: reality programs, formats, and the new business of television." In S. Murray & L. Ouellette (eds.). *Reality TV: Remaking television culture*. New York: New York University Press.
Maltby, J., Houran, J., R. Lange, D. Ashe, and L. McCutcheon (2002). "Thou shalt worship no other gods — unless they are celebrities: The relationship between celebrity worship and religious orientation." *Personality and Individual Differences*, 32(7), 1157–1172. Retrieved May 2, 2008, from http://www.sciencedirect.com/science/article/B6V9F-45HDDF2-5/1/8bab9ab7d5ed09b6ed955fb738e039ab.
Marshall, P. D. (1997). *Celebrity and power: fame in contemporary culture*. Minneapolis: University of Minnesota Press.
_____. (2006). "New media ? new self." In P. D. Marshall (ed.). *The celebrity culture reader*. London: Routledge.
Marston, G. (2000). "Metaphor, morality and myth: a critical discourse analysis of public housing policy in Queensland." *Critical Social Policy*, 20(3), 349–373.
Martin, G., and L. Koo (1997). "Celebrity suicide: Did the death of Kurt Cobain influence young suicides in Australia?" *Archives of Suicide Research*, 3(3), 187–198.
Marx, K. (1998). *Karl Marx's capital*. New York: Cominsane Press.
_____, and F. Engels (1956). *The German ideology*. New York: International.
Mathur, L. K., I. Mathur, and N. Rangan (1997). "The wealth effects associated with a celebrity endorser: The Michael Jordan phenomenon." *Journal of Advertising Research*, 37(3), 67–73.
McCabe, C. (1986). *High theory/low culture: Analyzing popular television and film*. Manchester: Manchester University Press.
McCourt, A., and J. Fitzpatrick (2001). "The role of personal characteristics and romantic characteristics in parasocial relationships: a pilot study." *Journal of Mundane Behavior*. Retrieved May 1, 2008, from http://www.mundanebehavior.org/issues/v2n1/mccourt_fitzpatrick.htm.
McCracken, G. (1989). "Who is the celebrity endorser? Cultural foundations of the endorsement process." *Journal of Consumer Research*, 16(3), 310–321.
McCutcheon, L. E. (2001). "Are parasocial relationship styles reflected in love styles?" *Current Research in Social Psychology*, 7(6), 82–93.
_____, D. D. Ashe, J. Houran, and J. Maltby (2003). "A cognitive profile of individuals who tend to worship celebrities." *J Psychol*, 137(4), 309–322.
McDonald, P. (2000). *The star system*. London: Wallflower.
McKee, A. (2003). *Textual analysis: A beginner's guide*. Thousand Oaks: Sage.
_____. (2007). *Beautiful things in popular culture*. Malden: Blackwell.
McQuail, D., J. G. Blumler, and J. Brown (1972). "The television audience: A revised perspective." In D. McQuail (ed.). *Sociology of mass communication* (pp. 135–165). Middlesex: Penguin.

Bibliography

"Megan Fox." (n.d.) Retrieved December 4, 2008 from http://coolspotters.com/actresses/megan-fox.

Mendelson, A. L. (2007). "On the function of the United States paparazzi: Mosquito swarm or watchdogs of celebrity image control and power." *Visual Studies, 22,* 169–183.

Mendible, M. (2004). "Humiliation, subjectivity, and reality TV." *Feminist Media Studies, 4*(3), 335–338.

Meyer, D. S. (1995). "The challenge of cultural elites: Celebrities and social movements." *Sociological Inquiry, 65*(2), 181–206.

Mills, C. W. (1956). *The power elite.* New York: Oxford University Press.

Mills, N. (2004). "Television and the politics of humiliation." *Dissent, 51*(3), 79–81.

Mirzoeff, N. (1998). *The visual culture reader.* New York: Routledge.

Monolescu, D., and C. Schifter (2000). "Online focus group: a tool to evaluate online students' course experience." *The Internet and Higher Education, 2*(2), 171–176.

Moynahan, R. (2004). "The intangible magic of celebrity marketing." *PLoS Medicine, 1.* Retrieved December 12, 2007, from http://medicine.plosjournals.org/perlserv/?request=get-document&doi=10.1371/journal.pmed.0010042&ct=1.

Murray, S., and L. Ouellette (2004). *Reality TV: Remaking television culture.* New York: New York University Press.

Nabi, R. L., E. N. Biely, S. J. Morgan, and C. R. Stitt (2003). "Reality-based television programming and the psychology of its appeal." *Media Psychology, 5*(4), 303–330.

"Name that do!" (2008, October 27). Retrieved December 4, 2008 from http://www.nbcbayarea.com/around_town/fashion/Name_That_Do.html.

"NBA salaries." (n.d.) Retrieved September 30, 2008 from http://www.insidehoops.com/nbasalaries.shtml.

"NBC's worst week?" (2007, June 6). Retrieved March 1, 2009 from http://www.imdb.com/title/tt0412142/news?year=2007;start=21.

Nesbitt-Larking, P. (2007). *(Almost) everywhere they are in chains: The political economy of communications in Canada.* Ontario: Broadview Press.

Nightingale, V., and T. Dwyer (2006). "The audience politics of 'enhanced' television formats." *International Journal of Media and Culture, 2*(1), 25–42.

Nordlund, J. E. (1978). "Media interaction." *Communication Research, 5*(2), 150–175.

Oliver, M. B. (1994). "Portrayals of crime, race, and aggression in 'reality-based' police shows: A content analysis." *Journal of Broadcasting & Electronic Media, 38,* 179–192.

Olsen, E. (2002, September 18). "Slaves of celebrity." *Salon.* Retrieved January 3, 2009, from http://dir.salon.com/story/ent/feature/2002/09/18/idol_contract/index.html.

Orbe, M. P. (1998). "Constructions of reality on MTV's 'the real world.'" *Southern Communication Journal, 64*(1), 32–48.

Park, J. H. (2004). "Television apparel shopping: Impulse buying and parasocial interaction." *Clothing and Textiles Research Journal, 22*(3), 135–144.

Pitman, B. A. (2002). "Re-mediating the spaces of reality television: 'America's Most Wanted' and the case of Vancouver's missing women." *Environment and Planning A, 34*(1), 167–184.

Pitout, M. (1998). "Reception analysis: A qualitative investigation of the parasocial and social dimensions of soap opera viewing." *In Communicatio, 24*(2), 65–82.

"Plot summary for 'An American Family.'" (n.d.) Retrieved September 13, 2008, from http://www.imdb.com/title/tt0211195/plotsummary.

Potter, W. J., R. Warren, M. Vaughan, K. Howley, A. Land, and J. Hagemeyer (1997). "Antisocial acts in reality programming on television." *Journal of Broadcasting & Electronic Media, 41,* 69–75.

"Prison Agony." (2008, January 18). *The New York Post.* Retrieved December 12, 2008 from http://www.nypost.com/seven/01182008/gossip/pagesix/prison_agony_596369.htm.

Bibliography

Raftery, B. M. (2000, June 16). "Got to be real." *Entertainment Weekly*. Retrieved September 9, 2008 from http://www.ew.com/ew/article/0,,85292,00.html.
Raphael, C. (2004). "The political economic origins of reali–TV." In S. Murray & L. Ouellette (eds.). *Reality TV: Remaking television culture*. New York: New York University Press.
Ray, G. (2007). "Avant-gardes as anti-capitalist vector." *Third Text, 21*, 241–255.
"Record plant." (n.d.) Retrieved February 13, 2009 from http://www.recordplant.com/history/index.html.
"Rebecca Romijn." (n.d.) Retrieved March 9, 2009 from http://www.boxofficemojo.com/people/chart/?view=Actor&id=rebeccaromijn.htm.
Reed, T. V. (2002). "Production analysis." In *Popular Culture*. Retrieved September 10, 2008, from http://www.wsu.edu/~amerstu/pop/prod.html.
Rein, I., P. Kotler, and M. Stoller (2005). *High visibility: The making and marketing of professionals into celebrities*. New York: McGraw-Hill.
Rojek, C. (2001). *Celebrity*. Chicago: Reaktion Books.
Roper, R. S. (2008). "Legal blur over celebrities' rights." *Broadcasting & Cable, 138*(27), 28–28.
Rose, G. (2001). *Visual methodologies: An introduction to the interpretation of visual methods*. Minneapolis: Sage.
Rose, R. L., and S. L. Wood (2005). "Paradox and the consumption of authenticity through reality television." *Journal of Consumer Research, 32*(2), 284–296.
Rubin, L. C., L. S. Brown, W. M. Robinson, A. Sikula, and L. P. Anderson (2003). "The forum." *Ethics & Behavior, 13*(4), 401–413.
Ryan, B. (1991). *Making capital from culture*. Berlin: Walter de Gruyter.
Schulman, N. (1993). "Conditions of their own making: An intellectual history of the centre for contemporary cultural studies at the University of Birmingham." *Canadian Journal of Communication, 18*(1).
"See you in hell, johnny bravo!" (2004). In L. Ouellette & S. Murray (eds.) & J. Sconce (author). *Reality TV: Remaking television culture* (pp. 251–270). New York: New York University Press.
"Simon Cowell Biography." (n.d.) Retrieved March 3, 2009 from http://tv.yahoo.com/contribs_print?id=293411.
Smith, M. J., and A. F. Wood (2003). *Survivor lessons: Essays on communication and reality television*. Jefferson, NC: McFarland.
Stamou, A. G., and S. Paraskevopoulos (2004). "Images of nature by tourism and environmentalist discourses in visitors books: A critical discourse analysis of ecotourism." *Discourse & Society, 15*(1), 105–129.
"Star search." (n.d.). Retrieved September 11, 2008 from http://www.imdb.com/title/tt0085093/.
Sternberg, S. (2008). "U.S. producers find their own reality." *Broadcasting & Cable, 138*(23), 38–38.
Summerfield, M. (2006, March 17). "'American Idol,' perverting dreams." *Associated Content*. Retrieved January 3, 2009, from http://www.associatedcontent.com/article/32573/american_idol_perverting_dreams_pg2.html?cat=7.
Summers, J., and M. J. Morgan (2008). "More than just the media: Considering the role of public relations in the creation of sporting celebrity and the management of fan expectations." *Public Relations Review, 34*(2), 176–182.
Sweet, C. (2001). "Designing and conducting virtual focus groups." *Qualitative Market Research: An International Journal, 4*(3), 130–135.
"2006 Yearly Box Office." (n.d.) Retrieved March 9, 2009 from http://www.boxofficemojo.com/yearly/chart/?yr=2006&p=.htm
Teo, P. (2000). "Racism in the news: A critical discourse analysis of news reporting in two Australian newspapers." *Discourse & Society, 11*(1), 7–49.

Bibliography

"The fabulous life." (n.d.) Retrieved September 20, 2008 from http://www.vh1.com/shows/dyn/fabulous_life_of/104772/episode_about.jhtml.

"The Nielson company measures the 'American Idol' phenom." (2008, May 15). Retrieved September 12, 2008 from http://www.reuters.com/article/pressRelease/idUS225052+15-May-2008+PRN20080515.

"The real world." (n.d.) Retrieved September 12, 2008 from http://www.imdb.com/title/tt0103520/.

"There can be only one." (2006, January 18). Retrieved December 13, 2008 from http://www.highlander-community.com/Forum/showthread.php?t=19792

Traube, E. G. (1996). "'The popular' in American culture." *Annual Review of Anthropology, 25,* 127–151.

Tulloch, J. (2000). *Watching television: Audiences, cultural theories and methods.* New York: Co-published by Oxford University Press.

Turner, G. (2006). "The mass production of celebrity: 'Celetoids,' reality TV and the 'demotic turn.'" *International Journal of Cultural Studies, 9*(2), 153–165.

Vaara, E., and J. Tienari (2002). "Justification, legitimization and naturalization of mergers and acquisitions: A critical discourse analysis of media texts." *Organization, 9*(2), 275–304.

Vancil, M. (1991). "Michael Jordan: Phenomenon." *Hoop Magazine.* Retrieved September 30, 2008 from http://www.nba.com/jordan/hoop_phenomenon.html.

Van Dijk, T. A. (2001). "Principles of critical discourse analysis." In M. Wetherell, S. Taylor, and S. Yates (eds.). *Discourse theory and practice* (pp. 300–317). Thousand Oaks: Sage.

Van Zoonen, L. (2004). "Imagining the fan democracy." *European Journal of Communication, 19*(1), 39–52.

Weber, M. (1978). "The Types of Legitimate Domination." In M. Weber (author), *Economy and Society* (Vol. 1). New York: Bedminster Press.

Weisman, L. (2008, November 14). "NFL salaries '08: Big Ben smiling as highest-paid player." *USA Today.* Retrieved December 15, 2008 from http://www.usatoday.com/sports/football/nfl/2008-11-05-salaries_N.htm.

"'When will I be famous?': Reappraising the debate about fame in reality TV." (2006). In D. S. Escoffery (ed.) and S. Holmes (author). *How real is reality TV? Essays on representation and truth* (pp. 7–25). Jefferson, NC: McFarland.

Williams, J. A. (2005). "On the popular vote." *Political Research Quarterly, 58*(4), 637–646.

Witkin, R. (2000). "Why did Adorno 'hate' jazz?" *Sociological Theory, 18*(1), 145–170.

Wodak, R. (2001). "What CDA is about." In R. Wodak & M. Meyer (eds.). *Methods of Critical Discourse Analysis.* Thousand Oaks: Sage.

Wyatt, E. (2008, May 1). "'Idol' judge admits rehearsal guided her." *The New York Times.* Retrieved May 11, 2008, from http://www.nytimes.com/2008/05/01/arts/television/01idol.html.

"You Tube Fact Sheet." (n.d.) Retrieved September 9, 2008 from http://www.youtube.com/t/fact_sheet.

Index

Abdul, Paula 9, 45, 107, 111, 112, 113, 115, 116, 121, 124–125, 127, 128, 132, 136, 141, 142, 146–147, 160, 162, 168, 170, 178, 204, 205
academic *celebrity* 70–71
achieved *celebrity* 2, 8, 11
Adamic hero 56, 72, 181, 191, 192, 197
Adorno, Theodor 6, 19, 36–38, 180
aesthetic dissonance 37
Aiken, Clay 136, 139, 144
album sales 7, 145
Alexander, Alaina 169
Alexander the Great 54–55, 203
American celebrity system 58–61
American dream 40, 123; *see also* success myth
America's Most Wanted 6
Archuleta, David 139, 142–143, 188
Arête 164, 203
ascribed *celebrity* 2, 201
AT&T 173–174, 185, 186
attributed *celebrity* 2, 8, 11, 201
authentic *celebrity* 7, 11, 45
"authenticity" 123, 125, 126, 129–132, 183, 204
award shows 94–95

Barba, Antonella 108, 112
Barrino, Fantasia 112, 139, 141–142, 144, 145, 155, 156, 167, 182
Baudrillard, Jean 179
Bayer-Sager, Carol 178–179
Bennett, Paris 140
Berger, John 23
Berry, Colton 155, 167–168
Bice, Bo 106, 126–127, 129, 131, 132, 136, 139, 140, 144, 145, 167
Big Brother 7
"The Big Three" 110–114, 141, 171; *see also* Carey, Mariah; Dion, Celine; Houston, Whitney
BMG (Bertlesmann Management Group) 43

Bon Jovi, Jon 169
Boorstin, Daniel 1, 5, 39, 56, 68, 94, 98, 184, 197
Bordieu, Pierre 17, 23–24, 28, 32, 33
Bridges, Dale x
Brown, Baylie 129
Brown, Temptress 159–160, 192–193, 205
Burke, Kenneth 66–67

Caesar Augustus 55, 71
Candid Camera 6
"cannon fodder" 154–157, 184
Cardinale, Lindsay 140
Carey, Mariah 110, 112, 113, 137, 182
Carrey, Jim 175–176
Carrico, Robbie 132
Castro, Jason 151, 153, 169–170
categorical individuality 116, 182
celebrity as consumer 75, 98, 173
celebrity mentors 137–139
celetoids 3–4, 7, 8, 83–84, 99, 156–157, 160–161, 181, 186, 194, 201
charismatic authority 87–88
Clarkson, Kelly 7, 40, 42, 102–103, 105, 108, 109, 111, 112, 139, 142, 143, 144, 145, 149, 155, 156, 167, 182, 204, 205
class struggle 16, 21, 25, 180
Coca-Cola 173, 174, 185
conglomeration 26
consumer culture 22–25, 28, 35, 46, 75–76
contract 42–44, 85
Cook, David 139, 142–143, 145, 165, 167, 187, 188, 192
Cook, Kristy Lee 133, 170
Cops 6
Couldry, Nick 7
counterculture/counterhegemony 33
Covais, Kevin 127
Cowell, Simon 9, 44, 107, 108, 109, 111, 112, 116–117, 118–119, 121, 123, 124, 126–128, 129, 131, 132, 133, 134–135, 138, 141, 142, 144, 146–147, 150, 151, 155–156, 160, 161,

217

Index

162, 163, 164–165, 166, 167, 168, 169, 170–172, 185, 187, 195, 196, 204, 205
Cox, Heather 112
cultural artifacts 15, 25–32, 33–34, 99
cultural studies 19
culture industries 6, 28, 91–92, 135, 180, 186, 188

Dancing with the Stars 37, 99
Daughtry, Chris 7, 129–130, 139, 140–141, 143, 144, 145, 147, 165, 169, 187
Davis, Amy 155
Davis, Clive 138–139, 145, 146
DeGarmo, Diana 144
DioGuardi, Kara 196, 204
Dion, Celine 111, 112, 165
DIY *celebrity* 3, 7, 11
Doolittle, Melinda 177
dream fulfillment 157–160, 169, 184, 186
Dunkleman, Brian 107

Emerson, Ralph Waldo 67–68, 197; *see also* representative man
Ethos 68, 72, 203
exchange value 80
exploitation crews 59
Eze, Chikeze 188

Federov, Anthony 131, 140
Ferl, Ashley 163
fetishized labor 78–79, 149–150
finale 10–11
force, coercive and non-coercive 16
Ford Motor Company 173, 174–175, 185
format 9–11
Fort-Coutaz, Cecile 40
Franklin, Aretha 128, 135
Franklin, Benjamin 55, 72
Fremantle Entertainment 42–44; *see also* 19 Entertainment

Georgias 65
Gertz v. Robert Welch, Inc. 201
Goldberg, Sarah 178–179, 193
Gordon, Mikalah 101, 113, 140
gossip 52, 89–90
Gramsci, Antonio 16–17
Gray, Tamyra 144, 174, 175
Guarini, Justin 102–103, 108, 158, 176

Haelan Laboratories, Inc. v. Topps Chewing Gum, Inc. 62–63
Haley, Garrett 169
Hall, Stuart 16, 17, 18, 19, 20
Hazlitt, William 69
hegemony 17–18, 28, 32, 46, 92

Hewitt, Jennifer Love 81, 176
Hicks, Taylor 41, 108, 127, 139, 150, 167, 172
"high" culture 19, 24, 36
history of *celebrity* 53–61
Hollywood Week 9
Holmes, Su 49, 61–62, 89
Horkheimer, Max 6
Houston, Whitney 111, 112, 182, 186
Hudson, Jennifer 136, 139, 143–144
Hundley, Mandisa 116–117, 120, 194
Hurley, Elizabeth 79–80

identification 66–67, 92, 188
"Idol moments" 136, 141–143, 163, 165, 186

Jackman, Hugh 176, 206
Jackson, Randy 9, 107, 111, 112, 113, 121, 124, 128, 130, 131, 133, 134, 135, 156, 158–159, 161, 162, 163, 164–165, 168–169, 170, 178, 194, 196, 204
Jauss, Robert 66–67
Jay-Z 76–77
Jhalley, Sut 15, 21, 31, 32, 33
Johns, Michael 158–159
Jones, Lakisha 113, 144
Jordan, Michael 75

Kim, Paul 126
Kuzmich, Heather 193

Lampley, Jim 142–143
Lewis, Blake 132, 140, 168, 177
"likeability" 133–135, 183, 191, 192, 195
limited public figure 201
Lira, Melinda 178
"little fictions" 51, 202, 203
Lloyd Webber, Andrew 138
Locke, Kimberly 144
Lopez, Jennifer 176
Lynyrd Skynyrd 106, 140

Malakar, Sanjaya 160–163, 164, 184, 195, 205
Malloy, Kady 155–156, 169
Maroulis, Constantine 120, 133, 140, 170
Marshall, P. David 48, 73, 78, 80, 84, 88, 96–100, 181–182, 185–186, 197
Matchbox Twenty 169
Matlin, Marlee 193
McKee, Alan 20–21, 35
McKinney, Gedeon 130
McPhee, Katherine 41, 111, 112, 132–133, 141, 144, 168, 169, 170
"The Media" 51, 202
Mercado, Syesha 153, 158
Mills, C. Wright 5
Morton's Fork 187

218

Index

19 Entertainment 42–44

Olivarez, Vanessa 195
"originality" 123, 164–167, 172, 185
Overmyer, Amanda 153, 166–167

Pickler, Kellie 117–120, 123, 134, 139, 147, 183
Pop Idol 40, 44
post-structuralist approach to *celebrity* 93–96
Potts, Paul 193
power 16–17, 21, 32, 33, 46, 73
presentation of self theory 69–70
property rights 61–64
Protagoras 65
pseudo-events 2, 39–40
"public persona" 63

Queen 132, 137, 175

Rascal Flatts 140
ratings 8, 11, 35–36, 40, 41, 189
Ray, Selina 130, 156, 171
The Real World 6, 180
reality television archetypes 38–39, 180
The Record Plant 104, 146
Red Hot Chili Peppers 130, 165
"relevance" 123, 164, 167–169, 172, 185
representative man 67–68
revenue 8, 41
Richardson, Chris 177
Robinson, Anwar 140
Robson, Wade 37
Rojek, Chris 2, 4, 55, 69–70, 75, 77, 82, 83, 86–96, 197
Romijn, Rebecca 176, 206

Savol, Scott 140, 149, 171, 195
Scarnato, Haley 150
Seacrest, Ryan 9, 101, 102, 106, 107, 108, 109, 110, 113, 114, 118–119, 124, 134, 137–138, 140, 142–143, 144, 145, 146, 150, 151, 152, 157–158, 159–160, 163, 174, 175, 179, 186, 204
Seinfeld, Jerry 64
Sierra, Jessica 134, 140, 195
Sligh, Chris 165–166, 167, 168

Smith, Nikko 140
Smithson, Carly 111, 132, 155–156
So You Think You Can Dance 36–37, 99
Solomon, Vonzell 103, 106, 111, 127, 140, 149
Sparks, Jordin 139, 144, 145, 167, 177
Starr, Ryan 102
structuralist approach to *celebrity* 90–92
Studdard, Ruben 139, 145, 167, 195, 204
studio contracts 59–60, 85
subjectivist approach to *celebrity* 86–90
subsumption, real 26, 31, 32, 46
success myth 50, 52, 71, 91, 152, 158, 160, 181, 186, 189, 191, 194, 195–196, 197
symbolic degradation 155–156, 160–163, 166, 184, 195
symbolic functions of *celebrity* 73–86
symbolic recovery 156–157

theme nights 10
311 (band) 168
tour 10
Turner, Graeme 3, 4, 201
Turner, Nadia 130, 132, 140, 157

Underwood, Carrie 7, 8, 104, 106–107, 116, 120–123, 126, 129, 139, 140, 141, 143, 144, 145, 151, 156, 167, 169, 173, 182–183, 187, 192, 205
use value 80–81
"Uses and Gratifications" 202

Velasco, Camile 195
viewers, number of 8, 11
voters 44–45

wardrobe 132
Weber, Max 87–88
weight 116–117, 127–128
West, Cornell 70–71
White, Brooke 104, 115, 123–125, 129, 132, 140, 144, 183, 188
Williams, Ted 60–61
Witherspoon, Reese 78–79
Wonder, Stevie 130, 137–138, 161, 165, 184

Yamin, Elliott 132, 137, 139, 140, 152
Young, Ace 133

www.ingramcontent.com/pod-product-compliance
Ingram Content Group UK Ltd.
Pitfield, Milton Keynes, MK11 3LW, UK
UKHW041918140426
5217IPUK00013B/209